ASIAN FOOD

The Global and the Local

ConsumAsiaN Book Series

edited by

Brian Moeran and Lise Skov

The Curzon Press and The University of Hawai'i Press

Women, Media and Consumption in Japan (*Published 1995*)
Edited by Lise Skov and Brian Moeran

A Japanese Advertising Agency (*Published 1996*)
An Anthropology of Media and Markets
Brian Moeran

Contemporary Japan and Popular Culture (*Published 1996*)
Edited by John Whittier Treat

Packaged Japaneseness (*Published 1997*)
Weddings, Business and Brides
Ofra Goldstein-Gidoni

Australia and Asia (*Published 1997*)
Cultural Transactions
Edited by Maryanne Dever

Staging Hong Kong (*Published 1998*)
Rozanna Lilley

Asian Department Stores (*Published 1998*)
Edited by Kerrie L. MacPherson

Consuming Ethnicity and Nationalism (*Published 1999*)
Edited by Kosaku Yoshino

The Commercialized Crafts of Thailand (*Published 2000*)
Hill Tribes and Lowland Villages
Erik Cohen

Japanese Consumer Behaviour (*Published 2000*)
From Worker Bees To Wary Shoppers
John L. McCreery

Adult Manga (*Published 2000*)
Culture and Power in Contemporary Japanese Society
Sharon Kinsella

Illustrating Asia (*Published 2001*)
Comics, Humor Magazines, and Picture Books
Edited by John A. Lent

Asian Media Productions (*Published 2001*)
Edited by Brian Moeran

Asian Food: The Global and the Local (*Published 2001*)
Katarzyna Cwiertka with Boudewijn Walraven

ASIAN FOOD

The Global and the Local

Edited by

Katarzyna Cwiertka with
Boudewijn Walraven

UNIVERSITY OF HAWAI'I PRESS
HONOLULU

Editorial Matter © 2001 Katarzyna Cwiertka with
Boudewijn Walraven

Published in North America by
University of Hawai'i Press
2840 Kolowalu Street
Honolulu, Hawai'i 96822

First published in the United Kingdom
by Curzon Press
Richmond, Surrey
England

Printed in Great Britain

Library of Congress Cataloguing-in-Publication Data

Asian food : the global and the local / edited by Katarzyna Cwiertka
with Boudewijn Walraven.
     p. cm. – (ConsumAsiaN book series)
     Includes bibliographical references and index.
     ISBN 0-8248-2544-6 (alk. paper)
     1. Gastronomy. 2. Diet–Asia. 3. Food habits–Asia. I. Cwiertka, Katarzyna Joanna,
1968- II. Walraven, Boudewijn, 1947- III. Series.

TX641 .A788 2001
394.1′095–dc21   2001046284

CONTENTS

CONTENTS

LIST OF FIGURES

LIST OF FIGURES

ACKNOWLEDGEMENTS

The cradle of this volume was the workshop 'Asian Food in the Twentieth Century' which took place at Leiden University in February 1998. This meeting was rather unconventional in that it brought together scholars from very different disciplinary backgrounds, including anthropologists, sociologists, nutritionists, cultural historians and even an entomologist. This unusual gathering proved to be most rewarding, both academically and in terms of individual contacts between the participants, which have flourished ever since. The workshop was made possible by generous funding provided by the Japan Foundation, the International Institute of Asian Studies, and the CNWS Research School of Asian, African, and Amerindian Studies at Leiden University. The Centre for Japanese and Korean Studies of Leiden University hosted the workshop. We would like to thank these organisations for their support. We are particularly grateful to Jan van Bremen for his assistance in procuring funds. Unfortunately, not all the papers presented during this workshop could be included in the book, but we would like to take this opportunity to thank all the participants in the workshop, including the members of the audience who took part in the discussions. We feel especially grateful to the contributors who stayed with us until the end, for their patience and the promptness with which they responded to our requests. We are also indebted to Sidney Mintz, the series editors and an anonymous reader, who all provided valuable comments to earlier drafts of the manuscript.

INTRODUCTION

Katarzyna J. Cwiertka

In the twentieth century, the extent and speed of the global flow of people, commodities, and information has been magnified, driven at first by technological progress and later by the globalisation of markets, trade, and labour. During the last few decades in particular, the diversity of channels for global exchanges has continuously been expanding and the interconnectedness of people worldwide has intensified. Today, the global connectivity exerts an increasingly strong impact on the everyday life of people worldwide, penetrating various domains of their local lived experience.

Globalisation, as the complex global connectivity is usually referred to, has by now become both a mainstay topic in journalism and an important object of inquiry for practically every field of the social sciences.[1] An army of scientists, from political and economic analysts to media specialists and anthropologists, study globalisation not only because of the fashionable nature of the topic, but also due to the evident worldwide implications of global connectivity for various spheres of life. It has become practically impossible for scholars to deal with local issues of whatever nature without taking into consideration either the global forces that affected them, or the impact these linking issues will eventually have on global markets, politics and culture.

The main objective of this volume is to identify the diversity of issues and forces involved in dietary globalisation, and by doing so to underscore the omnipresent and multi-layered nature of the globalisation as such.[2] The focus on food that *Asian Food: the global and the local* consistently retains throughout the book will enable us to demonstrate the many realms of social action affected by global interconnectedness. Globalisation influences the production and processing of food, as well as the way in which it is sold, prepared and consumed. As integral components of local cultures, these practices are involved in shaping social relationships and cultural and national identities. Food also connects globalising markets with individually-perceived crucial life issues, such as health and religion. By identifying a variety of such links, the contributors to the volume underline an important theme in the study of globalisation – the continuous tension between homogenisation and heterogenisation, the inter-connectedness between the global and the local. By presenting different case studies illustrating the interaction between Asian and Western dietary cultures throughout the twentieth century, each chapter addresses the variety of ways in which commodities, practices and ideas coming from elsewhere become embedded in local life.

The increasing number of consumers worldwide finding the same foods produced by the same multinational companies on the shelves of the supermarket, itself a globalised phenomenon, along with fast-food restaurants serving similar menus all over the world, seem to signify a sense of culinary loss. However, there is much more to culinary globalisation than a bitter scenario of homogenisation facilitated by the worldwide expansion of Western food industries and the spread of Western commodities. Because dietary patterns and attitudes toward food are integral components of local cultures, introduced foreign foods, catering technologies, and consumption practices tend to become indigenised, resisting the homogenising power of global forces. Global influences, however strong and far-reaching, are experienced locally and in relationship to the geo-historical processes that have shaped specific localities.[3] In the circumstances of today's trans-national interconnectedness, the local cannot escape the global implications, nor can the global manage without its local articulation. As a result, not only do global brands spread worldwide diminishing the diversity of local cuisines, but also new hybrid cuisines are created and new identities embraced through the acceptance and rejection of new commodities and new forms of consumption.

Food as Culture

Similarly to other kinds of social action, food-related practices are embedded in the biological and ecological context, and are shaped by economic, political, religious, ideological and emotional relationships between people. However, the production, distribution, preparation and consumption of food, more so than other kinds of behaviour, reveal the complexity of human interdependence, and serve as a nexus for an unbounded number of issues concerning society and culture. In the following paragraphs, I will try very generally to describe this complexity.

Until very recently, ecology and human physiology used to be the most important factors determining the formation of diet. Ecological circumstances such as climate and geographical location (e.g. access to the sea) primarily determined the availability of food in every part of the world, so that the diet usually was composed of products available in the immediate vicinity. Human physiology prevents the digestion of all available fauna and flora, and physiological needs are also affected by environmental conditions, such as the climate. For example, people residing in areas with low air temperatures required a larger intake of fat than those living in the tropics.

During the last few centuries, the number of people relying entirely on local products in their diet has gradually been diminishing. From the late nineteenth century onwards, in particular, industrial societies became less dependent on local ecology, as far as their food supply is concerned. Due to the development of modern technologies for producing and processing of food, along with the advancement of modern modes of transportation, an increasing number of people acquired access to an increasing variety of new foods. At the same time, the once obvious seasonal variation of foods is becoming blurred, as they become available all the year through. Regional ecology is still reflected in culinary traditions and food preferences, as they evolved historically under certain ecological conditions. Nevertheless, today, socio-cultural and economic factors rather than ecological ones are chiefly responsible for dietary differences among societies.

As an indispensable component of our daily existence, food is very intricately linked to profit. Sidney Mintz is one of the first anthropologists who examined closely the relationship between eating habits and economic development. In his 1985 book entitled *Sweetness and Power: the place of sugar in modern history*, he described the history of sugar consumption in Western Europe and linked its popularisation to the rising supply of sugar provided by sugarcane plantations in the New World. Mintz argued that the transition of sugar from a luxury item to a daily food, between the 18th and late 19th centuries, had less to do with cultural and nutritional needs of the European populations than with the pressures in the pursuit of profit that were sustained among the producers and distributors of this commodity.

Culinary culture has always been affected by the pursuit of profit by those involved in the production, processing, and distribution of food, and that pressure only increased with the advance of capitalism (Achaya 1995, Jiménez 1995). Another powerful factor that was involved in the shaping of foodways at all time and regions was prestige.

Eating habits has for centuries been used as a means of social display, and a symbol of social status. As conflict and social competition often find articulation in social display, of which conspicuous consumption is a magnificent example (Mennell 1985:16), individual food choices serve as perfect indicators of social standing and mark the distinction between groups within society (Bourdieu 1986).

The case studies provided by Stephen Mennell and Jack Goody became classics in cultural studies on food. In *Cooking, Cuisine and Class* (1982), Goody compared the link between prestige and food in European, African, and Asian societies. Stephen Mennell, in turn, in his distinguished work *All Manners of Food* (1985) tried to find the reasons for the existence of considerable differences in culinary development between France and England, and linked them with the strength of social competition in the two countries. Goody and Mennell both concluded that prestige was the primary incentive and driving force for the progress of the cooking craft and the development of table manners, and that the social hierarchy was absolutely indispensable to the creation of culinary refinement. The two tendencies, towards social distinction from those lower on the social scale, and towards social imitation of those higher up on the social scale were largely responsible for innovations in diet (Wiegelmann 1974). The stronger the social hierarchy, the more emphatic the uniqueness of the culinary culture of the elite, and the sharper the social stratification, the greater the differences in diet one may expect (Goody 1982:97–99).

However, prestige plays a role in food choice only when the economic standing allows people the freedom of such a choice.

> A compulsive desire for social prestige is to be found as the primitive motive of action only among members of classes whose income under normal circumstances is substantial and perhaps even growing, and at any rate is appreciably over the hunger threshold. In such classes the impulse to engage in economic activity is no longer the simple necessity of satisfying hunger, but a desire to preserve a certain high, socially expected standard of living and prestige.
>
> (Elias 1994 [1939]:473)

Economical resources are thus an important factor in the desire for social prestige, and their absence interferes with having the food that one wishes to eat. Economic growth leads to an improvement in nourishment and advancements of cookery, whereas economic crisis has the reverse effect. However, like many other connections in the food system, this link is not always so straightforward.

The economic growth that followed the Industrial Revolution was undoubtedly the main contributor to the improvement of living conditions and removed hunger as a social problem in industrial societies. The advancement of technology led to greater efficiency in farming and husbandry, which in turn resulted in an increase of production and an improved quality of diet. New cooking equipment brought variety and diminished the workload of food preparation. The development of mass food-processing technologies allowed for the better preservation of food, or preservation of foods which could not be preserved before. Food processing technology brought new foods to regions where they had previously not been available, and provided cheap substitutes for luxury food products, such as margarine as a substitute for butter and condensed milk as a substitute for fresh milk.[4] The improved conditions and the enhanced speed of transport, together with food processing technology, lowered the cost of food not available locally, and stimulated the diffusion of food innovations. The cross-cultural flow of foods, cookery techniques, and consumption patterns, which accelerated in the second half of the twentieth century, brought variety to daily nourishment and has broadened the culinary horizons of ordinary people in industrial societies.

Nevertheless, although this economic and technological advancement generally led to an increased freedom in food choice, it has also been accompanied by new nutritional problems. The use of chemical additives and other harmful substances during the production and the processing of food, and the spread of diseases related to the excessive consumption of sugar and saturated fat, eating disorders and obesity, are among the most pressing health issues of the late twentieth century.[5]

The impact of certain food items, or a certain dietary regime, on the human organism is conceptualised in various ways in different cultures (Mennell et al. 1992:42–44). For example, all major religions attach symbolic meanings to food and drink by creating rules regulating their consumption, and often by including them in religious rituals (Goody 1982:108–129, 144–147). Many forms of belief in supernatural powers are somehow concerned with the consumption of food, most often in the form of forbidding the consumption of certain foods completely or only at specific times. Even if we follow Harris' questionable argument that religious food symbolism and internalised repugnances only perpetuated already established practices (Harris 1985), it remains the case that the food-related symbols and values propagated by religions and folk beliefs are deeply involved in moulding culinary traditions all over the world.

Consumption of the same kind of food may bring people together, just as the lack of common food habits may set them apart. For example, specific foods often serve as an expression of national identity, generate feelings of unity with other members of the same nation, and mark the distinction between the native and the foreign (Murcott 1995). Food may also be used as the mirror of the self (Ohnuki-Tierney 1993), what we eat, how we eat, and how we feel about it speaks eloquently to the question of how we perceive ourselves in relation to others (Mintz 1985:4).

Hence the variety of social functions and cultural meanings that food carries while it is produced, processed, distributed and consumed makes it a perfect means for the observation of local life. The study of globalisation through a focus on food enables us to underscore the interconnectedness between the global and the local in the diverse domains of social action.

Food and Globalisation

Any attempt to pinpoint the exact beginning of a major social transformation such as globalization is likely to prove misleading. On the one hand it is true ... that 'until our day, human [global] society has never existed' – but only in the sense that never before have all the possible actors been on stage at once. On the other hand, some of the processes which in this century have made the human world one have been at work in human societies as long as the species *Homo sapiens* has existed.

(Mennell 1990:359)

As far as the origin of globalisation is concerned, there seems to be a certain degree of ambiguity among the theorists. While they generally closely relate

5

globalisation to modernity and postmodernity, at times they admit that this process is not detached from the past.

> [T]he world has been a congeries of large-scale interactions for many centuries. Yet today's world involves interactions of a new order and intensity.
>
> (Appadurai 1990:1)

> Much of world history can be fruitfully considered as sequences of 'miniglobalization'.
>
> (Robertson 1990:20–21)

> [I]n a great many places, decades or centuries of contact and change, of many kinds and intensities, have already shaped that local scene which meet[s] the transnational culture industries of the late twentieth century.
>
> (Hannerz 1992:226)

Statements like these very pointedly indicate the ambiguity of globalisation as both a new process closely related to capitalist culture and a universal long-term development that progresses through the ages. An integral component of this ambiguity, as expressed in numerous theoretical studies on globalisation, is the generative source and the key force leading to the contemporary global interaction. Is it a process closely related to the West and its global expansion, as social scientists have let us to believe for decades (i.e. Weber 1958, Wallerstein 1974–1989, Braudel 1981–1984)? Or, as the newer approaches claim (Blaut 1993, Hodgson 1993, Perlin 1994, Goody 1996, Frank 1998), is it a more prolonged process of which Western domination is merely one of many stages?

In his recent book *Globalization and Culture* (1999), where he analyses the relationship between the globalisation processes and contemporary cultural change, John Tomlinson argues that a critical difference between the pre-modern global connectivity and the 'global modernity' that takes place today, is our consciousness of the world as a whole and the integration of this awareness into our daily local life.

> '[T]he global' increasingly exists as a cultural horizon within which we (to varying degrees) frame our existence. The penetration of localities which connectivity brings is thus double edged: as it dissolves the securities of locality, it offers new understandings of experience in wider – ultimately global – terms.
>
> (Tomlinson 1999:30)

The fact that people nowadays increasingly link mundane aspects of their lifestyle with global consciousness affects their 'context of meaning construction'; influences their sense of identity and other cultural values that have developed around locally situated life. The mundane nature of this experience, rapidly assimilated to normality, is achieved through the overwhelming global context in education, employment, consumer culture and mass media – agencies that are closely linked to the experience of modernity (Tomlinson 1999:20, 43). Therefore, Tomlinson argues, the sources of 'multivalent connections' that today bind worldwide practices, experiences and fates together, are of a different nature that the pre-modern globality.

The questions concerning the source and origin of globalisation will most possibly remain an issue in academic discourse, and involvement in this discussion is outside the scope of this volume. At any rate, it is hardly deniable that the expansion of Western capitalism has had a critical impact on the recent global developments. Western imperialism in political, economic and cultural terms is a well-documented phenomenon (Tomlinson 1991), and its consequences are vividly demonstrated by the modifications in lifestyles of many societies worldwide. However, this is not a one-way stream. Assimilation of influences from the periphery by the centre is another outcome of globalisation, and is regarded as an important source of innovation in the contemporary world (Hannerz 1996:77). Hence, the twentieth century may be generally characterised as a period of intensified flows of culture, in large part asymmetrical, between the dominant West and the rest of the world, leading to an increasing global interconnectedness.[6]

Cross-cultural Culinary Exchanges

> Despite the gradual diffusion of foods and food-producing methods worldwide, the large-scale movement of the earth's peoples across continents and oceans in the course of many millennia, and the enormous *total* variety of human foodstuffs, until recently most human beings subsisted on foods produced or acquired within a day's travel from home. ... Of course there are certain exception to these assertions. As long as human communities have been stratified, kings and their courts have gloried in their prerogatives to eat foods not available to others less privileged than they, and these were often foods that had been carried great distances.
>
> (Mintz 1997:185–86)

The existing expansion of the relationships between places and localities all over the world has been vastly intensified in recent decades. This acceleration of the movements of foods and culinary cultures has been often described as culinary globalisation, which would finally lead to the development of a *world cuisine*. It has today become commonplace for both professional and amateur cooks to mix foodstuffs produced thousands of kilometres apart in one dish, to adapt unfamiliar cookery techniques to deal with familiar ingredients, and to add unknown flavours to well-known tastes (*Figure 1*). Culinary globalisation does not only form the core of refined cookery, but has also evolved into a major trend affecting the everyday diets of increasing numbers of people around the world. It is no exaggeration to say that never before have such manifold varieties of food

Figure 1 A Multicultural Menu on a Flight of a Major Airline (Photo: Lennart Durehed).

been on stage at once, and never have so many people shared the same kinds of food.

On the other hand, it should be borne in mind that this global amalgamation of foodstuffs, cooking techniques and eating habits is by no means a new phenomenon. In fact, historical accounts suggest that the major components of many traditional diets originated somewhere other than where they were put into use (Goody 1982:97–153; Tannahill 1988; Davidson 1983). For example, the cuisine of ancient Rome was developed by Greek cooks whose forebears had refined their cooking by learning from the Persians (Roden 1985:30–31). Likewise, the food culture of Europe was greatly affected by foreign influences – for example in the Middle Ages by Arab cookery (Hieatt 1997; Roden 1985), from the seventeenth century onward by the numerous foodstuffs adopted from the New World, and in the nineteenth and twentieth centuries increasingly by Asian foodways (Driver 1983). Moreover, the worldwide dispersion of food plants, to mention only tomato, chilli peppers and maize, has had an impact on the diets of almost the entire human population (Ho 1955, Sokolov 1991).

Culinary cultures are, and have always been, geographically constituted through processes of displacement. Foreign foodstuffs and other components of consumption practices have always spread and have been adopted and domesticated by societies throughout all times and regions. It is mainly the

8

speed, intensity, and range of global culinary interaction that have successively increased during the twentieth century. Generally speaking, before the development of modern modes of transportation, such as the railroad train, the steamship, and later the aeroplane, food grown in distant places was expensive and therefore available to only the richest sections of the population. Even if the climate allowed for the production of an exotic food on a large scale outside its place of origin, as in the case of the potato and capsicums native to the Americas, it usually took two to three generations before the newly introduced foodstuff found a place for itself as a regular part of the domestic diet (Wiegelmann 1974). Nowadays, however, culinary novelties from abroad may spread through a society in less than a decade. Moreover, foreign foods are not necessarily expensive now.

Generally speaking, until the dawn of the twentieth century, it was only the richest sections of the population who were exceptions to the rule of locality. Kings and courts ate differently from commoners in order to validate their special status. Rare and costly exotic foods were the means of differentiating them from the rest of the society, and this explains the fact why the elite circles in hierarchical societies have, in principle, always been cosmopolitan (Goody 1982).

With the exception of certain foodstuffs, such as potatoes and maize, and certain condiments such as black and red pepper, which also reached lower orders of the populations worldwide, it is only since the dawn of the twentieth century that a growing interest in foreign food could be observed below the elite level. In Europe and North America, this sort of interest became particularly evident among the urban middle classes. For example, from the early twentieth century onwards, the eating habits of foreign nations were increasingly featured in the mass media, and growing numbers of foreign recipes appeared in cookbooks. Simultaneously, the rise of interest toward Western cuisines could also be observed among the middle classes of certain non-western societies. This curiosity about other people's foods was not directly followed by a large-scale adoption of their consumption practices. In fact, the majority of dishes that appeared in restaurants and cookbooks, and were claimed to be of foreign origin, were rather products of the imagination of their creators. Nevertheless, this trend foreshadowed the culinary globalisation that has become so characteristic of the late twentieth century. The growing emphasis on the cross-cultural theme in food during the last decades was closely related to a smoother worldwide flow of information, commodities and people. The increasing intensity of exchanges between Asia and the West signifies this connection.

In centuries past, consumer preferences, such as a penchant for Asian spices, had already stimulated the creation of far-flung trade networks and inspired colonial expansion. However, in the nineteenth century, and even more so in the twentieth century, when food began to play a more important role in the political economy of global trade, Asian and Western culinary traditions became embedded in increasingly complex economic structures.

During the twentieth century, the diffusion of new crops, adoption of new foods, and the development of food industries constituted the major trends in the dietary changes in Asia. Although the transformation of food habits in various Asian societies took different paths, the most powerful incentive for the change came from a single source – Western colonial expansion. The impact of the West often facilitated and accelerated modifications and innovations in local foodways which, however, were never mere changes in diet, but also reflected the reformulation of economic and social conditions in these societies.

This doesn't mean that in the twentieth century the impact of the West on Asian culinary cultures was much stronger than the influence of Asia on Western eating habits. From the 1950s onwards, following the earlier spread of food items of Asian origin such as rice, sago and spices, the expansion of ethnic restaurants in Europe and the United States fascinated the further diffusion of Asian cuisines in Western societies. By the 1980s, Asian food, although often in a modified form, has become a mainstay of the Western culinary horizon. The popularisation of specific Asian cuisines in particular European countries was closely related to their past colonial relationships. For example, the introduction and diffusion of Indonesian food in the Netherlands, and of Indian cuisines in the United Kingdom depended to a large degree on the flow of immigrants from the former colonies.

Under the stimulus of tourism and the exposure to the culinary cultures of migrant communities, interest in foreign food increased steadily in the economically prosperous societies of Western Europe, North America, and some regions of Asia. Meanwhile, the expansion of global capitalism led to the cross-cultural spread of the products of the western food industry, such as breakfast cereals, condensed milk, fizzy drinks, and ketchup, and of American fast-food chains like McDonald's, Burger King, and Kentucky Fried Chicken (*Figure 2*). A general quest for novelty, inspired by the advertising strategies of food producers and inflamed by the mass media, made the fashion for multicultural cookery, or as it is often called 'fusion cooking', the major culinary trend of the 1990s.

There is, however, another factor that has played a crucial role in the contemporary culinary globalisation – imagination as a social practice. As Arjun Appadurai has pointed out, 'the imagination has become an organised field of social practices, a form of work (both in the sense of labour and of culturally organised practice) and a form of negotiation between sites of agency ('individuals') and globally defined fields of possibility' (Appadurai 1990:5). In this context, food becomes increasingly invested with meanings, turns into a means of creating imagined worlds, to a much greater degree than was formerly the case. As Ian Cook and Philip Crang put it, nowadays foods 'do not simply come from places, organically growing out of them, but also make places as symbolic constructs, being deployed in the discursive construction of various imaginative geographies' (Cook and Crang 1996:140). For tourists, immigrants, refugees, guest workers, employees of multinationals and other individuals who move around the world, or simply for the customers of ethnic restaurants, foods

Figure 2 Pepsi-Cola Crossing Cultural Borders (Photo: Magnum).

are the building blocks of imagined worlds, that is, the 'multiple worlds which are constituted by the historically situated imaginations of persons and groups spread around the globe' (Appadurai 1990:7).

The Issues Raised by this Volume

In the framework of the growing interaction between Asia and the West within the last hundred years, the contributors to this volume collectively document and

11

analyse the transformations in the local diets of Asian peoples, and point toward the role of Asian cuisines in the transformation of European foodways. As mentioned earlier in this introduction, the focus on food that *Asian Food: the global and the local* consistently retains throughout the book will enable us to demonstrate the multiplicity of the realms of social action that are affected by the global interconnectedness, and the continuous interconnectedness between the global and the local.

As consuming is closely related to producing, buying and selling, our inquiry includes a focus on the agency of commercial interests in the transition of food habits within and outside Asia. Each chapter employs food as the focus for the different issues that follow upon the global spread of modernity and its consequences for both periphery and centre. The encroachment of Western capitalism, which remains the main incentive for globalisation, not only affects Asian foodways, but boomerang-like comes back to influence the tastes and customs of non-Asian peoples.

The chapters are arranged in chain-like fashion, each introducing a topic that is elaborated upon by the next contributor. We have also tried to present the cases in chronological order, with the aim of indicating how the interconnectedness between Asia and the West advanced throughout the twentieth century, how increasingly complex their relationship has grown, and how the impact of Asia on the culinary culture of the West has expanded. The reappearance of similar issues throughout the book, in chapters dealing with different Asian societies, suggests the global character of the forces at play, and similar local reactions towards these forces, in various processes related to the production and consumption of food in different parts of Asia.

The book opens with the issue of how cultural and national identity can be constructed by internalising foods and forms of consumption introduced from outside, illustrated by the case of Hong Kong. Cheng's chapter explores the origins of the diversity in Hong Kong's food culture, with the recent revival of Chinese tea restaurants as a point of departure. The overview of the culinary history of Hong Kong presented in Cheng's study shows how the development of a diverse food culture was intertwined with the specific political, economic and social conditions of the city. Cheng also demonstrates how food consumption was and still is engaged in the negotiation between internationalisation and nostalgic Chineseness in the process of the making of a Hong Kong identity.

The identity question reappears later in the book, in the two chapters concerning Korea by Pemberton and Walraven. Firstly, Robert Pemberton discusses the countercurrents to globalisation in South Korea, reflected in the revival of the consumption of wild-foods, such as wild-gathered food plants and rice-field grasshoppers. The author argues that alongside the increasing presence of foreign food in Korea a clear tendency towards resisting internationalisation of food habits can be observed. Associations of local food producers, for example, are largely involved in creating and disseminating the popular belief that Korean-grown foods are better for Korean bodies. Moreover, the extensive, and continuously growing, market presence of wild-gathered foods indicates a tendency towards a return to 'traditional' Korean foodways. Contrary to the fact that in the past, food-gathering was caused by necessity, in the contemporary situation eating wild-gathered foods is an expression of nostalgia and the yearning for cultural distinctiveness.

Similarly to the case of Hong Kong, Korean cultural identity is constructed by, at times, absorbing foreign culinary elements and modifying local habits and, at other times, rejecting foreign foods – taking pride in traditional native foodways and yearning nostalgically for their return. The eagerness to join the rest of the world by consuming symbolic representations of the West in the form of Coca-Cola, hamburgers, breakfast cereals etc., is in conflict with the sense of loyalty towards one's own food culture, and the need to cope with the homogenising threat of western economic imperialism. These contradictory inclinations represent the 'homogenisation-heterogenisation' tension so characteristic of contemporary global interaction.

Boudewijn Walraven describes Korean 'cultural nationalism' using the examples of rice, *kimch'i* pickles and dog meat. Walraven argues that despite the decline in the quantity of kimch'i eaten by Koreans in recent decades, its symbolic connotation of national identity has been strengthened. In the instance of the dog meat eating, which is elaborately examined in this chapter, the author demonstrates how certain local customs, even though controversial, manage to resist global pressures. Campaigns of the western animal rights activists against this 'barbaric habit' are seen by many Koreans as an attempt to destroy their culture and are resisted, despite the fact that dog meat is not a very important item in the Korean diet. Walraven's example illustrates not only how food may be used for self-identification, but also how it serves to stigmatise others in multicultural contacts.

The issue of cultural identity presented in these two chapters should not be viewed in complete separation from Korean commercial interests. In fact, farmers and other groups that suffer from the expansion of foreign food imports in Korea are often among those who support and often initiate the local resistance towards the global pressure of competition in international trade.

The relationship between dietary transition and economic profit is extensively examined in the chapter by Adel Den Hartog, where he describes the efforts of the Dutch dairy industry in the early twentieth century to create a new market for their products in colonial Indonesia. Den Hartog explores in detail the health issues involved in this development, pointing towards the increasing influence of governmental authorities on public nutrition at that time. This case study dealing with an early stage of globalisation illustrates the impact of the western food industry on the transition of local foodways in Asia, an issue also raised by the next contributor, Pat Caplan.

Caplan's analysis of middle-class households in Madras deals with the expansion of the western food industry into non-western markets. Caplan's study illustrates the impact of multinational food concerns on patterns of eating in

13

middle-class households in India and consequent changes in local culinary traditions. She argues that India is undergoing 'a revolution in food consumption patterns', which is due mainly to the government's economic liberalisation policies, which enable multinational food companies to enter this large market. On the other hand, the incentives for Indian people to try new kinds of food are very diverse: search for quality and convenience, peer group pressures and the urge to differentiate, but above all, a sense that India has joined the rest of the world.

The following chapter accentuates a strong connection between food, home, and women. Merry White describes young women in contemporary Japan, who demonstrate both the power of marketing and their own agency as they follow food trends and engage in behaviour antithetical to the culturally approved model of nurturance, service, self-denial and domesticity. White deals with the case of an Asian society, one which has already undergone culinary internationalisation, and her main focus is on the social messages that food-related practices transmit, rather than on the culinary changes themselves. In her examination of three sites of food consumption – a cooking demonstration, an Italian restaurant and a convenience store – she exemplifies the rejection or delayed accommodation of the realities of domestic roles, which are seen as unsatisfying.

The last three chapters in the volume follow Asian food as it leaves Asia and travels westwards. Helen Bush and Rory Williams, and Katarzyna Cwiertka describe the foodways of Asians residing in Europe. Anneke Van Otterloo, in turn, explores the transfer of Asian food habits to the native European population, drawing upon the example of the development of the taste for the exotic among the Dutch.

Bush and Williams' case deals with the consumption habits of South Asian migrant communities who have settled in Glasgow. They investigate how considerations of health compare with the social and symbolic importance attached to family hospitality in these communities. A prodigious emphasis on foods and forms of hospitality that migrant and British-born South Asians report as traditional, and which in fact are different from the original habits in South Asia, lead to both excess energy and increased fat intake, and eventually to heart diseases. The case presented in this chapter perfectly illustrates how food serves as a link between identity, health and post-colonial migration.

The emphasis on identity expressed through foodways seems to be characteristic of Asian communities residing outside Asia. This issue, although without the focus on health, is raised again in the next chapter, in which Katarzyna Cwiertka describes the consumption patterns of Japanese expatriates in the Netherlands. She argues that though a stay abroad may enable Japanese people to become better acquainted with foreign foodways, many Japanese residing in the Netherlands tend to make their diet more conservatively 'traditional' than it was in Japan. By consequently removing western-style elements from their meals, they try to assuage the identity crises that they experience abroad, and at the same time they reinforce their Japaneseness, avoiding the future problems of re-accommodating to Japanese life after their return home.

The volume closes with a chapter by Anneke Van Otterloo, in which a new dimension of Asian food is presented – its diffusion among the European population. The case of the assimilation and adaptation of Indonesian and other ethnic cuisines in the Netherlands, described by Van Otterloo, illustrates two social phenomena. In the first place, it demonstrates the transformation of immigrants from Asia from the status of 'outsiders' to 'established' citizens. Secondly, the embracing of Asian food by European consumers symbolically represents, next to the intensification of the global commercial network and the diffusion of Asian cultural elements in the western world, the acknowledgement and enjoyment of ethnic exoticism. One may borrow the phrase of bell hooks: 'within commodity culture, ethnicity becomes spice, seasoning, that can liven up the dull dish that is mainstream white culture' (hooks 1992:21).

Notes

1 See the bibliography for the representative theoretical studies on globalisation.
2 For the contribution of this volume for the study of globalisation see the Afterword.
3 This point has been emphasised by a number of globalisation theorists. See, for example, Tomlinson 1992, Hannerz 1996, and Watson 1997b.
4 For more detailed information concerning the emergence of food industry see, for example, Driver 1983, Den Hartog 1995 and Pyke 1970, 1972.
5 For details on dieting and eating disorders see Levenstein 1993, chapter 3 in Beardsworth and Keil 1997, chapter 5 in Warde 1997, and chapter 6 in Mennell et al. 1992.
6 Of course, the schematic character of the terms 'the West' and 'the rest' should be borne in mind.

1

EATING HONG KONG'S WAY OUT[1]

Cheng Sea-ling

> In understanding the relationship between commodity and person, we
> unearth anew the history of ourselves.
>
> (Mintz 1985:214)

A mixture of tea and coffee blended with condensed milk may not be everyone's
cup of 'tea', but *yùn yèung* – as the mixture is called in Hong Kong – is one of
the things that have survived like a shared secret in the ex-British colony in
South China. Often not listed on the menu, it can be ordered at any of the *chàh
chàan tèng* (lit. 'Tea Restaurants'), or Chinese cafes (Wu 1996) that have become
the icons of the Hong Kong way of life. Chàh chàan tèng can now be found
amongst the Hong Kong migrant communities in, for example, Toronto, New
York and Sidney. With an inexpensive menu and quick service, these restaurants
are very popular among Hong Kong people also for the variety of food that one
can order: a rice dumpling in lotus leaves with a cup of boiled coke with lemon,
or stir-fried spaghetti served with yùn yèung. The cultural significance of yùn
yèung, as well as these restaurants, is maybe their epitomisation of the crossing
of boundaries on both institutional and individual levels.

The readiness to explore across cultural boundaries that has given rise to the
diversity of food culture in Hong Kong should be understood in the context of
Hong Kong's history. As a British colony and a receptacle for migrants from
different parts of China for over 150 years, the populations in Hong Kong have
been engaged in processes dating from 1400 (Wolf 1997 [1982]), in which
'populations impinged upon other populations through permeable social
boundaries, creating integrating, interwoven social and cultural entities. (Wolf
1997 [1982]):71)' It is *not* just a place where 'East meets West', a rhetoric
astutely critiqued by Evans & Tam (1997). It is far more complex than that. The
flows of people, capital, knowledge and skills from different directions into
Hong Kong have expanded and contracted along with the political, social and
economic developments. These diverse forces have worked themselves out in
and onto the social and cultural landscapes of Hong Kong.

This chapter seeks to portray how the development of a diverse food culture is intertwined with the rapid political, social and economic changes in Hong Kong, and how these developments impinge on the way in which the Hong Kong identity has been constructed and negotiated. The first part outlines a history of Hong Kong in relation to the development of food consumption, with reference to political forces such as colonisation, wars and diplomacy; economic developments from an entrepot trade to manufacturing industries and subsequently service industries; changes in social conditions with ethnic division, influx of immigrants, developments in medical services and housing, and the emergence of a locally born middle class. The diversification, stratification, syncretisation and transformation of Hong Kong society and its people find expressions in the patterns of food consumption.

The second part examines the search for a Hong Kong identity that began in the late 1960s and how it has been manifested in the arena of food consumption. The development of herbal tea shops reveals divergent historical and structural forces on the one hand, and the engagement of food and drinks in identity construction on the other. Herbal tea, or *lèuhng chàh* (lit.: 'cooling tea'), is a folk practice of the Chinese medical system, which emphasises the balance between dichotomies of 'hot/cold' and 'wet/dry'.[2] Herbal tea shops provide a convenient venue for people who subscribe to the folk ideas of Chinese medicine to consume the traditional concoctions. The unfolding history of herbal tea shops is an example of how food consumption is engaged in the negotiation between modernity, internationalisation, and a search for nostalgic Chineseness for Hong Kong people, in particular towards the historic return of Hong Kong to China in 1997.

Eating Out Hong Kong's History

Before 1841: The Fishing Village

Hong Kong was only a quiet fishing village with a population of around 4,000 before it was taken over as a British colony. In 1821, the main settlement on Hong Kong island was along the western coast, where lobsters and fish were found in abundance in the area of Sui Hang Hou (*sèui hàang hàu*). This is also the spot where the British fleet landed and raised the first Union Jack in 1841.

Colonialism in South China started in the sixteenth century with the Portuguese taking over Macau as its trading post in East Asia. A large number of East-West exchanges of natural and human resources thus first took place through Macau. In particular, European culinary skills were spread to the Chinese population by missionaries, merchants and Portuguese officials, this occurred through socialising with, and marriage to, Chinese people or through their employment of Chinese individuals as cooks. These people became a valuable source of culinary expertise for their Hong Kong compatriots and were seen to be responsible for the first generation of western cuisine in the British colony.

Hong Kong: The Nineteenth Century Colony

In its initial century as a colony, Hong Kong remained largely a 'refugee city' where the mainland Chinese came for refuge before either returning to the mainland or, after entrepot trade was established, continuing to North America or South East Asia. Waves of immigrants poured into the colony regularly, in particular after unrest such as the Taiping Rebellion in the 1870s. After the founding of Hong Kong, the first wave of immigrants boosted the population to 30,000 by 1845, reaching 110,000 in 1867, and 151,000 in 1881.

The first arrivals from the mainland in the 1840s included labourers and petty merchants. Two immigrants founded the Màhn Móuh Temple on Hong Kong Island in 1847. This became the main communal centre for the Chinese until the Tung Wah Group of Hospitals emerged in late nineteenth century as the unofficial Chinese leadership. One of the two immigrants who founded the temple gained wealth and influence by provisioning the British forces during the Opium War and thereafter investing in local dwellings, gambling houses and brothels (Smith 1971:81 quoted in Lang 1997:253).

In the area west of Sui Hang Hou, where the original settlements were found, the district of Sai Ying Pun (*sài yìnhg pùn*) became the base for these sojourners from the mainland. They frequented the small tea houses, tea stalls and inns, as well as the brothels. In most tea houses, stratification was organised according to the floors: the second and third floors charged double the price of that on the ground floor, which was frequented by labourers and was known as a 'squatting house' (*deih mauh gùn*). More elaborate institutions such as Hahng Fà Làuh, a famous brothel established in 1845, facilitated business transactions and merchant-official agreements by providing food, alcohol and the company of women. Customers would host banquets, called 'drink flower wine' (*yàm fà jàu*), which involved dining, drinking and gambling in the company of courtesans.[3] Sai Ying Pun, westwards to the communal centre in Màhn Móuh Temple, thus thrived with these restaurants and brothels and became a hub of vigour for the Chinese along the western coast of the island.

Foreigners could occasionally be spotted in these predominantly Chinese establishments.[4] Writings and records show that western-style dishes were provided in these restaurants. Residents from Macau arrived in Wanchai (*wàan jái*) opening bars and inns, as well as brothels catering mainly to sailors. Amongst these Chinese migrants were experienced chefs with western cooking skills. Due to the strong ethnic boundaries, the Chinese population in Hong Kong was thus introduced to western cuisine not directly from their colonisers, but by Chinese compatriots who had already been exposed to these external influences.

Hong Kong Before 1941

The expansion of social and culinary lives took place socially and geographically. The flow of people and resources from the mainland increased, in particular from Guangzhou (*gwóng jàu*) but also from northern cities like Shanghai. Europeans and Americans arrived not only from their own countries, but also via China. The tram system was laid in 1904, connecting the western and eastern parts of the island along the coast, boosting expansion towards Central and Wanchai. The food scene in the beginning of twentieth century was thus marked by 1) the enrichment of local foodways from both Chinese and Western influences; 2) the stratification of eating and drinking establishments along both ethnic and class boundaries.

The first century of colonial rule had been marked by strict racial distinction between the Chinese and Europeans in terms of economic activity, residence and entertainment. The Chinese community was geographically separated from the European community, with the former's economic activities being limited to the western part of the island, while the latter community being free to expand into Central. In 1867, Chinese merchants established Na Pei Hong (*nàahm bak hohng*), a company that focused on North-South trade with mainland China, marking the realisation of their economic ambitions. In the 1870s, the Chinese were allowed to purchase the failing businesses of foreigners, and the fiercely guarded ethnic boundary gradually became blurred. The Peak, however, where a panoramic view of the harbour and the Kowloon Peninsula could be enjoyed, was an exclusively European residential area (with the exception of servants) with its own church, club and hospital (Lethbridge 1969:89–90). A District Reservation Ordinance of 1904 stipulated that no Chinese could reside in the Peak area. While foreigners were free to roam the Chinese parts of the island and visit their restaurants, the Chinese were not admitted to the Hong Kong Club, founded in 1846 in Central which served the social and welfare needs of all 'non-Chinese'.[5] The distinctions and hierarchy of colonialism could here be clearly seen.

After 1900, many Guangzhou restaurateurs started businesses in Hong Kong, bringing with them specially prepared abalone, shark's fin and other Guangzhou delicacies. They opened tea houses which served delicacies in small portions called *dim sum* (lit. 'touch heart') with tea. The Luk Yu Tea House, still a famous institution today, was opened in 1923. A whole dim sum culture evolved, indulging customers with an ever-changing range of creative dim sums. Weekly specials of dim sum were the basis for inter-restaurant competition. Chinese restaurants began to be found in Sheung Wan (*séuhng wàahn*), Des Veoux Road, and Wanchai. The Ying King Grand Restaurant in Wanchai was frequented by the Chinese elite. The foundations of 'Cantonese cuisine' were thus laid with large-scale importation of capital, skills and human resources from Guangzhou.

The government sought to clear Central of the influence of the 'vices' in 1903 and ordered the brothels to move westwards to Sek Tong Tsui (*sehk tòhng jéui*). The restaurants followed. Businesses continued to thrive and thus the period known as 'Indulgence West of the (Sek) Tong (Tsui)' (*Tòhng sài fùng yuht*) began. Yet a further decree in 1935 outlawed prostitution in Hong Kong, subsequently ending the colourful life of this part of the island. The fall of the west thus contributed further to the spread of activity towards the east.

While the Chinese elites, like those from the Tung Wah Group of Hospitals, frequented Ying King Grand Restaurants and famous tea houses and brothels, the less fortunate found their niche in ordinary tea houses and street stalls. During the 1910s, a type of tea stall with dressy young girls arose in Fourth Street in Sai Ying Pun, where the male customers could find piecemeal satisfaction for their sexual and culinary appetites. Though these tea stalls were soon wiped out after repeated complaints of indecency to the government, they illustrate how food and sex were related across class levels, and how both were accessible to different consumers.

Western-style restaurants catering to Chinese (meaning smaller number of dishes and smaller portions) also sprouted. Examples include the Wellington Restaurant and Man Yuen (New) Restaurant in Central, with daily set meals as their major attractions. Advertisements for these restaurants' set meals[6] boasted eight items, always including soup, a fish special and a rice dish, and ending with tea or coffee. These items remained at the core, while trimmed versions of the set meal developed later on. Meanwhile, westerners arriving from Shanghai opened restaurants catering to Europeans and Americans. Jimmy's Kitchen (founded 1928), still as robust and famous as the old enclave of the colonial elite, was opened first in Wanchai, then in Central.

A blurring of the ethnic boundaries thus took place through food, mainly in the form of the Chinese adoption of non-Chinese foodstuffs, the syncretisation of Chinese and European traditions, and the consumption of these foods. Foreigners imported exotic foodstuffs and attempted to reserve exclusive access to them before a process of localisation or popularisation by Chinese merchants, as in the case of ice (the first batch of which was imported in 1843), carbonated drinks (brought in by the Dutch in 1850) and ice cream (first arrival from Manila in 1900). Merchants and the middle class, while not admitted to places of European exclusivity, started patronising both western-style restaurants like the Wellington and grand Chinese restaurants such as Ying King in Wanchai. From the exclusive European meals served at the Hong Kong Club to the differentially syncretised western style restaurants around the island, a decentralisation and stratification of cuisine could be seen together with much incorporation and modification by the Hong Kong Chinese.

For the majority of the Chinese population, however, health was a constant problem and medical services were never adequate. Another influx of refugees caused by Sino-Japanese hostilities only led to the further 'aggravation of the various public health problems such as overcrowding, malnutrition and epidemic disease' (Hong Kong Report 1938:23). The masses relied on traditional Chinese herbal medicine for their health problems. The Taoist temple honouring Wong Tai Sin, the 'Refugee God' (Lang and Ragvald 1993), gained a large following by offering prescriptions with limited free herbal medicine (Lang & Ragvald 1993:44). Wong Lo Kat herbal tea shop, first founded in Guangzhou, went into business in 1897 in front of the Màhn Móuh Temple and moved to Aberdeen Street in Central in 1915. Wong Lo Kat appealed to the masses with its medicinal concoctions at the affordable price of one cent per cup. Making a name for itself, packaged tea was sold as Wong Lo Kat Medical Tea locally and overseas to 'Europe, England, America, Holland, and various ports of the South Pacific' (Wong 1987:44).

The first hundred years in the colony thus saw the concretisation of an ethnic boundary establishing the superiority of the British colonialists over the Chinese. Active trading and exchange brought wealth and material advancement to the people, who had access to a much greater range of foodstuffs than a century before. Such expansion was accompanied by the internal diversification of the two growing communities, as can be seen in the hierarchy of the eating venues that were established.

1941–1948: The Japanese Occupation and its Aftermath

The Japanese occupation not only caused further aggravation for the masses, but also interrupted British colonial rule and provided a new impetus for members of the Chinese population to strive for their own control.

In many ways, the Japanese occupation caused great misery to more than 1,846,000 people, many of whom tried in vain to escape from Japanese aggression on the mainland (Lethbridge 1969). Food was scarce and medical services dwindled. Government rations were severely limited and became non-existent towards the end of the occupation. Starvation and cannibalism were recorded in many memoirs of the period. People added to their very meagre diet of congee by fishing, eating sweet potatoes and their roots, or buying leftover food from the Japanese military, which often included cigarette butts, toothpicks etc. Wong Lo Kat herbal tea shops' business thrived during this time of collective crisis: 'Ordinary hospitals, both private and public, were fully occupied, and most people could not afford the costs of private doctors, naturally they came for a glass or two and bought some packaged tea home in case of sudden needs' (Wong 1987:120). Even 'Japanese soldiers and their families relied on Wong Lo Kat herbal tea to cure diseases' (Wong 1987:120). Herbal tea thus became the only substance the masses could depend on for managing their own health.

The defeat of the British, however, helped erode the supremacy of the colonialists over their Chinese subjects. The British surrender of Hong Kong to Japan and the internment of the British as prisoners of war for almost four years were certainly a blow to their pride and sense of mission. The Japanese propaganda campaign against (western) colonialism and colour prejudice boosted the Chinese, or at least the powerful businessmen's, sense of confidence. The Chinese flags that waved to the incoming British fleet in 1945 (Donnison 1956 quoted in Lethbridge 1969) may be interpreted as an implicit rejection of the British.

Those who emerged relatively unscathed from the occupation gained a new sense of power, like the local deity Wong Tai Sin and the Wong Lo Kat herbal tea shops. The Chinese, who witnessed the humiliation of the British, were now more ready to defend and assert their rights and interests. They found that the most effective way to gain power and status was by developing their economic strength. It was on this basis that rapid developments took place in the next two decades, marking an era of rapid change initiated by the Chinese population.

1949–1969: Rapid Diversification and the Beginning of Modernity

The post-war influx of immigrants in the 1950s from different parts of China and Southeast Asia brought with it a diversity of knowledge, skills, capital and culinary patterns. The economic structure underwent drastic changes with the end of entrepot trade, as a result of the trade embargo on Chinese goods following the outbreak of the Korean War, and the beginning of local industries. With added investment from the new waves of migrants fleeing China, the growth of an industrial economy supported a permanent labour force rather than casual workers, and a white-collar middle class began to emerge. Agriculture declined in relation to industrial development. Traditional wet-rice cultivation changed to the cultivation of vegetables and pig and poultry husbandry. The influx of people into the city further reduced the proportion of the rural population. Less than 7% of the working population was engaged in farming, forestry and fishing in 1961. Economic stability improved material conditions and social mobility. Thus a diversified urban society developed with increased yearnings for modern tastes and comforts.

Regional and class diversification was necessarily reflected in the food scene. Diverse culinary skills and knowledge came with well-trained chefs from other regions. The first high-class Pekingese restaurant, Yin Wàahn Làuh was opened in 1950. Many Shanghainese restaurants were also founded, and some of their names like Lo Ching Hing (*lóuh jing hing*) have persisted until the present day. Szechuanese, Fukienese and Hunanese also found their own markets. Malaysian cuisine was also brought by the wave of Chinese people who fled from the anti-Chinese movements in Malaysia in the 1950s. Restaurants serving Malaysian and Nonya (Chinese-Malaysian) cuisine were opened, introducing a South East Asian flavour to the Hong Kong food scene. These variant Chinese cuisines not only broadened culinary choices, but were also sources of syncretisation for the Cantonese cuisine in Hong Kong.

Shanghainese immigrants brought with them much capital, skills, entrepreneurship, as well as Russian and European foodways. Russian foods like borscht and chicken Kiev have retained their importance into the 1990s in most local western restaurants. The White Russians and their culinary skills came with the influx from Shanghai. The 88-year-old owner of Queen's Cafe, one of the two Russian restaurants left, learnt his art from a Russian chef in Shanghai in the 1920s (*South China Morning Post*, 20 October 1994). Russian restaurants, with names like Cherikoff, Chantecler, and Tkachenko, became prominent in the 1950s. Grills, curries and barbecues at Victor's Restaurant, European food and Italian and French wines at the Parisian Grill on Queen's Road, American steaks at Gingle's on Nathan Road, as well as the cuisines of the many hotel restaurants and bars, constituted the range of modern 'western-style' establishments that the city spawned. The localisation of western cuisine in various Chinese-owned restaurants was epitomised in the term *sih yàuh sài chàan*, literally meaning 'soy sauce western meals'.

A new leisure pattern and a leisure class emerged. An advertisement for the Dairy Farm chain of restaurants and soda fountains in a 1950 guidebook boasted of their 'variety of foreign-style dishes' across Hong Kong Island, the Kowloon Peninsula and the New Territories.[7] This geographical spread of eating venues reflected the extension of people's mobility as well as their leisure patterns. More people in Hong Kong could afford a trip beyond the city centre and enjoy a soda or coffee at a fashionable restaurant. Beer also became a popular drink and was manufactured by San Miguel locally as well as imported from the mainland from Tsingtao, where the Germans first set up a beer factory. The first regular gourmet column[8] by Chàhn Muhng Yàn in *Sing Tao Daily News* further confirmed the rise of a leisure class and a greater sophistication in the appreciation of food.

Yet lower down the hierarchy, the majority of Hong Kong people were struggling to make a living in cramped tenement housing in the fifties. The influx of immigrants brought even greater population pressure to the already poor living conditions. Overcrowding made the 'home' most unattractive and literally forced people onto the streets. Street stalls arose to cater to those people who did not have their own cooking space. Entertainment and other services came among these food stalls, giving rise to the 'Poor People's Night Club' on Hollywood Road. Herbal tea shops became an important social centre for the masses in search of space and connections to others as well as to the world beyond.

The installation of radios since 1948,[9] jukeboxes in the 1950s, and television sets since 1958 made herbal tea shops a favourite place for the common people for whom little entertainment was available. Radios and television sets were luxuries beyond the means of ordinary people. By paying ten cents per drink, people old and young could enjoy their favourite broadcast programmes in the company of others. Jukeboxes were a major attraction for the younger generation who would socialise and dance to western music played at their choice for ten cents a record. With these modern technological devices being made accessible at herbal tea shops, people gathered and shared a glimpse of their own society and the outside world.

This was the time when Hong Kong seemed to have suddenly taken over the role of Shanghai as the 'nerve-centre of western enterprise in the Far East,' where status could be gained more by money than by position or rank (Lethbridge 1969:79). Local manufacturing and export became major economic activities and ended Hong Kong's role as a transit lounge for goods and people. Media productions increasingly drew on local experiences, the exposure through trade and media to the international world and western ways of life as models of modernity stimulated an awareness of Hong Kong identity. Communist virulence exposed in the Cultural Revolution further prompted a rejection of mainland China. Hong Kong people started to identify their place as a modern international city in the making, a development foretold by the range of food offered at the Gold Fish Restaurant in 1950 (Ng 1988:13): 'dim sum, snake soup, game, roast duck, Portuguese chicken, smoked fish, shark's fin, comprador soup,[10] ice cream, cream cake'.

1969–84: The Rise of the Modern Metropolis

This was the era when the first generation of locally born Chinese matured and participated in the economic boom. It was the time when a local Hong Kong identity was substantiated. Their vague sense of Chineseness had a more imagined quality than that of their parents, who had actually lived on the mainland, and had experienced all the political upheavals. Instead, they were the ones who had been exposed to images of James Dean, The Beatles, hippies, miniskirts, Lucky Strike cigarettes and other icons of modernity in the 1960s, a genre of icons that continued to proliferate with the popularisation of television in the 1970s. The Government initiated programmes for the improvement of social conditions, in particular housing. Hong Kong entered the spotlight of international stage as a financial centre. Prospects for economic development were promising and overall living conditions improved. Television sets became a necessity rather than luxury. The grounds for the search of a modern cosmopolitan Hong Kong identity were laid, as shown in the vigorous diversification and internationalisation of the eating out culture of Hong Kong people.

Icons of modernity in the form of fast food shops began to pop up around 1970. Both local and foreign corporations joined the race. The first fast food shop with bright, clean and modern decor was Cafe de Carol, opened in 1969 serving both Chinese (e.g. soy sauce chicken wings and thighs) and western snacks (e.g. sandwiches). Maxim's fast food followed suit in 1971. Self-service was not introduced until 1974 and special personnel had to be appointed to guide customers with the procedures. The first golden arches of McDonald's arrived in 1974, followed by Kentucky Fried Chicken and Burger King.

At local western restaurants, 'western meals' were popular as a set with cream soup served with a roll and butter, sizzling steaks served on hot grills, followed by tea (with milk or lemon) or coffee in air-conditioned restaurants. At Christmas and New Year, western restaurants became immensely popular by serving up set menus with ten to twelve items – soup, salad, cold cuts, turkey, steak, jelly, cake – all in small portions, together with a present for every child customer. As a child then, instead of praying to Santa Claus for a Christmas present, I would be praying frantically every year that my father would take me to a Christmas dinner. And that if this happened, let him bring me to a 'proper' western restaurant, not one of those Singaporean and Malaysian restaurants that started dishing up Christmas dinners in the late 1970s. These eating rituals were important in popularising a consumerist consciousness, especially among the young, of these western festivities and foodways.

Internationalisation was the theme of the 1970s. Experiencing new things became a continuous goal and a possibility for the economically sound. The number of outbound tourists spiralled and was complemented by the influx of visitors. Diversification and specialisation became necessary to satisfy the appetite for new dining experiences to match an international orientation. Hotel grillrooms started to open up to non-hotel guests, catering to the 'westernised' and the well-to-do. French restaurants represented the finesse of taste in the 1970s and were commonly found in upper-class hotels. From 1980 onwards, a series of food events initiated the catering industry to continuously search for special cuisines or specialists. In 1980, representatives from Shandong, Hubei, Yunnan, Chekiang, Tientsin and Kwangsi were invited by the Miramar Hotel to exhibit their culinary skills. The Hilton Hotel, the Mandarin Oriental Hotel and Maxim's Restaurants organised various Szechuanese and Hangchou banquets. European and American restaurants, in and out of hotels, began to invite world famous foreign chefs as guest chefs. A range of Asian cuisines – in particular Japanese, Korean, Vietnamese and Thai – also found their own niche in the local market in the 1980s.

Conspicuous consumption thrived with burgeoning economic growth. Ostentatious décor plus expensive tastes became another winning formulae. The Jumbo Floating Seafood Restaurant in Aberdeen became a symbol of Hong Kong extravagance, where diners could enjoy the local catch in the glamour of a floating palace. Abalone, shark's fin and high-priced seafood were consumed in great quantity and frequency, giving rise to numerous sharks' fin and seafood restaurants.

A Hong Kong identity distinct from that of the mainland Chinese or Taiwanese could be discerned in the mass media. Cantonese pop songs triumphed over mandarin tunes and gained popularity with lyrics that signified a local identity and a common aspiration. Television drama series represented Hong Kong's success as a result of its hardworking, intelligent and virtuous people. In 1979, in a television drama series, the character A Can, a mainland immigrant, was ridiculed as a dumb and greedy country bumpkin. In one scene, he was challenged by his Hong Kong friends to eat 30 hamburgers in one go. They promised him a sum of money if he accomplished the feat. A Can devoured the hamburgers in mounting pain as his friends watched on and roared in laughter. The blind pursuit of modernity and money stereotypically associated with the mainland Chinese in the 1970s was personified in A Can – the glutton, the avaricious and the fool all in one, all that Hong Kong people were not. The pejorative stereotyping of mainlanders evident in the 'A Can syndrome' arose out of a new local consciousness, embedded in a new relationship with the mainland – the sense of identification and accommodation before the Cultural Revolution vanished, 'replaced by a resentment of economic migrants from the Mainland who became objects of mirth' (Cheng Yu quoted in Lilley 1993:278).

In less than a decade, Hong Kong was successfully transformed into a cosmopolitan city with a mixture of high and low cuisines from various corners of the world. Fast food, eclectic tastes, fine dining and ostentatious decor are the diverse façades of a modern palate with an international orientation. Dominant discourses of internationalisation, scientism and conspicuous consumption were fundamentally opposed to the folkloric and traditional as represented by the herbal tea shops. This was also a period when the boundary between the public and the private was strengthened as household space and resources increased. Public space, communal television sets, and neighbourhood community as once provided by herbal tea shops became less necessary and attractive. The quest for a modern Hong Kong identity necessarily led to the rejection of the traditional.

1985–1997: The Modern Chinese in Hong Kong

Hong Kong underwent a political and cultural awakening with the signing of the Joint Declaration by the British and Chinese governments in 1984. The search for a Chinese identity, which Hong Kong people could comfortably hold onto while maintaining their international profile finds expression in consumer culture. As the approach to the handover drew closer, these impulses were soon joined by an urge to rediscover 'authentic' Hong Kong. In the same period, spiralling estate prices created immense pressure on eateries to minimise food costs and maximise customers' spending. A new health consciousness reified 'natural' foods and advocated a modern approach to the body. As a result, Hong Kong people found consolation in a nostalgic Chineseness that accommodated vigorous diversification.

Economics governed certain ways in which the catering industry developed. Increased food costs coupled with skyrocketing rents led to the employment of economies of scale and the high turnover of customers as the way out. High-status delicacies became even less affordable, and a general shift towards cheaper, but more exotic tastes was witnessed. Eateries serving Chiuchow cuisine, with their use of simple and low cost ingredients, rose from the ruins of many seafood and sharks' fin restaurants. Chain restaurants run by large corporations have replaced many independent establishments. With bulk purchases and packaging, restaurateurs teased appetites with previously inaccessible delicacies, as chains of sharks' fin restaurants boasted: 'Mixing shark's fin with rice?'[11] Shark's fin and birds' nest set meals at low prices became the essential family dine-out experience and were immensely popular between 1994–1996. Food festivals and promotions of various exotic culinary ideas have become a must for many to attract customers, while buffets of all sorts have been introduced to save costs. The popular desire for what was

Figure 1.1 A neon sign of Hong Kong's cosmopolitan palate in Lan Kwai Fong.

considered good and exotic persisted if not intensified, but was to be fulfilled only on the condition of reasonable prices.

A consciousness of health and body figure mounted in scale and influence towards the 1990s and Chinese medicine was looked at more positively than ever before in the 1990s. Eating 'healthy' and 'natural' means a diet free of fat, sugar, cholesterol, MSG (monosodium glutamate), artificial colouring, and so on. Health clubs and gyms proliferated and set up a new regimen of body management. Many Chinese restaurants began to advertise their MSG-free cuisine with 'lite' dishes, often detailing the medicinal effects of their dishes according to Chinese medical beliefs. Yat Chau Health Restaurant – with its own restaurant, Chinese herbalist to consult and prescribe medication, and herbal medicine shop – was an institutionalisation of the Chinese concepts of health and diet, proclaiming a legitimate status for Chinese medicine not available at a governmental level.

The emergence of a syncretic 'New-Style' Chinese cuisine can be interpreted as a culinary response to the need for negotiation between the global and the local in the context of Hong Kong. Gaining popularity in middle and high-end restaurants, this New Style Chinese cuisine was analysed by a prolific gourmet writer (Ng 1988) to have the following features: 1. creativity with ingredients from cuisines of different ethnicities and nationalities; 2. the use and distinction of utensils and general aesthetics in eating different foods; and 3. the health qualities of food, especially concerning the use of natural and light ingredients. A look at the menus in Chinese restaurants since the early 1990s supports his analysis of the new trend, as most contained at least one or two exotic dishes like 'Strawberry Spare Ribs', 'Kiwi Fruit Stir-Fried with Chicken', or 'Macadamia Nuts stir-fried with diced Chicken and Vegetables'.

However, there was no explanation of the prominent trend for Chinese nostalgia that began with the new eateries. Gone are the conspicuous symbols of grandeur – crystal chandeliers, huge golden dragon and phoenix sculptures with glittering red bulb-eyes dancing against an auspicious background of crimson velvet. In came the icons of gentility – modest mahogany furniture, Chinese calligraphy and paintings of mountains and rivers. Chinese motifs and literary classics are increasingly mobilised to market modern consumer products. The theme of 'romancing with the past' is so dominant that a thesis of diversification and syncretisation fails to explain this development adequately. It is necessary to examine such changes in the light of an ambiguity towards Chineseness in the construction of a Hong Kong identity.

Nostalgia and Cultural Identity

Herbal tea shops made a come back in the 1980s as one of the pioneers of the nostalgic movement, which usually blends in an appeal to Nature. The new wave of herbal tea shops adopt names reminiscent of a traditional world that customers could be assured of their Chinese origins – Hui Lau Shan (*héui làuh sàan* – a famous herbal tea shop in Yuen Long, New Territories before the 1970s), Hung Fook Tong (*hùhng fuk tòhng*),[12] Po Chi Lam (*bóu jì làhm* – a famous charitable Chinese clinic in Fo Shan) are some prominent ones. Motifs of Chineseness abound – gold-plated name tablet hung high at the centre of the shop's front, golden bell-shaped Taoist urns, wooden furniture, Chinese calligraphy and paintings constitute an unmistakably 'Chinese' feel. Décor that foregrounds nature is also common, suggesting a rustic life of peace and simplicity. The chain of Best Herbal Tea Shops adopts a dominant green shade, displays medicinal herbs and has a running waterwheel in every shop front. Such décor creates an illusory world of leisure, refinement and harmonic coexistence with Nature, where enchantment in a 'disenchanted world' (Weber 1958) can be found.

Health concerns guided the diversification of herbal tea shops, while high rents demanded a constant flow of customers who are always on the look out for the new and trendy. The old repertoire of herbal tea shops was revolutionised to fall in line with the global health trend. Papaya milk with Chinese herbs and turtle jelly with American ginseng are just some of the new variations. Herbal teas have been sidelined by freshly squeezed and blended fruit juices and desserts. Hui Lau Shan prospered with their sago fruit mix and expanded to almost 40 branches between 1992–94. Herbal tea shops have turned into health food halls that combine previously distinct businesses – herbal tea shop, fruit stall and dessert store all-in-one.[13] A diversified palate, increased consumption of snacks, modern health concerns, and a demand for stylish décor made herbal tea shops *the* place to visit in between shopping trips, after movies or between meals for the modern consumer.

Simultaneously, the romance with Chineseness and Nature found its way into not only the restaurant trade, but also into the architectural and fashion businesses. The traditional décor typified by herbal tea shops was replicated to different degrees in Chinese restaurants like Ah Yee Leng Tong (lit. 'Great Soups of No. 2 (wife)') and Big Bowl Congee. Chinese literary and medicinal classics are increasingly cited as evidence of the 'natural' and 'traditional' goodness of their delicacies. The chief targets of all these eateries are local Chinese; foreigners are conspicuous by their absence. This nostalgia soon spread to those businesses that have a significant share in the foreigners' and overseas market. An upmarket transnational department store also played with motifs of Chineseness – on one hand adopted the look of a grand Shanghai tailor shop and the name of 'Shanghai Tang', redolent of the glories of the old metropolitan, on the other used simplified Chinese characters (popularised under the Communist regime) suggestive of another 'Chineseness'. Their products include clothes with cuttings of the late Ching and Republican period, but modified into glaring bright yellow, green and other glistening colours.

The 'Chinese' image is more important than the content for these enterprises. It is the 'Chineseness' – rather than the efficacy of a tea or authenticity of a design – which is cherished in the consumption experience. In this 'new trend', one can witness an active reconstruction of the 'past', a kind of fantasy world in which Hong Kong people could find an affirmation of their Chinese identity. The owner of Po Chi Lam insisted that the décor is not a return to the past, but part of the 'new trend'. Herbal tea shops are no longer 'old-fashioned' – they have been renewed and transformed by embracing nostalgia. As Robert Nisbet writes, 'Nostalgia tells us more about present moods than about past realities' (cited in Davis 1979:10).

The mood since the Joint Declaration in 1984 has been one of 'fears, discontents, anxieties, or uncertainties', as witnessed by the rise of *fùng séui* (geomancy) and astrology that have sprung up from the depths of popular culture to become dominant discourses in the search for meaning and control (Evans 1997). Nostalgia is part of 'an attempt to abort or, at the very least, deflect' the threat of identity discontinuity (Davis 1979:108). The Hong Kong metropolitan identity has to be renegotiated with its Chinese 'roots'. Those who are most affected by the uncertainty of the transition, namely the younger generations whose futures are closely bound up with the political future of Hong Kong, are also the most active participants in the nostalgia. That there is no active discovery of what contemporary China has to offer is a sign of reservation about the impending identity. What has been retrieved from the archives of Chinese culture is the familiar and the folkloric, 'stereotypes which endow present reality with ... the spell and distance of a glossy mirage' (Lilley 1993:267). It is nostalgia for a fictional rather than a specific past. It is also a collective nostalgia removed of any political or nationalist sentiments or content. Hong Kong's colonial experience is unique in that the end of colonialism does not engender much prospect of independence or autonomy, but a mere transfer of sovereign power to a state that most have learnt to distrust. When reality has little to offer, it seems, Hong Kong people take the active step to search for the folkloric and idyllic.

That is not to say that the shaping of a Hong Kong identity is consummated by the search for Chineseness alone in the run-up to the 1997 handover. Identity is a relational process in which individuals draw on available resources and symbols in the course of interactions with others within broader cultural parameters. In addition to the search for a Chinese cultural identity, cosmopolitanism and localism are two other paradigms that modern Hong Kong people draw on in the construction and experience of a Hong Kong identity. Cosmopolitanism, with all its varieties and levels (Hannerz 1990:239),[14] operates in such a way that individuals set out to seek diverse cultural experiences, whether for the internationalisation of the self, or to enjoy eclectic consumption and greater plurality of lifestyle (Clammer 1997:99). The development of Lan Kwai Fong into the hub for expatriates, young urban Chinese professionals and aspiring trend-setters since the 1970s is an illustration of cosmopolitanism as well as patterns of cross-cultural relations in Hong Kong (Cheng 1996a). Lan Kwai Fong (*Fig 1.1*) is known not only in its vast range of 'ethnic' bars and restaurants, from Thai and Vietnamese street stalls to exquisite Italian restaurants, but also as a place for assuming and experiencing a different lifestyle, even temporarily. Popular fascination with Lan Kwai Fong can be seen in the New Year's Eve tragedy in 1993. 23 people were trampled to death as 10,000 people crowded into the two streets that made up Lan Kwai Fong. Most of these people were young people and non-regulars who went to experience a different 'culture'.

In the march up to the transfer of sovereignty from the British to the Chinese on 1st July, 1997, the media, the arts, and the academia were saturated with debates on 'Hong Kong identity' and 'Hong Kong culture'. Historical archives were dug up, pictures, first and second-hand narratives of historic events like the Japanese occupation and confrontations with the colonial government in the 1966–1967 riots paraded for public consumption and reflection, reminding the audience of a history forgotten, giving depth to both a public memory and the question of 'Who are we?' As with all identity rhetorics, a specific past is recalled and reinterpreted in the present so as to conjure a vision for the future. Localism concerns itself with a search for what is 'unique' and 'authentic' in Hong Kong in relation to the larger corpus of Chinese culture, elements that defy the state discourses on a Chinese national culture emanating from Beijing (Siu 1993 quoted in Evans 1997:14). The Chàh chàan tèng (tea restaurant) finds a spruced up version in the Dai Pai Dong (lit. 'Street stalls') chain of restaurants, this time with yùn yèung (tea mixed with coffee) clearly stated in the menu that talks of 'old Hong Kong'. Local traditions have also been 'invented' to give uniqueness to Hong Kong's history. Watson (1998) examined the marketing of *sihk puhn* ('eating-pot'), a communal eating ritual practised only in the villages of the New Territories (Watson 1976), re-invented as an 'authentic' local tradition. Marketing professionals repackaged and rearticulated *sihk puhn* as *the* traditional Hong Kong food. The ingredients of the 1970s – turnips, huge pieces of pigs' skin and pigs' fat have been replaced by abalones, oysters, sea cucumber and other delicacies. A sanitised and upgraded version of the common pot as the 'authentic' Hong Kong experience has thus been ushered into five-star hotels and high-class Chinese restaurants since 1996, drawing in curious consumers, both local and foreign.

However, under the impending re-unification with China, the underlying theme in all these developments is the negotiation of a Chinese identity to which the Chinese-nationals-to-be could lay claim. In this way, the phenomenon that has been illustrated should be understood in the following light: 'nostalgia is a distinctive way ... of relating our past to our present and future ... nostalgia is deeply implicated in the sense of who we are, what are we about, and ... whither we go' (Davis 1979:31).

We are More *and* Less Chinese...

Mintz has argued that there is no American cuisine as such because of the heterogeneity of origins and thus the lack of a 'background of commonly recognized foods' (1996:116). In the US, the consumer impulse to try new things for sophistication and the entrepreneurial vigour to introduce novelty foods for profit conjures up a cornucopia of exotic food choices. Yet this diversity does not create a cuisine that needs 'a community of people who eat it, cook it, have opinions about it, and engage in dialogue involving those opinions' (1996:117). Similarly, Hong Kong people are proud of our food culture, but rarely do we speak of a 'Hong Kong cuisine', a term which interestingly is finding its way into the sea of Chinese restaurants abroad. The pride lies in the availability of quality food, especially Cantonese Chinese, as well as the diversity of choices that mirrors Hong Kong's international profile, *not* in a distinct cuisine unique to Hong Kong. It is an assertion that we are more *and* less Chinese in Hong Kong. This echoes Evans & Tam's interpretation of the Hong Kong people's self-description as *Heung Gong Yahn* (Hong Kong people), a term they found so 'redolent with local meaning' that made it 'ultimately untranslatable into English': 'It not only signifies a life-style, but also something more than a resident yet less than a people' (1997:9).

At different nexuses of history, a different dialogue and debate of culture takes place, informing individuals of their multiple positions and possibilities. In the post-handover era, the boundaries between Hong Kong and the mainland have become more blurred than ever. The flow of people and resources across the border escalated in volume and frequency – Hong Kong people are not only crossing borders for business, but are also shopping and dining, even commuting to work everyday on the Kowloon-Canton Railway; housewives go for cheaper food and groceries; families go for sumptuous meals at much lower prices. The psychological distance between 'here' and 'there' has become much shorter compared to twenty years ago, when 'going back to China' was a major event usually for family reunions. Does this, however, also shorten the distance between 'us' and 'them'?

Just as the early migrant population identify differently with mainland China from their children born and bred in Hong Kong, the cultural identity of those brought up in the transition will also differ. Colonial Hong Kong before the handover has never entertained a nationalistic agenda. Re-unification with China has necessitated changes in the apolitical nature of Hong Kong culture: for a start, the Chinese national anthem (Revolutionary Song) and flag-raising ceremony have been introduced into primary and secondary schools. While I grew up in the 1970s rejecting herbal tea shops, craved for 'western meals', never learnt *Putonghua* (Beijing Chinese) at school and did not sing the national anthem until 1989, my youngest brother, who was born in 1986 and became an active consumer in the 1990s, loves the sago fruit mix from Hui Lau Shan, has a taste for ravioli and paella, speaks passable Putunghua and was singing the national anthem at the age of 11.

The 1998 television commercial of Wong Lo Kat carton herbal tea may illustrate some of the subtle changes that are taking place. In the commercial, four university graduates (in graduation gowns) were discussing their post-graduation travel, each holding a beverage in hand. As three of the students holding canned beverages shared their plans to go to Paris, Japan and New York for career development, the remaining (male) student replied, looking skywards after a sip from his carton of Wong Lo Kat herbal tea, 'Talking about good things. China has everything that others have, so why don't we stay in our own place?' The commercial finished with two lines written in large Chinese characters on the right side of the screen, 'Looking Out to the World, Linking Our Hearts to the Fatherland' and on the left, 'The Spirit of the New Times'. In this new era, the romantic engagement with a Chinese past is gradually transformed into a recognition of the Chinese nation and its rich resources, as well as one's own role in its development. A new dialogue has begun with the past, the world, and 'Chineseness' in the shadow of the old.

Notes

1 This chapter is rewritten from a chapter of the author's Masters thesis 'Hong Kong on a Plate' (1996) and a publication on the cultural history of herbal tea shops (Cheng 1997).
2 Medicinal as well as thirst quenching, herbal tea is commonly consumed in the southern coasts of China where hot and humid weather predisposes its inhabitants to 'overheating'.
3 Similar practices were found by Hershatter (1997:94–5) in her study of prostitution in Shanghai in the early twentieth century.
4 Travel records of Chinese official Ho Siu Kei include an observation of 'red hair' – Caucasians – in these restaurants.
5 Only a selected few, e.g. Sir Robert Ho Tung, who had substantial financial and social capital, could move freely between the top of the two worlds.
6 For example, in *Wah Kiu Yat Po* (14/1/1927).
7 Namely, Gloucester Hotel, Windsor House, Repulse Bay, Shek O, Castle Peak, Airport, Hong Kong Ferry Pier and Nathan Road.
8 Goody (1984) has examined the importance of writings about food and recipes in the formation of elite culture.
9 Rediffusion (Hong Kong) Limited received a government franchise in 1948 to operate a wired broadcasting system.
10 Comprador soup gained its name by being a favourite of the go-betweens for Chinese and foreign traders. One way to demonstrate their wealth and status was to enjoy the western cream soup with the Chinese delicacy of shark's fin. This information was provided by Mr. Harold Yung, who has worked in the hotel and catering industry for over 20 years, and was a general manager at a major hotel in Hong Kong during 1996.
11 A parody of the saying 'Mixing soy sauce with rice' which denotes poverty. Shark's fin is a banquet food that should be consumed without a staple. Referring to someone who eats 'shark's fin mixed with rice', reducing shark's fin to the status of a side dish, means that s/he is extremely rich.
12 The word *tòhng* means hall, as used in *chi tòhng* – ancestral hall.
13 Diversification took place at the expense of violating the Urban Services Department's regulations on herbal tea shops, which permitted the sale of a limited range of traditional concoctions.
14 'In its concern with the Other, cosmopolitanism thus becomes a matter of varieties and levels. Cosmopolitans can be dilettantes as well as connoisseurs, and are often both, at different times. But the willingness to become involved with the Other, and the concern with achieving competence in cultures that are initially alien, is related to considerations of self as well. Cosmopolitanism often has a narcissistic streak; the self is constructed in the space where cultures mirror one another' (Hannerz 1990:239-240).

2

ACCEPTANCE OF MILK PRODUCTS IN SOUTHEAST ASIA

The case of Indonesia as a traditional non-dairying region

Adel P. Den Hartog

Introduction

This chapter deals with the question of the introduction of milk products, in particular the sweetened condensed milk in a traditional non-dairying area, Indonesia. Export to and use of milk in tropical regions is often criticised from various sides in Europe. Common arguments against export to and the use of milk in tropical regions are, for example, that milk is not a part of the local food habits and cannot easily be digested because of lactose intolerance; that milk products are a threat to breast-feeding; and that milk is a relatively expensive protein-rich food and therefore it is more sensible to use cheaper local foods.

Is there an insuperable prejudice against milk among non-dairying populations? Marvin Harris (1985) even goes so far as to divide the world into lactophile (milk loving) and lactophobe (milk hating) populations, the latter mainly being found in tropical regions and China. Despite all these factors against milk, there is an increase in the use of milk and milk products in traditional non-dairying areas.

This chapter is a case study demonstrating the diffusion of an industrially processed food product from Europe – sweetened condensed milk – to Indonesia in the period between 1875 and 1914. This was the time that Hobsbawm (1991) called the age of empire and strong economic expansion of Western Europe and North America into the un-industrialised world, and was the beginning of an intensive dietary exchange between Asia and the West.

The process of food diffusion has two levels; a geographical diffusion, which is the spread of the food or food product from its place of origin to other parts of the world, and a social diffusion, which is the rate at which the new food is adopted into the diet by various categories of the recipient society. This chapter will examine a diffusion of sweetened condensed milk in Indonesia from the both perspectives.

The historical data for the study were obtained from published literature, such as studies and reports of Indonesia issued during the colonial area, in particular

1880–1940, and material on marketing activities during the period of 1929–1940 found in the archives of the Cooperatieve Condensfabriek Friesland (CCF), now Friesland Dairy Foods. Archival sources for the period between 1901 and 1945 available in the State Archives, the Ministry of Colonies, The Hague, were also used.

Milk and Non-Dairying Areas

As far as the place of milk in the diet and dairying in general is concerned, a distinction can be made between traditionally dairying populations and populations without a dairy tradition.

The concept of dairying and non-dairying regions was introduced by Eduard Hahn in 1896 in his classical study on domestic animals and their economic significance for man. When, in the 1960s, lactose intolerance and milk avoidance first began to receive attention, it was Frederick Simoons who explored the cultural historical aspects of dairying (Simoons 1970). Empirical data, however, indicate that the high incidence of lactose intolerance does not prevent a positive attitude towards and consumption of moderate quantities of milk (Scrimshaw and Murray 1988:1083–1159; McBean and Miller 1998:671–6).

It is most probable that cattle dairying (employing *Bos taurus* and *Bos indicus*) and the use of milk as a food gradually spread from the region of origin, the Middle East and North Africa, to Europe and to West and East Africa, Central Asia and the Indian Subcontinent (Simoons 1971, 1974). After 1500, acceleration in the process of milk diffusion took place as a result of European expansionism. Mass migration from Europe to the American continent brought dairying to the New World. British and Irish settlers introduced it into Australia and New Zealand. European settlers considered milk to be an essential part of their food habits and took cattle with them to overseas territories.

However, tropical Africa, South East Asia, and the Far East remained more or less untouched by dairying during the seventeenth and eighteenth century. Only in those regions with a relatively large European population was some dairying introduced (*Figure 2.1*). By the end of the seventeenth century, the Dutch had

Figure 2.1 Places with Major Dairying Activities in Java, 1920–1940 (Den Hartog 1986).

introduced it for their own needs in some places on Java (Den Hartog 1986:72–73).

Ecological conditions in the humid tropics do not favour cattle raising, particularly dairying. Apart from serious cattle diseases, tropical pasture of average quality has no great value (Gourou 1959:53–5; Huitema 1982:288–290). However, the main difficulty for milk production in the tropics is that animals are often unable to keep their body temperature within normal limits. This has a negative impact on lactation (Huitema 1982:262).

Although the Indonesian archipelago is without any doubt a typical non-dairying region, there were however some populations who were already using milk long before the arrival of the Dutch. For example, a number of populations using buffalo (*Bubalus bubalis*) milk were found in Sumatra and Sulawesi (*Figure 2.2*). As far as can be ascertained, the indigenous Banteng cattle were not used for milking. However, with the strong Hindu influence of the first centuries AD, Zebu cattle (*Bos indicus*) were introduced by the Indians. Cross breeding with the Banteng (*Bos javanicus*) resulted in a new breed, the Java cattle. Furthermore, there are indications that milk was used in old Java for ritual purposes (Dupuis 1970:538–39; Wheatley 1965:587). It is however likely that milking disappeared in Java after the decline of Indian influence.

The Arrival of Tinned Milk

Milk is a perishable product and cannot be transported over long distances or over a long period of time without first being processed. Prior to the Industrial Revolution, surpluses of milk had to be made into butter, cheese, curds or yoghurt in order to be preserved. When the Dutch established themselves in the

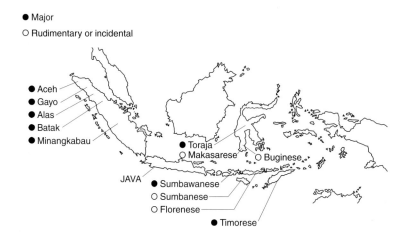

Figure 2.2 Populations with a Tradition of Using Buffalo Milk in Indonesia in Late Colonial Times (Den Hartog 1986).

East Indian archipelago during the seventeenth century, they introduced some dairying to meet their need for fresh milk (Den Hartog 1986:72–8). The demand for other dairy products, like butter and cheese, could be satisfied by importing them from the Netherlands in the ships of the VOC, the United East Indian Company. Needless to say these products generally arrived in a very poor state.

At the end of the nineteenth century, modern dairying was initiated on the island of Java. Milk stables were set up in towns with sizeable European populations and dairies were established in the cooler mountains (Den Hartog 1986:82–3). The consumption of fresh milk was largely confined to Europeans. It was too expensive for the Indonesian population. In the 1920s, a litre of fresh milk cost about 50 Dutch East Indian cents, while the average household income was estimated at 81 cents a day (Van Laanen 1979:135–6). An additional problem was that milk could not be kept fresh for long under tropical conditions. It was almost impossible to keep milk cool in the home. Milk, in the form of either a drink or as an ingredient, was an unknown foodstuff among the Indonesian population.

During the nineteenth century in Europe and the United States, a number of important innovations in the field of food preservation took place. In 1806, the French confectioner Nicolas Appert succeeded in preserving meat, vegetables and milk in bottles by means of heating. Problems with the fragility of glass jars were eventually solved when, in England, Appert's methods were adapted to tin-plate canisters or cans (Morris 1958:42).

After Appert's innovation, several attempts were made to preserve milk by evaporating the water and keeping the product in sealed bottles or tins. This product was rather unattractive to consumers (Hunziker 1946:34). In the 1860s, however, two major inventions changed this situation. In the United States, Gail Borden succeeded in condensing milk in tins by the addition of sugar. He was granted a patent for this process in 1856. Adding sugar was necessary because in high concentrations it inhibits bacterial growth. The increase in the availability of sugar in the UK, Western Europe and the USA, particularly after 1850, extended the use of sugar as a food preservative (Mintz 1986:147, 187–8).

Industrially processed foods, such as tinned milk, were originally developed to meet the needs of the armed forces, seafarers and later the urban consumers of Western Europe and North America. With the rise of modern imperialism after the middle of the nineteenth century, industrial products, including processed foods, reached Africa and Asia. The development of mass transport and cooling techniques made it increasingly possible to diffuse foodstuffs far beyond their original ecological zones.

By the 1880s, the food manufacturers Nestlé and the Anglo-Swiss Company were already very active in Africa and Asia (Heer 1966:68). The export of processed foods to these regions was originally intended to satisfy the needs of Europeans residing there, but it eventually led to the gradual diffusion of processed foods and other European foods from the colonial elite to local populations. Around 1883, most of the condensed milk used in Indonesia was Swiss condensed milk imported from the Anglo-Swiss Company in Cham (Van de Burg 1883:136). Other forms of preserved milk imported to Indonesia can be traced back to as early as 1835 (De Haan 1935:529).

Sweetened condensed milk had several advantages compared to fresh milk. It was relatively safe and unadulterated. It possessed qualities that allowed it to be kept for a relatively long time, even after the tin was opened. This was due to the conserving properties of the added sugar. Equally important was the price, which although originally high, was gradually lowered.

The Spread of Tinned Milk

How did the use of milk products spread from the top layer of European colonial society to the Indonesian population? This mainly occurred through those Indonesians who had close contact with Europeans, for example, those employed by the colonial government, the army, on plantations, in industry, and those who had received some form of Western education. The relatively better-off Indonesians and Chinese were the first to accept European commodities and habits, including the idea of milk as food. After 1900, within the framework of the colonial power's ethical policy to improve the welfare of the Indonesian population, a modest start was made in the field of education.

Towns played an important role in the spread of new foods among the population. In the towns, the Indonesian population was confronted with European ideas and habits. It was in the towns that a modern Indonesian elite gradually developed – intellectuals and the middle class (Wertheim 1951:34–5). Commodities from overseas, including foodstuffs, were imported to satisfy the needs of the resident European communities and the better-off Chinese and Indonesians. In towns, and of course particularly in the capital city of Batavia (Jakarta), offices of trading firms and major stores could be found. From the towns, commodities were further distributed to the interior. Chinese-owned shops (*toko*), the market (*pasar*) and to a lesser extent street vendors became sales outlets for these imported commodities (Wertheim 1958:24–5, 30–1, 37–8; Boeke 1931:2).

In this process of the spread of tinned milk into Indonesian society, a wide variety of institutions acted intentionally and unintentionally as agents of change: European-oriented school systems, the army, public health services and the retail outlets.

During the period of 1920–1940, milk products were diffused throughout the Indonesian population, particularly on Java. The spread of tinned milk took place through two main agencies: firstly, governmental and mission hospitals and clinics set up as part of a modern public health system for the Indonesian population, and, secondly, the marketing activities of the agencies and sales offices of the condensed milk industry, which were focused at a new potential market, an emerging local middle class and a wage earning class.

Public Health Services and Tinned Milk

During the early 1920s, a change took place in the Public Health Service. Until that time its activities had been directed towards combating major tropical diseases. However, the Public Health Services now began devoting increasingly more attention to maternal and child health care and the general nutrition of the Indonesian population (Den Hartog 1989:105–18). Hygiene centres and child health centres (*consultatie bureaux*) were established in major towns and places on Java (Nationaal rapport 1937:128–30).

In contrast to European women, Indonesian mothers universally practised breast-feeding. At these centres, breast-feeding was always encouraged, but the question remained of what to do if this failed or if the mother died. In general, wet nursing was not practised. Infants were instead given gruels or porridges of mashed rice and banana. Due to poor hygiene and diets with a low protein content, the chances of survival were small. In view of this, hospitals and later the consultatie bureaux began feeding these infants on milk products and, when available, on fresh milk. In general, however, sweetened condensed milk diluted with water was used. When, around 1918, evaporated milk appeared on the market in the Dutch East Indies, some physicians began to advocate its use.

In 1927, buttermilk and sour milk were also introduced by a number of physicians for infant feeding. In a hot and humid climate, sour milk can be kept for 24 hours, is hygienic and young infants can digest it better than fresh milk. Milk kitchens (*melkkeukens*), belonging to the Medical School in Weltevreden, Batavia, became well-known under the leadership of Dr. J.H. De Haas (De Haas 1932:58–60; 1936; Meulemans and De Haas 1940:2466–67). In Batavia, infants received sour milk feeding from the milk kitchens when it was considered to be medically necessary. The use of milk as part of infant care was practised by the medical staff in the Dutch East Indies only in cases where breast-feeding had failed or was insufficient. As mother and child care centres initially developed in towns, artificial milk feeding on medical grounds was mainly restricted to urban and peri-urban areas.

Early Marketing Activities for Tinned Milk

Before the outbreak of the First World War, the European condensed milk industry had already made serious efforts to include Indonesian consumers within its marketing activities. Around 1910, Nestlé began to penetrate into the Javanese market. Nestlé's special salesmen were occasionally sent to villages (*kampung*) to distribute free tins of sweetened condensed milk. This created some demand and the firm did everything to maintain the quality of the product under tropical conditions (Den Hartog 1986:136). Other firms who could not afford their own sales network made use of an importing firm. Imported milk products were distributed to the consumers by Chinese wholesale dealers through an extensive network of retail traders.

Milk products were not only used for infant feeding, but also in coffee and tea, and as an ingredient in ice lollies and ice cream, which led to the development of a local ice-cream industry. One clear difference between Indonesian and European consumers in their use of milk was that the former did not use it as a beverage. Milk products consumed by the Indonesians were derived from sweetened condensed milk and, later, in the 1930s, the cheaper sweetened condensed skimmed milk. Evaporated milk remained a product used almost exclusively by the European consumer. Given that opened tins of unsweetened milk products were subject to rapid deterioration, they were unsuitable for local consumers. Sterilised milk was sometimes used as medicine (*obat*). Milk powder was not important in the total milk supply during the period covered by the study. The quality of milk powder at that time made it unattractive for domestic consumption.

An insight into how Indonesian consumers were influenced by the marketing activities of sales agencies can be gained by examining the efforts of the Dutch-based condensed milk manufacturer CCF (known under the name of Frisian Flag) to secure a place in the Indonesian market in the 1930s. Earlier efforts of the firm were less successful (Tjepkema 1963:132). The strategy was based on two approaches: the introduction of a relatively cheaper milk product, sweetened condensed skimmed milk, instead of the more expensive full cream product; and a close association with a well-established importing firm, Internatio of Rotterdam. A suitable importing firm had to be chosen because, unlike Nestlé, CCF lacked the resources to set up its own sales network.

In order to speed things up, the CCF consulted the then well-known advertising agent A. De la Mar of Amsterdam, who had a branch office in Batavia. In 1931, De la Mar reported on milk marketing in Indonesia, particularly on Java (Den Hartog 1986:139–43). According to this report, the European population was the pace-setter for any new brand of imported products on the market. The fact that Europeans preferred tinned milk proved it was of good quality and that the Chinese and Indonesians would most likely keep abreast of their preference for certain brands. A clear brand name had to be chosen, with a symbol easily recognisable to illiterate consumers. The outcome was the still well known brand name, Frisian Flag or in Bahasa: *Ciap Bendera* (*Figure 2.3 and 2.4*). Although CCF could not afford its own sales network, De la Mar recommended that it should have its own sales manager in Indonesia. Such a manager would be expected to visit the various importing firms, wholesalers, European shops, tokos and stalls (*warung*). One of the major tasks would be to check the quality and prices of the milk products and to report on a regular basis by means of marketing reports.

It was obvious that only a limited number of consumers could be reached through advertisements in the Dutch and Malay language press. Due to the limited distribution of newspapers, De la Mar suggested that illiterate consumers could be reached through advertisements in railway stations and at train stops. Placing advertisement boards at the side of major roads was

Figure 2.3 Advertisement for Sweetened Condensed Milk on a Delivery Van in Batavia (Jakarta), 1935 (Photo: Courtesy of CCF).

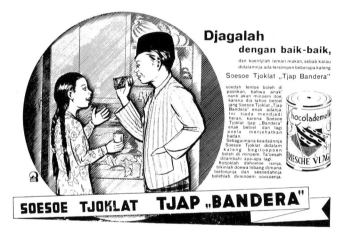

Figure 2.4 Chocolate Milk Poster Directed to Indonesian Consumers, 1936 (Photo: Courtesy of CCF).

deemed too expensive; limited results were expected in towns from bill boards, enamel plates and cards in the shops and tokos. Cinemas were already fairly common in various parts of the archipelago and were very popular with Indonesians, both rich and poor. Advertisements by means of slides or films were thought to be an excellent means of reaching all strata of the Indonesian population.

41

Another way of reaching a great number of potential consumers was through the *pasar malams* of *pasar gambirs*, a kind of annual fair that was very popular in the various towns and villages. De la Mar, however, did not favour the display and sale of products at these events due to the expenses involved. He felt that the sale of products should be left to the retail trade, which was largely in the hands of the Indonesian Chinese.

Notably, De la Mar's report advised that medical recommendations on the purity and nutritional values of the condensed milk products be obtained from physicians. Most of the report's recommendations were put into practice by the CCF. The marketing activities of the condensed milk industry in pre-independent Indonesia included the advice that sweetened condensed milk, a full-cream product, could be used for infant feeding. However, it was not explicitly stated that it could substitute breast-feeding. Compared with that for the full-cream product, there was far less advertising for skimmed milk, the relatively low price being the main factor for its success. As far as can be ascertained, tinned skimmed milk was not promoted for infant feeding as such. It is very likely that a move from full-cream milk to skimmed milk for infant feeding took place because of its low price. During the economic depression of the 1930s, imports of the cheaper skimmed milk increased (*Figure 2.5*).

A Skimmed Milk Public Health Problem

The relative success of directly marketing a skimmed milk product to Indonesian consumers created a public health problem. In 1937, a rather emotional discussion flared up within public health circles on the dangers of using

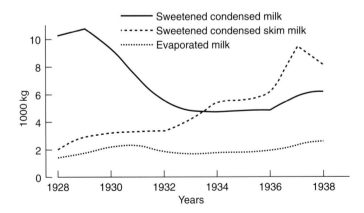

Figure 2.5 Import of Tinned Milk to Indonesia in 100 kg, 1928–1938.
Source: Centraal Kantoor voor de Statistiek, 1928/38

sweetened condensed skimmed milk for infant feeding and the risks of blindness (De Haas 1937; Den Hartog 1986:159–63; Donath 1938). Those working in the field of food and nutrition regarded the imports of sweetened condensed skimmed milk with suspicion. A food product deprived of the important vitamins A and D by skimming off the cream caused anxiety. Vitamin A deficiency could lead to night blindness and eventually result in a drying of the conjuctiva and cornea and the onset of blindness. Nutrition studies revealed vitamin A deficiencies in children living in the archipelago. At the same time, government medical and agricultural officers became more interested in the well-being of the population (Van Veen 1950ab).

Further to this, it was known that authorities in neighbouring countries had already limited or even prohibited the import of sweetened condensed skimmed milk. In Singapore, the well-known nutritionist Cicely Williams launched an attack on the use of all kinds of tinned milk for infant feeding in 1939. She spoke of 'milk and murder' (Craddock 1983). In this respect, the Dutch East Indies government lagged behind other countries in the region. There was no food law as such, nor did a food control system exist. Only in larger municipalities were there day provisions for the veterinary control of meat and dairying.

The skimmed milk affair went beyond professional circles. The issue was raised in the *Volksraad*, or People's Council, an advisory body to the government with the right of interpellation. Some concerned members of the Volksraad approached the government by posing a number of questions on the issue, and urging the administration to take appropriate measures (Den Hartog 1986:167–72). The government, however, was reluctant to make any decision on import prohibitions, sales restrictions, or food labelling. It is likely that it was not convinced of the severity of the situation and was more inclined to take into account the possible negative effects of import restrictions on the Dutch condensed milk industry during a period of economic depression.

At first, the industry tried to argue that the skimmed milk question was out of proportion and that the milk was not used for infant feeding. However, the CCF decided to take positive steps by re-vitaminising its skimmed milk products. On the label it was stated, in both Dutch and Malay, that the contents were unsuitable for infant feeding. Other manufacturers followed suit. The outbreak of the World War II in Asia in 1941 put an abrupt end to the skimmed milk question.

Milk Products and Milk in Present Indonesia

After the Dutch left in 1949, the Indonesian government took a great interest in the development of a national dairy industry based on local fresh milk production and condensed milk manufacture. The government obliged foreign dairy firms to set up a condensed milk industry using both local and imported raw materials. Tinned milk products, particularly sweetened condensed milk are more popular than fresh milk, which is an expensive beverage that is highly perishable. Tinned milk products have found their way not only into the urban and peri-urban markets, but also into the tokos and warungs of rural areas.

Nowadays milk is used as a beverage, but also as an ingredient. Tinned milk products are used in make-shift coffee shops as ingredient in tonic drinks such as Ovaltine, Horlicks and Milo. They are also used in traditional recipes. Advertisements, for example, suggest that sweetened condensed milk can be poured over green beans or over a black glutinous rice porridge. Another advertisement presents breakfast as being bread covered with sweetened condensed milk. The coming of UHT milk (ultra high temperature treatment) in carton containers in the 1970s has also had an impact in Indonesia. Long life milk in small handy carton containers with various flavours can now be found in all major cities.

In May 1978, the Indonesian government announced that milk processing factories (tinned milk and milk in cartons) must exclusively buy locally produced fresh milk, in order to substitute milk imports. This has been a good development for small Indonesian dairy-holders (Leake 1980:65–74).

Accurate data on milk consumption are not available. The food balance sheet for Indonesia indicates an availability of milk, 5.7 kg per capita a year in milk equivalents (FAO 1996). Milk is mainly consumed in the urban and peri-urban areas and only in small quantities. For the island of Java, it has been estimated that in the 1980s 65% of the rural population never consumed milk. The percentage of non-milk consumers in the total urban population was estimated at 10% (Den Hartog 1986:189).

A recent study among low-income households in Jakarta indicates that milk is reportedly consumed at least 11 times a week (Pudjilestari 1995). It is greatly used in infant feeding. At the age of 3–5 months, infants receive a rice-and-milk porridge from their mothers as weaning food. About 20% of the mothers give older infants sweetened condensed milk.

Concluding Remarks

No indications of a fundamental and insurmountable prejudice against milk as food in Indonesia could be found in the available sources. The price, rather than unfamiliarity, remained a major obstacle for its popularity. It seems that the occurrence of primary lactose intolerance among a traditional non-dairying population does not deter the limited adoption of milk into existing consumption patterns.

Milk condensing made it possible to bring relative cheap milk products from the temperate zones to zones where prevailing ecological conditions made the production of fresh milk scarce and expensive. The foundation for the present demand for milk products and fresh milk in Indonesia was laid in the late colonial era. The spread of milk products among the Indonesian population continued to grow after independence. In this respect, there was no break with the past. Milk once unknown as a commodity suitable for human consumption is now a common food, adopted to a limited extent into the foodways of the higher and middle class of the Indonesian society.

3

FOOD IN MIDDLE-CLASS MADRAS HOUSEHOLDS FROM THE 1970s TO THE 1990s

Pat Caplan

This chapter considers foodways in middle-class households in the city of Madras in the period between 1974 and 1994. It begins with a discussion of pan-Hindu ideas around food, showing the exceptionally heavy symbolic load which it carries in this culture. It then moves to a consideration of material collected from informants during the 1970s, 1980s and early 1990s. During this period, Indian economic policy moved from import substitution to economic liberalisation, and, by the time of my last visit in 1994–5, it was plain that major changes in food processing and marketing were taking place. The question raised is how a cuisine which is so tightly constructed allows new food items and new dishes to penetrate and be accommodated, even domesticated, an issue which has been well explored for Japan by Cwiertka (1997 and 1999).

Hindu Ideas on Food

For Hindus, food is closely related to notions of bodily substance, health and well-being, and to religious conceptions of purity and pollution (for particularly Tamil ideas see Daniel 1984). Food is subjected to division into humoral categories of 'hot' and 'cold' which have nothing to do with temperature, but are concerned with its supposed heating or cooling properties on the body (Beck 1969). Such categories are not absolute – they vary according to a person's own qualities, which are in turn affected by gender, age, and by particular states such as menstruation, pregnancy, and the puerperium (see Ferro-Luzzi 1980).

Secondly, concepts of purity and pollution, which are closely related to the hierarchy of sub-castes, play an important role in determining what can be eaten, and who can prepare what for whom (see Mayer 1956, Marriott 1968, Selwyn 1980). Here the dual division into *pacca* (cooked) and *kacca* (raw) foods is significant, since the latter do not act as a vehicle of contagion, and hence can be relatively freely given and received, whereas pacca foods are highly susceptible to the contagion of pollution (Cantlie 1981). These again are not absolute categories, but there is a continuum ranging from foods totally 'unopened' and unprocessed, such as paddy, to foods which have been opened by husking, skinning, grinding, soaking and boiling, of which the most extreme example is boiled rice. In Hindu south Asia, among the high castes, this is cooked in the inner kitchen, an area used only after bathing and changing into ritually pure clothes (Tamil *maadi*), and which is not entered by outsiders, or by women when they are menstruating.

In the course of processing and cooking foods, they may be rendered relatively impure by the status of the person who carries out such work, hence while all can accept cooked food from Brahmins, the latter can only accept it from their caste equals. However, some cooked foods are less susceptible to pollution than others, and thus can be given and accepted by a wider status range. As will be seen, this has implications for the possibility of neighbours of different caste backgrounds being able to establish commensal relations.

Third, there is an important distinction between meals, on the one hand, and snacks, usually referred to as 'tiffin', on the other. For south Indians in general, and Tamilians in particular, a meal consists of boiled rice, a meat or vegetable *sambar*,[1] *dahl* (lentils), *rasam* (a kind of peppery soup), *puriyal* (a dry vegetable dish) and some kind of salad, such as *raitha* (raw vegetables in yoghurt). These are served together. Tiffin, on the other hand, consists of a variety of snack dishes such as *dosai* (rice/lentil pancake), *iddly* (rice/lentil dumpling), *upma* (thick porridge), often served with milky coffee. Breakfast consists of coffee and, usually, iddlies with sambar. Lunch, which may be eaten any time between ten a.m. and one p.m., is the main meal of the day and always includes rice. On return from school or work, tiffin is served, and a second, less elaborate rice meal, often consisting of curd rice and a vegetable dish, forms supper.

A fourth important point is that the relationship between humans and deities is expressed through food (Ferro-Luzzi 1977). Worshippers present offerings of food to the deities, and through a process of transsubstantiation, this becomes *prasad*, the sacred leavings, which are then taken and distributed back to worshippers, who themselves may distribute it further to others who were not present at the devotions.

In this chapter, I consider how the classical notions concerning food, described above, are observed, adapted, or disregarded in a middle-class multi-caste setting of the suburbs of south Madras, and ask what are the likely effects of the recent dramatic changes in the availability of highly processed and packaged foods, many of them imported from abroad.

The Area and Methodology

In 1974–5, I carried out research on women's organisations in Madras City, during the course of which some 200 middle-class women were interviewed (see Caplan 1985). Some of these were re-interviewed in 1981–2, and contact maintained during short visits between that time and 1994.[2] As part of the study, questions were asked about time budgets, and it was apparent that the vast majority of women, except the minority who employed cooks, spent a good deal of time preparing and serving food. Few of the women active in women's organisations had paid jobs outside the home. In addition to interviewing such women, participant observation was undertaken in the homes of a number who became friends, and a dozen such women agreed to keep diaries for two-week periods in 1975. Much space in the diaries was occupied by accounts of food preparation. Several of these women also wrote accounts of festivals which they observed, and this often included the preparation of special food. In addition, a number of group discussions, some pertaining to food, was taped and transcribed. Although most of the organisations had the practice of charity as their *raison-d'etre*, several of them also ran classes, including cookery classes, for members.

Food in the 1970s

In the 1970s, food was usually purchased in its raw state from shops, including ration shops, markets, and street vendors. It was rarely packaged. Some families I interviewed obtained some of their supplies, particularly rice, direct from the countryside where they either still owned land themselves, or had relatives who did so. Some processed food was available, including bread, biscuits, cake, and canned food such as jam and baked beans, while bottled soft drinks (Limca, Fanta, Thums Up) were ubiquitous. Most of this processed food and drink was made by Indian companies, although there were some joint ventures or products made under licence such as Horlicks.

Here are some extracts from a taped discussion between a number of women in 1975 on how they spent their day:

Mrs. K.K. The corporation water comes only at five or six a.m. Then I take bath and go to the kitchen. I will be busy preparing [breakfast] tiffin for about an hour: iddlies or puris or something like that. I also have to cook lunch – rice, sambar and so on. Everything has to be finished by nine a.m. Only after then do I have leisure to attend these [English conversation] classes. Then after four p.m. I go to the kitchen again to prepare coffee for the children coming home. In the evening, we eat what is left from lunch – sambar or puriyal or whatever ... How much time do I spend in the kitchen? Three hours at least, five hours maximum.

(Kallar caste, husband retired, three adult daughters, all employed, living at home)

Mrs. S.S. Usually I get up at 5.30 a.m. and then I say a few words of prayer. Then I make breakfast: iddly or dosai or something like that. Then I go for a walk and do *puja* (worship) for ten or fifteen minutes. (...) Then I prepare lunch to be eaten about one or 1.30 p.m. My husband and son both come home for lunch, but my other son takes his lunch [with him] and my daughter also sometimes takes iddlies or dosai with her to college. Then

I listen to the radio and then have a rest. Then I have to prepare tiffin [for their homecoming] and sometimes we have a heavy tiffin [rather than a rice meal again] at night [for supper]. How many hours do I spend in the kitchen? In the morning from 7–9 a.m. then from 10.30–12.30, then again for tiffin, and finally for the evening meal – about 5–6 hours altogether, I'd say. (...) It doesn't take so long in the kitchen because they (husband and children) come at different times, but because they eat different things: my servant is a vegetarian, my husband a diabetic. Then on Sundays they demand meat, which requires long preparation, so Sunday means a long time in the kitchen. Sunday is a heavy day for me.

(Kallar caste, non-vegetarian, three teenage children living at home)

Mrs. M.S. I usually get up at 4.30, have my bath, and go to the kitchen and prepare coffee. If it is a school day for the children I have to prepare lunch early at eight a.m. Usually I have all my work finished by nine a.m. Then my husband has tiffin and goes off [to work] at ten a.m. and comes in again at 1.30 p.m. At 3.30 he has his coffee and goes to work again. At four p.m. my eldest daughter comes back from her college and at 4.15 my second daughter comes home from school. I will have made some sweets for them. At six p.m. my husband comes home and I will prepare chutney and dosai. At night [for supper] he takes only curd rice, so I don't cook at night. I cook everything in the morning and keep it in the fridge. It only takes me about one and a half hours to cook in the morning ... and total cooking time is about two hours, but that is excluding time spent on making sweets and things like that. I do make fresh rice in the evening – he likes only curd rice [for supper] after his [tiffin] dosai. But the children and I eat the rasam and sambar left over from lunch.

(Brahmin, vegetarian, two teenage daughters living at home)

The above extracts reveal a number of points:

(a) The prevalence of unprocessed foods in domestic cuisine

Food is cooked from its raw state, and indeed, several women recorded in their diaries how they would sit down with their maid servants and pick out the grit and dirt from rice grains, a tedious job. In these middle-class households, however, there were usually refrigerators, and 'mixies' – food processors – which lightened the load, as did the presence of servants.

In the diaries, it is rare to find reference to consumption of ready-processed food except on particular occasions. One such is as follows: 'My daughter came home from school with her friend. They wanted to finish their homework. I gave them sandwiches, cakes, banana and milk.' Here it is apparent that sandwiches and cake was associated with having a young guest for tea, since cake is not mentioned on any other occasion except one – a visit to a relative in hospital: 'On the way we bought fruits (banana, apples, oranges), cakes, biscuits etc.'

Only one of the diaries recorded that bread was consumed regularly, and that was because the children demanded toast for breakfast. In this house, there is even a mention of the toddler consuming cornflakes for breakfast.[3] One woman, when asked why she did not cut her morning cooking time down by serving bread instead of iddlies or dosai, replied that on a tight budget, bread was too expensive, and in any case, people preferred iddlies.

(b) In all of the above households, women were responsible for cooking food.

Most such households would have domestic servants, usually a part-time maidservant who would cut up vegetables and wash dishes in addition to cleaning the house and washing clothes. Women, as wives and mothers, were not only responsible for cooking, but also for serving food to the household members before they went to work or school/college, as well as on their return. The notion that people might make their own coffee or snack, or help themselves from the fridge, was quite alien, and, given that most maidservants were of lower caste than their employers, so too was the possibility of them actually cooking and serving food.

Women often mentioned that they found cooking a chore, as in the following case:

Mrs. S.K. Here begins my headache, to think, to programme the day's menu. For instance, every day we require three types of vegetables: one for puriyal, one for sambar, one for salad or raitha. If we have one for sambar, I can't have it for curry the next day or my daughter says 'I have been eating *brinjal* (aubergine) for three days now' or 'Is this drumstick week then?' So I plan and buy the vegetables in Pongal Park (a big market in the west of the city) the previous day.

(c) The diaries made frequent mention of hospitality.

Mrs. M.R. My sister had invited us for food, so I did not prepare anything [for lunch] but I prepared some custard in the morning and took it and went to my sister's house. We had very elaborate food: coconut rice, tamarind rice, sweet *pongal* (a kind of rice pudding), potato curry, buttermilk *koyambu*, *appalam* (rice pancakes), chips, vermicelli *payasam* (a sweet dish cooked with milk, spices and cashewnuts), pickles.

But having guests means a lot of work:

Mrs. S.K. I had a hectic day. I started to prepare some snacks for my friend [who was visiting] with the help of my cook. Oh, it took nearly five hours. I was helping the cook now and then, supervising her cleaning ... I prepared five or six items like cashew cake, *thathai* (small savoury chapati), *poli* (sweet dosai), papaya fruit cut up, iddli, chutney. These things are quite time-consuming dishes, but they do keep for a few days.

On another occasion, the same woman had dinner guests:

> I hardly had time to breathe ... [I served] carrot salad, cucumber and curd rice, *pappad* (poppadums), chips (crisps). Everything was ready for 8.30. I was really feeling proud because all of them liked the food and really complimented me.

> *Mrs. K.K:* Sunday. Got up at 5.30 a.m. Had coffee and tiffin (iddly) at 7.30. Started preparing different kinds [of food]: *kootu* (spicy curry), puriyal, sambar, rasam, mutton – since I expected my married daughters and their husbands for lunch.

In the middle-class suburbs, guests for a meal might not all be of the same caste background, and thus care would be taken about the kind of food to be served. Women of the Brahmin caste could cook and serve any vegetarian food for non-Brahmins, but the latter would have to avoid serving foods such as boiled rice to Brahmin guests. On occasion, food was exchanged between neighbours:

> *Mrs. A.N.* While (we were) having our food, my neighbour sent in some of her dishes, and in exchange, we sent in some of ours.

Here again, only certain kinds of food, usually sweetmeats, would be exchanged.

(d) special food is cooked for religious festivals:

> *Mrs. M.R:* We celebrated Sri Rama Navami day. From 9–10.30 a.m. I prepared a special *payasam* (a kind of milk pudding), *vadai* (dumplings), green gram *kari* (curry), *panakam* (sweet drink used on ritual occasions), and fruit. First I had my head bath (hair wash)[4] and wore new clothes and made food.

> *Mrs. M.V.:* Today is the commencement of Adi, the fourth month in Tamil. I got up, took [a] bath, prepared coffee. My husband left for [the] factory and I started cooking. Menu: curd and buttermilk sambar, lemon *rasam*, potato curry, *thengaipal* (extract of coconut juice, mixed and boiled with jaggery, with cardamon added), and vadai.

In the 1970s, middle-class urban women were beginning to incorporate new dishes into their culinary repertoires. Most of the women's organisations ran classes of one kind or another, and cookery classes were popular, especially in cake-making. Cakes involve the use of wheat, rather than rice, they usually incorporate eggs, which vegetarians would not normally eat (although I did come across recipes for 'eggless cakes'), and they necessitate the use of an oven, which few south Indian kitchens possessed at that time. Cakes were either served on special occasions such as children's birthdays (although never at weddings), or, if served at home, as part of tiffin, not meals.

Middle-class households had for some time made use of commercially-produced jams and cordials, and some women were learning to make these things for themselves, even on occasion to sell to their neighbours.

Families sometimes ate out, but if they did so, it would usually be in restaurants where the cooks were known to be Brahmin, as in the famous Woodlands restaurants, and where the cuisine was Tamil fare. Only a few of the upper-class non-Brahmin families belonged to clubs such as the Madras club or the Gymkhana club, where Western food (pasties, mixed grill, cutlets, puddings and pies) has long been available. To some extent, a distinction was thus made between food domestic and non-domestic contexts, but within fairly narrow limits. For example, people at this class level rarely purchased food from street vendors and when travelling would carry their own home-cooked food with them in 'tiffin carriers' (interlocking metal boxes).

There were gender differences in consumption between men and women. Men would sometimes admit to having eaten rather unorthodox food outside the house in the course of their work-related activities, but would hasten to add proudly that their wives were PURE vegetarians. To some extent, this difference is also linked to the domestic-non-domestic distinction mentioned above, but not invariably. For example, in some high-caste non-Brahmin households, women would be willing to cook food for their husbands, including meat, which they would not themselves eat. Similarly, they might cook eggs for children on nutritional grounds, but would not eat them themselves. Thus the purity of the home was very much dependent upon the eating habits of its adult women-folk. A single household could be both orthodox and unorthodox, with differences of inside/outside the house, male/female, adult/child.

Changes in the 1980s and 1990s: Accommodation and Resistance

During the 1980s, profound economic changes began in India, with the loosening of some restrictions on its 'import substitution' policy, a process which has accelerated since 1991. Indian food manufacturers have moved increasingly into more elaborate packaging of their products, and, since the success of Maggi Noodles, the first western-style convenience food, into the production of a range of such foods. In addition, more western-based companies have begun operating in the country, including PepsiCo (from 1989), Coca-Cola, and Kellogg's (see Abbott 1995). What effect, if any, has the availability of these new kinds of food had upon domestic consumption among the middle-classes in Madras?

By 1994, there was a dramatic growth in self-styled 'supermarkets' in the city which contained a wide variety of processed food, some of it imported, such as Kellogg's breakfast cereals and California seedless raisins. Even those items produced in India were by now often elaborately packaged, a practice which stressed hygiene. Such supermarkets were obviously patronised by the wealthy upper middle classes, often young couples shopping together, although one which I visited had a set of chairs at the entrance 'for the husbands' to sit and wait for their wives. The indigenous soft drinks industry had largely been bought out and replaced by Coca-Cola and Pepsi-Cola, both of which advertised heavily, and bottled water was also widely available.

A second change was in the restaurants. There were now many more of them, and they included multi-cuisine restaurants, often serving Chinese and Western as well as Indian food. In addition, there were specialist local restaurants such as one to which I was taken which served Chettiar food.[5] The decor played a good deal on the culture of place, with dramatic Ayyanar horses[6] outside, and much use of carved wood, like that adorning Chettiar houses, in the interior. Several restaurants specialised in North Indian cuisine. In this way, as Appadurai has shown for cookbooks, 'a national cuisine is being constructed from regional or local traditions' (Appadurai 1988:21).

In addition, there were new forms of fast food: especially noticeable here was a chain of snack bars called 'Hot Breads' which sold vegetable pasties in addition to buns, bread and cakes, while all over the city were vans labelled 'Hot Chips' selling chick peas with rolls, dosai (a Tamil dish), *papri chaat* (a north Indian snack) and potato chips.

A third change was in hospitality. A friend invited me to a dinner at her house at which there was a lavish spread, served buffet-style, but with separate courses. The first course consisted of a soup, which was served after we had been offered drinks of a cola type. Although the family is non-Brahmin, most of the food which followed, with the exception of one dish, was vegetarian: dahi iddly, curries, biriani, puris. People ate with spoons and used paper napkins, rather than the more usual practice of eating with their hands, which would have

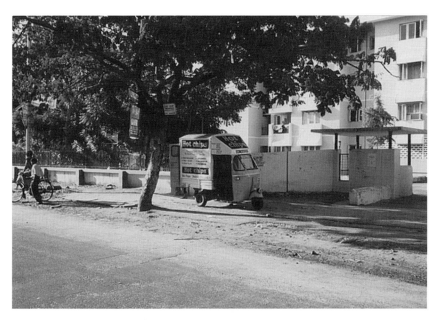

Figure 3.1 New kinds of fast food, including some sold from vehicles, appeared in the 1990s: 'Hot Chips' van became ubiquitous (1996).

Figure 3.2 By 1999, pizza 'joints' were found throughout the city. Much of the advertising linked eating pizzas and drinking Coke, Pepsi or Fanta (1999).

necessitated washing them both before and after food. The hostess had enlisted the aid of her married daughter and a friend. None of these three women ate at all, but busied themselves serving the guests. The friend who had helped to cook took food for her own consumption away in a tiffin carrier at the end. This was an interesting meal, with a mixture of Indian food and customs (e.g. women who cooked not eating with guests) as well as 'western' (e.g. use of spoons and napkins, the introduction of courses).

However, at the engagement ritual for the son of a Brahmin friend, which took place at her house, the food was cooked on the premises and served by Brahmins who wore dhotis to indicate their ritual purity and who operated in a cordoned-off area which precluded entry by others. In contradistinction to other cultures which have often adopted western customs such as the ubiquitous wedding cake, Hindu weddings in India, which are already highly elaborated, have not done so. Most weddings take place in specially designated *kalyana mandapam* (wedding halls), where the food is cooked and served by Brahmins, and only in a few cases do Hindus use western-style hotels for such events.

On another occasion in 1995, at a dinner given by a women's organisation, food was again served in buffet style by caterers but men and women ate separately, some with spoons, some with their hands. Here, however, there were no courses, but an elaborate variety of dishes from which to choose (dahi vadai, coconut chips, *polli* (sweet chapatis), chapatis, savoury rice, sambar, payasam), most of them Tamil.

In short, then, although changes are apparent in forms of hospitality provided in some homes, and in practices involved in eating out, there is considerable continuity in patterns of food consumption within the home, and on ritual occasions such as weddings. We may choose to interpret these as forms of everyday resistance to the forces of westernisation and globalisation analogous to the political protests which have taken place throughout India since accommodation with the IMF was signed, and economic liberalisation began to proceed apace.

Conclusion

Recently, I received a letter from an ex-student now working in the research department of a major multinational concerned with food, inviting me to their annual Consumer Science Symposium, and to speak at an innovative panel which she was organising on cross-cultural research. She noted that colleagues were increasingly interested in 'new perspectives for understanding cultural influences and differences', and that the questions currently being raised in the regional innovation centres in such areas as India, Thailand and Brazil included:

- How do you measure how easily people will accept a new product into their culture?
- Why do certain products travel successfully across cultures and not others?

Anthropologists can of course suggest many possible answers to these kinds of questions, although whether we may wish to do so is another matter.

Thus in answer to the questions posed above, and at the beginning of this chapter, I would suggest that there are various contradictory factors involved in changes on food consumption. Processed food is seen as time saving, a plus in a situation in which servants are not as easily and cheaply available as they were a decade or so ago. They are seen as more 'modern' and up to date, a factor which is heavily played on by advertising, as is their hygienic state.

Yet other factors make it less likely that they will be adopted on a large scale. Gender roles lay down that a woman's proper role is to cook good food for her family – nutritious, full of variety, and conforming to ideas about meals and snacks, hot and cold, purity and pollution. At the same time, ideologies of nationalism, and Gandhian notions of the importance of self-sufficiency, mean that for many Indians, the entry of Coke and McDonald's spells the end of economic independence.[7]

Epilogue: Madras in 1998–9

I returned to Madras for three weeks in December 1998 to January 1999 to make a further study of the ways in which middle-class households have incorporated the new forms of food, which have become available since economic liberalisation began in India in the 1980s. I found that there had been a mushrooming of 'supermarkets' selling packaged and processed food, and an increase in a wide range of new kinds of food outlets, ranging from expensive restaurants to mobile vans and stalls. Who buys such food (age, class background), when and where they eat it and with whom, and to what extent it is integrated into the existing cuisine raises interesting issues of accommodation and resistance to the forces of globalisation.

Changes

(a) Changes in kinds of food available

It was frequently said to me that 'You can get anything in Madras nowadays', and contrasts were drawn, implicitly or explicitly, with the situation prior to the late 1989s when most foodstuffs were either purchased from vendors and provision stores in their raw state, or were packaged in a rudimentary way by Indian companies. This situation has changed dramatically in a number of ways.

First of all, there has been a very visible entry of large multinational food and drink companies, such as Kellogg's, Nestlé, Coca-Cola and PepsiCo, into India. Even food companies that are entirely Indian-owned, now market in a more sophisticated way. Packaging has become much more elaborate, and brand names, which are heavily advertised in the mass media, significant.

Such companies have been skilful in drawing on local ideas about desirable qualities in food: one brand of cornflakes, for example, which is fortified with iron, not only claims that 'dieticians have shown that teenagers are mostly anaemic' but also call their product Shakti, a term which means 'spiritual power/ energy' in Hindu thought. Many packages proclaim proudly that their contents are 'egg-free' or 'suitable for vegetarians', of whom there are many among the middle classes in Madras.

(b) Changes in shopping patterns

While provision shops continue to be popular, and street stalls selling fruit and vegetables remain visible, there has been a proliferation of self-service supermarkets during the 1990s. In the Adayar area where fieldwork was conducted, which consists of a cluster of suburbs in the south of the city, there are over a dozen of these of varying sizes within one square mile. Supermarkets sell a wide range of convenience foods, ranging from ready-ground *masala* (spice) pastes, to 'ready-mixes' of dosai and iddlies which require minimal cooking. There are also new products such as pizza bases, and a wide range of breakfast cereals. As yet, there is only a small demand for ready-cooked food which has only to be heated up, or for frozen food, whether cooked or raw, but most supermarkets do carry some frozen goods. Some have begun to sell (wrapped) fruit and vegetables, so that the affluent are able to indulge in

Figure 3.3 'Fast foods' of all kinds are found everywhere. Chinese food became widespread in the late 1990s, serving a wide range of castes and classes. This stall in Besant Nagar, which serves beef and pork, would probably not have been patronized by most caste Hindus or by Muslims.

'one-stop' shopping. Most supermarkets will also deliver goods to houses, and accept telephone orders.

Indeed, supermarket shopping is beginning to be thought of as a leisure time activity in which some husbands also take part, and for which, as one informant noted, 'You have to dress up'. Some of the larger supermarkets incorporate snack bars and drinks bars which are particularly popular with young people.

Figure 3.4 Many foreign food companies moved into India in the 1990s and proved adept at catering to local sensibilities: here 'Baskin Robbins' (an American ice-cream company) emphasizes its use of cows' milk, and lack of egg (forbidden to vegetarians) in its products.

(c) Eating out

While mobile stalls selling ready cooked food, as well as eating houses serving a *thali* (meal of rice, lentils and vegetables), often on a banana-leaf, have long been a feature of the city scene, there were until recently few up-market restaurants, other than in the big hotels. This situation has also changed considerably. Eating out has become a huge and heavily-advertised industry

Figure 3.5 Fruit and vegetables, suitably wrapped, had moved inside supermarkets.

Figure 3.6 Although some people continued to buy fruit and vegetables from street stalls.

catering to a wide range of classes, with a variety of outlets. Although traditional south Indian food continues to be popular, there are also numerous places serving food of foreign origin especially Chinese (mostly cooked by Indians), with Thai, Mexican, Vietnamese and Italian also being found. In addition, north Indian foods, notably chaat and *tandoori* (food cooked in a clay oven), have become extremely popular. Restaurants specialising in Indian regional foods have opened. Pizza 'joints' (as they are termed locally) have become ubiquitous, and there are many places offering telephone orders and a pizza delivery service. Some restaurants offer 'multi-cuisine' menus, hoping to cater to all tastes.

(d) Drinks

Drinks too have changed. The uses of aerated soft drinks, notably Coca-Cola and Pepsi-Cola, has become widespread, with the virtual demise of the local soft drinks industry. Hoardings and advertisements are found throughout the city, attesting to the 'Coke-Pepsi' war. Bottled water is now widely available in supermarkets and in fast food outlets, and is popular because it is supposed (not always entirely accurately) that its quality is safe. Whereas few informants purchase bottled water to drink regularly at home, most now rely on a built-in water purification system, whereas such households would have boiled and filtered their drinking water to make it safe a few years ago.

Responses to Change

The responses of middle-class informants to these developments have been varied. Few of them remain unaffected, even if they are not in favour. 'The grandchildren like pizzas', 'Young people today want all kinds of food' were frequent remarks. Many families eat out regularly: 'We go out on weekends, to eat something different, because the children/grandchildren like it, to have a break from cooking' etc. Many informants pointed out that with most upper middle class women now holding paid jobs dual income families could afford both to eat out from time to time, and also to purchase the more expensive packaged, convenience foods available in supermarkets. A strikingly high proportion have added micro-wave ovens to their kitchen equipment, and most now have double-door refrigerators with small freezer sections.

Some informants noted the welcome saving in time provided by, for example, ready-made masala pastes, or the convenience of keeping a stock of iddly-powder in case of unexpected guests. Many also welcomed the additional packaging of modern foods, stating that it guaranteed standards of quality, especially hygiene and lack of adulteration: 'People these days are willing to pay for quality' was a frequently used phrase.

But many also regretted the innovations: 'Nothing tastes like fresh home cooking', 'Aerated drinks are bad for health'. There were clearly often tensions between the generations in this regard, and in many three-generation families, considerable differences in taste had to be catered for. Most children and young people now eat cereals (cornflakes, 'chocos' etc.) for breakfast, but older people continue to prefer their iddlies.

A few informants extrapolated from the kinds of food changes they observed to make observations on the changes in lifestyle of which they were symptomatic:

> I don't know if my son is going to find a girl [wife] who will be willing to cook for him in the way that I did. All the girls [women] these days are working and want convenience foods.

Others stated that they were unsure how much India's economy was benefiting from the use of imported foods, or foods produced in India with foreign licences or under collaborative arrangements.

Two issues which were frequently raised spontaneously by many older informants concerned the large-scale emigration of their children to the USA and their own process of ageing. Scarcely a family in this area does not have at least one child living and working there, and many have visited the West themselves, and have eaten non-Indian food there. They also receive visits from children and grandchildren, who may demand that they be served non-traditional food during their stay.

Yet while success in obtaining a 'green card' is much desired, older informants are also beginning to realise that the prospect of old age without the support of nearby children and grandchildren can be problematic. Some elderly couples have begun to rely on the new cottage industry of 'home caterers' who supply cooked food to households for very reasonable rates on a regular basis, and who advertise in the local press, often discreetly indicating that the food is only handled by Brahmins (the highest and most ritually pure caste). Others continue to rely on the still-cheap supply of servants to cook and care for them, although bemoaning the 'rising' demands of domestics for better pay and conditions.

Conclusion

Although I have not yet had an opportunity to analyse in any detail the data which I collected, it is clear that middle-class Madras, and indeed other parts of India, is going through a revolution in food consumption patterns. These changes are related to the government's economic liberalisation policies, the desire of multinational food companies to enter this large market, and the use of mass media to sell food, especially to the young. Many people want to try new kinds of food for a variety of reasons: quality, difference, convenience, peer group pressures, and above all, a sense that India has (finally) joined the rest of the world. At the same time, there is great pride in the complexities of Indian regional cooking, and south Indian food continues to be served on important ritual occasions, such as marriages and *upanayanam* (sacred thread ceremonies) which, even for green card holders and US citizens, usually take place in India.

Notes

1 A kind of thin stew/soup made on the basis of lentils with vegetables and/or meat. Brahmins are invariably vegetarians, as are some other of the higher castes.
2 Fieldwork in 1974–5 was funded by the Social Science Research Council, and in 1981–2, fieldwork and writing up time was funded by the Nuffield Foundation.
3 Cornflakes were manufactured locally at that time.
4 'Head bath' means washing the hair as well as taking a shower and confers greater ritual purity.
5 Chettinad is an area in southern Tamilnadu with a distinctive culture (see Nishimura 1998).
6 Ayyanar is a protective deity whose statue, along with those of his horses, is often seen at the entrance to villages in Tamilnadu.
7 There have been demonstrations against multinationals such as Coca-Cola and Kentucky Fried Chicken in various Indian cities (Swamy and Singh 1994).

4

LADIES WHO LUNCH

Young women and the domestic fallacy in Japan

Merry I. White

The novel *Kitchen* by Yoshimoto Banana (1990) attracted young female readers through its focus on the kitchen as a symbol of nurturance, nostalgia, and subversion. The fractionating and alienating experiences of family, society and the workplace were epitomised in the life of its young protagonist, and the heroine uses food to align herself in unconventional places and attachments, counter to the norms of her society.

Young women in Japan today, like Mikage, the heroine of *Kitchen*, use food as a means for engaging in relationships, organising their participation in consumption, and expressing themselves creatively – whether in tune or at odds with conventional behaviour. Here we will examine some contexts in which middle class young women interactively receive and create the food cultures in which they participate. We use here three kinds of information: what one might call the 'culinary curriculum' contained in the magazines they read;[1] ethnographic observations of behaviour and practice in three locations where young women purchase, eat and learn about food; and survey and interview data collected in 1997 and 1998 from a sample of twenty-five Japanese women aged seventeen to 29.[2]

Consumer trends and fads occur in clusters and are moved in predictable cycles, allowing trend-followers an illusion or semblance of choice in their engagement in purchased identities and life-styles (Skov and Moeran 1996). This '*trendo būmu*' (trend boom) effect is amplified for several demographic segments, most particularly for young people in their early twenties. Within this group, it is young women especially who receive and react to the blandishments of the market. They have three attributes that make them available to trends, namely money, time and a competitive need to be *au courant*. Trend creation is a two-way phenomenon – market sensitivity is high on both sides of the cash register in Japan; young people feel the need to be on top of or ahead of waves of trendy things and activities – what marketers call *infomaniakku* (information maniac) become skilled in watching and creating those waves.

An analysis of the food booms phenomenon in Japan reveals the elements that create an especially potent marketing relationship with the audience of young women. These include: a tendency to combine the socially legitimated context of learning with the less 'responsible', more self-indulgent pleasures of entertainment; an intense focus on female friendships, fuelled and supported by participation in trends, overshadowing the more traditional focus on the male-dependent role of home and family-building; and an active role in engaging and domesticating the 'international' which activates their relationships with food and each other. In all these aspects of the self-expressive bond between young women and food, they participate in, and help create, a complex bundling of extra-familial, counter-nurturant, self-indulgent, and in traditional Japanese terms, un-feminine acts and expressions, which one might see as small resistances to the contradictions of the 'domestic fallacy'.

Nostalgia and Duty: Food and Family

A young woman before marriage is in training for the life of a housewife, and while the Meiji Period's (1868–1912) encapsulation of the 'good wife, wise mother' (Uno 1991) may not be invoked today, the residue in terms of identity, life goals and roles still influences a woman's lifecourse trajectory (Brinton 1993). She is engaged in schooling and work, just as her male peers are, but the goals and applications of her study and work are different: everything underlines her identity and role in household and childrearing. The nostalgic references to the virtues of home cooking emphasise this in magazine articles on 'the taste of mother's cooking' (*okāsan no aji*) (Christine Yano, personal communication); advertisements for more traditional Japanese food products, and a popular *enka* song[3] all refer to Mom's cooking – the song is a tearjerker about 'the taste of Mother's *miso*[4] soup'. Mother's cooking is by definition not *haute cuisine*, not the refined aesthetic eye-inspiring *kaiseki*[5] creations considered quintessentially Japanese, but rather stews and other comfort foods or snacks such as *ochazuke*, the 'green tea over rice' invoked in the 1950s movie of the same name by director Ozu Yasuhiro. Nor is it 'international': the closest this 'mother's cooking' gets to imports is the thoroughly Japanised 'curry-rice', made usually from prepared sauce bases with 'international', but not Indian, brand names such as Vermont Curry or House Curry.

Training for the role of home cook may include schooling in other forms of food – not necessarily lessons that are expected to be translated into foods served at the family meal, training which is in itself seen as character- and role-building. A young woman's membership in the 'life-long learning society' both in school and in post-graduate learning is part of her apprenticeship to this role as she undertakes to accumulate social capital that will land her a worthy husband through educational credentials and through *okeikogoto*[6] such as cooking classes, tea ceremony and flower arrangement that symbolise her nurturant, service-oriented, selfless role as housewife. These classes, even traditionally, offered women something more. An escape from home, an arena to engage friendship, a way to learn trends including the exotic and international, a personal sense of accomplishment are all contained in this culturally approved mode of learning. Housewives too engage in such classes which are more about accredited leisure than a direct contribution to the performance of their role at home – and the foods would rarely be served to husbands in any case (Mori 1996).

The young woman before marriage is a working woman. Such a young woman conventionally uses her period of single working womanhood after graduation from high school, junior college or university to accumulate more merit as a future bride (as well as an income which will help defray the cost of her wedding) and experience in serving others. The work itself does not usually define her but it may support and emphasise her future home roles while providing some working women with an opportunity for creative consumerism. For the 'office lady' or OL, as the women working in Japanese offices are referred to, the workplace may also directly provide her with a spouse: managers are said to hire young women with the expectation that a certain percentage will marry the young men they work with and for.[7] The common wisdom is that a young male worker sees the four women seated closest to him in the office plan as key targets – and office managers plot with this in mind. The young woman worker has more time and disposable income, much of both going for self-indulgent food consumption and use of timesaving, but high quality prepared foods.

There are indications that women participate less in the fulfilment of older normative roles and more in the fulfilment of other goals and lifestyles that seem to contradict the models offered them by their families, and by the cultures of education and workplace. Or at least try to delay their enactment. First, the age of marriage is rising – now averaging 28 or higher in urban areas. Second, more women live alone before marriage, a practice until recently frowned upon by parents, employers and women themselves, and they have extended their working years well beyond the conventional two to four years of the 1970s and early 1980s. Third, women are having fewer children, and as the birth-rate per woman declined from 1.57 in 1990 to the current 1.32, delaying marriage and not having more children have become problematised by officials and policymakers. Some young women say they will never have children – some, because their hopes for a career seem to preclude having families. The Equal Employment Opportunity Law, promulgated in 1986, has not served to help them combine work, especially professional and career work, and family. Finally, the economic downturn and 'recessionary thinking' has led, some commentators say, to an increase in expenditure for entertainment and personal indulgences in place of long term investment in personal savings towards larger consumer goals such as home purchase. These factors all contribute to the current engagement of young women in food trends, both as responses to marketing blandishments – what

Kondō Sumio has called 'trend slavery' – and as expression of subliminal resistance to societal expectations for feminine and familial behaviour (Kondō Sumio, personal communication).

Hobby learning and self-improvement classes extend women's learning well past their student years in which the strictures of the examination system and the credential-focused learning of official schooling dominated their lives. Released into the workplace for a moratorium period before starting the life work of 'good wife and wise mother', they use this time to explore realms of life that have less to do with credentials and accomplishments and more to do with experience – whether related or totally irrelevant to their future roles. Just as in their teen years learning about pop stars and trendy goods focused their friendships, so in their twenties learning about food is also about fashion, friendship and fantasy, and it is still validated as learning. A huge industry of cooking classes and schools teaching such things as table settings, food etiquette and culinary history are available to support accredited 'feminine' areas of expertise. Some seem to parody the female role through extravagant and demanding perfectionism, but seldom in any case do the young women who engage in them employ the skills trained outside the classroom.

There is, however, within this elaborated domestic paradigm, similar in some ways to the domestic science movement in the west, a countervailing movement to appeal to women looking for an arena of self-expression and creativity in the home. Kurihara Harumi, a media 'tarento' (a term used for media celebrities) has recently achieved prominence for advocating the easy, enjoyable and creative aspects of domesticity rather than rigid perfectionism. She has a very popular television show and publishes a monthly recipe magazine, encouraging flexibility and experimentation. Her first foray into changing the housewife image was designing a stylish 'Armani'-type apron. As she put it, 'Why should I look like a frump when I carry out the trash?'. This is not an apron to wear while cooking. She has become a guru for women redesigning their home lives – some call her the Martha Stewart of Japan; as one woman said, 'She's an angel guiding my life' (Amelia Newcomb, personal communication).

More overtly feminist in her 'domesticity' is the writer Kirishima Yoko. She characterises the new woman's kitchen as a place of potential liberation, in which women who have forsworn their culinary skills in resistance to the servitude of their familial roles may indeed make revolution by mastering their kitchens, not forswearing them, and calls for women to embrace cooking, engage their talents as a means for self-expression, and abhors the negligence and passivity of women in a realm they could command (Kirishima 1995).

With friends, food serves several functions: a young woman shares information about food trends and locations with her friends, gives food related gifts, and uses eating as shared entertainment as well. Being seen and eating in the right places (as one of my informants said, the 'right places' may not have the best food, but the food quality doesn't necessarily drive the choices) is important. Articles guide women through wine selection too, one noting that you should never let others choose for you and you should select the glass of wine (note they are only choosing a glass, not a bottle) to go with the food, though red wines are trendy now with any food. Young women today know where and what to eat: knowing where the newest, hippest Italian restaurant is before the magazines feature it is important to at least one of my informants, who prides herself on being ahead of the curve as a specialist on the Italian restaurants of Shibuya and Akasaka districts of Tōkyō – her friends who don't are considered a bit *dasai* (country bumpkin). Those in the hinterlands complain that they are behind, and one girl estimated her city had a cultural time gap with Tōkyō of at least three weeks.

Eating together has now replaced going shopping or to the movies together as the favourite entertainment among these young women. One woman cited the recession of the early 1990s as a factor, saying that it is cheaper and more satisfying to arrange to meet at a restaurant than it is to wander the department stores after work or on the weekends. They do so an average of three times per week, and they say they prefer eating with other women to eating with men, whose tastes need training. When the economy was booming, people saved for their own homes. Now consumers look for choices on the small-scale level as a substitute for the lack of choice they have at higher levels.

Service is quite definitely not on the food agenda of young women: they say they prefer to eat out rather than to cook at home: they enjoy thinking about food, engaging in new trends, and participating in competitive gourmandiserie with their friends, but there is a strong preference for being served over preparing a repast to serve to others. Even the cooking classes are more about getting together under the guise of a socially-approved mode of 'learning' than about applying what is learned at home. The total engagement of the heroine of *Kitchen* in cooking and feeding others is part of what the young woman reader realises is a romantic fantasy (Treat 1996); she combines traditional nurturance with footlessness and non-traditional relationships and gender identities. In her own life, engaging in food in counter-traditional ways, she plays with the fantasy of the 'total woman' but at the same time she doesn't pretend it can be realised.

Young women are also encouraged by their magazines to DIS-engage from food: to develop their body-consciousness to a high degree, and like some of their counterparts in the West, to join the ranks of dieters (*Figure 4.1*). In the same magazines presenting trendy desserts and recipes for home-made high caloric treats, there are also treatments: presentations of fad diets (such as the 'oolong tea' diet in which you drink five or six cups of oolong a day and its diuretic effect creates the illusion that you are shedding real pounds) similar to those found in American popular magazines, some very surreal and punishing. One is well-known by my informants as the 'apple diet' (everyone had a 'friend' who'd tried it): this consists of four days of eating nothing but apples or other fruit followed by a cup of olive oil on the fifth day. Then you slowly add rice or bread to the diet. The newspaper article went on, 'you may get a headache as your body cleanses itself of toxins (...) Drink a lot of water and don't plan to do

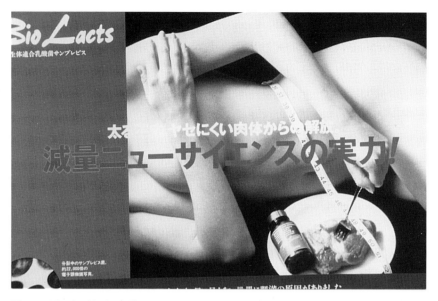

Figure 4.1 The ideal of sliminess, and various ways to achieve it, are featured constantly in the media.

anything stressful during these diet days'.[8] Some informants mentioned the opposite approach, restricting the diet to only rice or bread, supplemented with physical exercise. Several had tried Chinese herbal diets and a few had a water-only day every week. While there is some discussion about anorexia and bulimia in popular media, there is comparatively low public awareness of the problem and many young women are painfully thin or engaged in unhealthy bingeing and dieting practices. Controlling the body through food use and diet appears to be one 'management' function contained in young women's relationships with food, one which needs further investigation.

Looking at how the traditional relationship between women and food has been turned on its head, we will here observe young women in three sites where they learn about, buy and eat foods.

Scene One
Food Theatre: The Chef on Show

Ten women, all between 25 and 30 sit and stand around three sides of a long table set up in a well-appointed home kitchen-dining area in Setagaya, Tōkyō. They are well-turned out, their tailored dark skirts and silk blouses in contrast to crisply ironed frilly pastel aprons. The chef, on the working side of the counter, is the only man in the room, all business, with a striped, mannish, professional cook's apron. The cooking operations are performed by the chef alone, with one or another of the guests acting as assistants awkwardly and giggling as they hand him, various implements on demand, and the other young women have placed their identical clipboards on their laps as they hold glasses of red wine, rather than pens, in their hands. When the chef makes a stirring flourish or flips sautéing mushrooms in the air, the women stop chatting and make appreciative noises. When the dish is assembled, it is portioned out and the women eat happily, their notebooks untouched.

Are they students or invited guests at a party? Are they audience or participants? The cachet attached to inviting (at considerable expense) a chef from a trendy restaurant (in this case, Italian, the rage of the moment) to a private home for a party is considerable. The events combine the culturally validated structure and premise of learning – a combination of the bride training lessons in tea ceremony or flower arrangement – with home-based entertainment, a recessionary (but still very expensive) response to the lavish entertainment outside the home of the pre-crash 1980s. Yet, hardly ever will one of these young women translate this experience into a meal she will cook at her own home for husband and family.

Men too engage in the cooking class boom, but separately, in classes devoted to men, cooking ethnic or Western food – and occasionally renting special cooking/dining rooms where staff prepare all ingredients ahead of time. Men thus are engaged more in performance cooking for their male friends – cooking as 'hobby' and entertainment, rather than as part of domestic duty or an activity shared in families.

Scene Two
Mangia, Mangia: Aoyama Italiano

Three young women, elegantly dressed in high black boots, long slim black skirts and all with long straight hair, consult the menu on a small table on the sidewalk outside an Italian restaurant and are soon joined by two friends. They carry a guide to Italian restaurants in Tōkyō, an insert pulled from *Hanako* magazine. This place was a French restaurant only a few months before but the current boom in Italian food sent the owner-chef of the French bistro to Tuscany where he adapted his skill to the uses of *pappardelle*, *cinghiale* and *porcini* mushrooms. The women check their guide before ordering, each choosing a different dish so as to be able to taste and compare.

With line drawings and photographs (*Figure 4.2*), the manual instructs the young women in the right way of eating pasta, and tempts them with romantic, lavish illustrations of restaurants in Florence and Venice, each photo showing a pair of young Japanese women, 'just like us' enjoying a meal. These young women are today practising for the ultimate experience of *trippa* at Cibreo in Florence. The international aspect of eating out is not insignificant to these young women, both as preparation for actual travel (Italy now tops the list of favoured vacation spots) and for the cachet of the (safely domesticated) exotic it

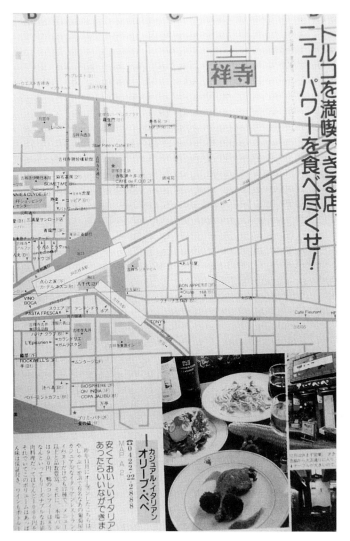

Figure 4.2 A typical young women's magazine's information on trendy restaurants, including a detailed map and photographs of the food.

provides. All things Italian are cultivated: recent issues of *25Ans* and *Veri* featured Italian fashion, interior design and travel as well, integrating *ishokujū* (clothing/food/living) as a total lifestyle.

Taking part in the Italian boom is thus a multimedia event, supported by television programs on Italian food and by department store food hall demonstrations. Isetan Department Store's large Shinjuku site has had Italian food festivals in its 'Queen Chef' departments featuring imported ingredients,

70

demonstrating food preparation, and offering sample tastes. Above all, the adventure is supported, enhanced – and managed – by the magazines the young women use as texts to guide experience.

The Italian boom has been fed by the perception that it is both an elite, developed European cuisine, and inexpensive – at least in comparison with the prices charged for French food in Japan. Young women say that they are attracted to it because it is *kigaru de yasui* (cheap and cheerful), casual compared to the more off-putting formality of French cuisine as it is presented in Japan. They also say it is healthier, based as it is on olive oil rather than butter, and Italian red wine is seen as almost a health food. As a result of its popularity, Italian food is trendy to cook as well as to eat, though, as noted earlier, most cooking classes are undertaken more for social and entertainment purposes than for functional learning. There is a shortage of teachers and schools providing classes in Italian food preparation and those available are booked early.

There is now some indication that French foods, of a new and stylish sort, are returning to the trend list in Japan, adding to and not displacing Italian foods. These foods and restaurants, unlike the older French restaurants, have emphasised, like the Italian ones, youth, style and lightness, rather than the predictable and conservative formal French mode of the past.[9]

Scene Three
A *Kombini*: Convenience and Anomie

At six-thirty in the evening, the line at the counter of the twenty-four-hour convenience store in Hiroshima reaches nearly to the door, in spite of the very efficient work of the two cashiers. First are four dark-suited young women, talking animatedly together as they pay for their boxed and canned fruit juices (tropical mix, apple, peach, and tomato), calorie-coded packaged prepared meals in styrofoam containers, and glossy fashion magazines. Next two high-school boys in school uniforms pay for their barbecue-flavoured potato chips, cokes and comic books. A middle-aged woman with an apron over her blouse and skirt buys a small bag of fresh pods of young soybeans (*edamame*), two large bottles of beer, and a plastic bottle of dishwashing liquid. Finally two older men come in together and confer over the steaming heated box of *oden*[10] on the counter, choosing several pieces while others behind them wait rather impatiently. The oldest person in line, a woman perhaps in her seventies, carries plastic-wrapped portions of *hōrensō no hitashi* (cooked seasoned spinach), *gobō* (burdock root), *kabocha* (pumpkin), grilled fish, and some *hōjicha* (roasted tealeaves) in teabags.

The convenience store, or *kombini*, is so much part of people's lives that people wonder how they ever lived without them, only a few years ago (Kennard 1997; Washida 1997). Few use a convenience store for staple foods or for the ingredients of a family meal, except in emergencies. Older people prefer patronising the neighbourhood's shopkeepers for rice, fish, vegetables and groceries, and younger working housewives might use the department store basement food halls on their way home from their jobs. Middle-aged full-time housewives are likely to use a combination of local shops, larger supermarkets, food halls (for special treats like cakes, pastries and high quality pickles) and kombini only when the former are closed. Kombini are very sensitive to their clienteles, and are often computerised so that instant notations of the approximate age and type of customer can be recorded and analysed, as well as the purchases made, so that stocking can be consumer-responsive. The quality is relatively high, even if shelf storage demands preservatives and heavy salting of some prepared foods.

Using kombini, however, presents a different image from that of other suppliers of the sources of family meals. Kombini food tends to be more processed – ready-to-eat foods – than foods bought for home preparation elsewhere (*Figure 4.3*). The labour (service) of cooking and presentation is provided outside the home, and the kombini (or the department store food hall) takes care of this component of a woman's role. Other kinds of services are provided in kombini too: you can send faxes, packages, buy plane or concert tickets, have film developed or use an ATM. One young woman called it her 'office'.

A phrase exists in current usage to describe a housewife who purchases readymade foods – she is a '*tenuki okusan*', a 'no-hands' housewife. According to Miyanaga Kuniko, the guilt a woman feels at buying prepared foods at

Figure 4.3 A shelf of a Japanese convenience store, displaying ready-to-eat snacks and meals. They may be microwaved on the spot if required.

the kombini depends on the degree of labour added to the food, corresponding to the labour she saves herself: something, it is felt, should be done to the purchased food at home to make the purchaser feel she has been engaged in its production (Miyanaga Kuniko, personal communication). For the working housewife, however, the kombini is indispensable: you can rely on it at any hour for the elements of a passable, nearly instant meal.

The kombini also offer young women a wide range of foods – and the chance to experiment in a modest way with trends and international products – usually on impulse. Depending on the neighbourhood or clientele, a shop will offer varieties of chilli or spaghetti, Oreo cookies, or new and seasonal or ephemeral items such as plum-flavoured potato chips or 'California tofu' with herbs (a case of the return from overseas of a local product transformed).

Of the three sites, kombini may be the most explicitly supportive of 'unfeminine' life styles and behaviour, as it makes it possible to double ones roles, taking on full-time work outside the home is no longer out of the question – as far as provision of meals goes, anyway. It also supports the status quo as it maintains the woman's capacity to be the main provider of food, along with other jobs – and doesn't force the issue of duplication.

Conclusions

In these three contemporary scenes of food marketing, consumption and trend enactment young Japanese women are playing out old roles and new realities as they transform themselves and their food culture. These engagements in learning and experiencing food and its preparation are validated as they conform to traditional role expectations, but these have been turned on their heads as the young women are served rather than serving others, engaged in entertainment more than in family roles, and in friendship rather than in nurturance. The new images deny the older equations of food/home/mother and reveal women co-opting food for their own pleasure and self-expression. These young women are not merely 'trend slaves' nor are they completely independent agents – their participation in the new food cultures is located where culture and social change intersect, as well as influenced by their economic status as earners and managers of their own disposable income.

To state the case more strongly, conventional, culturally approved housewife-role-building doesn't compute for many young women. Education, the economy, marriage and childrearing are all problematised for them. The facts of life for a young woman today are that for her the meritocracy based on elite educational credentials doesn't work to provide her with a place on the corporate ladder. The economy has let them down too – but also has released them into a world of micro-pleasures. Marriage promises not companionship with a husband, whom the young woman can lovingly serve, but isolation, and not the opportunity to nurture children creatively, but, because of economic constraints and the rigidity of the educational system, merely a background role subject to the demands of institutions beyond her control. It is no wonder that in 1995, 50% of women between the ages of 22 and 29 were unmarried, no surprise to find those who marry producing very few children.

Learning and apprenticeship have become entertainment, exposing the post-war fallacy of educational credentialling, service in marriage has become having others serve you, taking advantage of a faceless service industry and exposing the separation and disconnection in middle class marriages, and nurturance has turned to exchanges between friends rather than within a family.

Women who neglect the demands of the role are still stigmatised, however: the mother who doesn't prepare a home-made lunch but buys one for her child at the kombini; the wife who leaves her husband to buy instant noodles for himself when she spends evenings out; the woman who is not available to make tea for an elderly parent at home, bear burdens of guilt, reinforced by negative reactions from the *seken*, the watchful community of behaviour monitors governing behaviour. Social commentators have blamed 'poor mothering' as the root of contemporary social ills (Jolivet 1997) calling women selfish who use disposable diapers or try to combine career and motherhood. Avoiding this role patrol may seem preferable.

Food has come to be the commodity by which these women express themselves, cement their relationships with each other, and involve themselves in a complex and paradoxical play between marketed consumer cuisines and culturally validated home cooking. Their relationship with home (mother's taste), with friends (food as fashion and social exchange) and with men have strong food referents. Marketers and developers of products for middle class young women have focused on them as they negotiate these relationships and manage both 'body consciousness' and the need for indulgence.

Notes

1 Several magazines for young women were consulted: *Tanto, JJ, CanCam, Figaro, Nonno, Esse, Orange Page, Croissant, 25Ans, AnAn, HotDog, Oggi, Veri, Hanako, Vogue, Lee, ViVi.*

2 Thanks to Rico Mochizuki, Nakamura Noriko, Miyanaga Kuniko, Christine Yano, Amelia Newcomb, Kondō Sumio and Hirose Yōko for their expertise and suggestions, and to the many young women who contributed through their responses to my queries.

3 Sentimental popular ballads in Japan with origins in early twentieth century music, accompanied by primarily Western instruments.

4 Fermented paste of soybeans and usually either barley or rice, with salt.

5 Highly refined genre of cooking, with the emphasis on the seasonality of the food and the suitability and beauty of the vessels.

6 Okeikogoto: training, lessons in various arts and civilities aimed at improving one's overall 'culture', especially for elite young women in the recent past, who would take classes in tea ceremony, flower arrangement etc. as enhancements for their 'marriageability profile'. Cooking classes are a kind of okeikogoto which now can also be training for a 'hobby', and not just for marriage. Children's okeikogoto might be foreign languages, crafts, and the like.

7 Miyanaga Kuniko reports that Japanese managers now expect that a high percentage

of young men will marry the young women whose desks are positioned closest to theirs and make up the room plan with this in mind (personal communication).

8 *Daily Yomiuri*, October 1997.
9 'From French to Italian' in *Asahi Shimbun*, 7 October 1997.
10 A variety of ingredients simmered in stock, served with mustard.

5

WILD-GATHERED FOODS AS COUNTERCURRENTS TO DIETARY GLOBALISATION IN SOUTH KOREA

Robert W. Pemberton

Korea's agriculture and flora are similar to nearby areas of China and Japan, but its foodways are distinct.[1] Since the division of Korea at the end of the Second World War, North and South Korea (the Republic of Korea) have developed very differently. South Korea, the focus of this chapter, through its industrialisation and trade-based economy, has become one of the four Asian tigers. This Korean tiger is a meat eater with a diet greatly influenced by globalisation, but it remains very interested in the foods of Korean fields and forests.

Globalisation of Korean Food

South Korea's rapid economic development increased the per capita income from $150 in 1960 to $10,548 in 1996, and enabled the country to become the eleventh largest economy in the world (Foreign Agricultural Service 1997). Commensurate with this economic development, significant changes in the country's diet and food ways have occurred.

Change in Dietary Materials

Perhaps the most striking change has been the large increase in domestic animal foods eaten. In 1965, only 5.5kg of animal products (beef, pork, chicken, eggs, and milk and dairy products) were consumed per person.[2] By 1996, consumption of domestic animal foods had risen to 93.7kg/person, more than 18 times the 1965 level. Although Buddhism has strongly influenced Korea and still has many followers, the Buddhist prohibition against eating meat, unlike Japan, has been limited largely to the clergy. Historically the common people consumed little meat, but it has had high status. Korean beef cookery (mainly *kalbi* and *pulgogi*, often called Korean barbecue outside Korea) is, with *kimch'i* (spiced pickled cabbage) the best-known Korean food. Before Korea's trade based economy developed there were not many domestic animals produced and the ones that were produced were very expensive relative to average incomes. Korea is a mountainous country with almost no pasture. Livestock are confined and fed with feedstuffs brought to them. Traditionally these feedstuffs were hand cut grasses and other wild plants, and local agricultural by-products. These factors severely limited production. With the growth in the economy and trade, it became possible to import foreign feedstuffs, which increased production dramatically. From 1977 to 1997, the number of beef cattle produced doubled and the number of sows and hogs more than tripled. Almost all animal feed is imported. In addition, large amounts of meat and meat products are imported – almost one billion US dollars worth in 1996.

The consumption of milk and milk products has increased even more dramatically than that of meat products. Many Koreans older than 40 did not know milk when they were children, but there was some use of milk historically. One of the 190 annual Korean customs (Choe 1983), which were part of the formal rites and ceremonies practised during the Chosŏn Dynasty (1392–1910), was the Milk-Product Present (*t'arak chinsang*). From the first to the fifteenth day of the tenth moon, specially produced milk was presented to the Palace and to the Home for Superannuated Officials. In 1965 the per capita milk and milk product consumption was only 400 grams. In 1996, however, 54.5kg/person were consumed, while from 1978 to 1996 cheese production increased from 83 metric tons to 20,843 metric tons. The dairy cattle inventory grew accordingly from 90,000 head in 1977 to 551,000 in 1996. These cows also eat imported feed.

The consumption of cereals and other starchy foods (rice, wheat, corn, soybeans, and potatoes) declined somewhat, from 188kg/person in 1965 to 158kg/person in 1996. The relative importance of individual starches shifted somewhat. Rice is still by far the most important starch and overall food, but consumption of rice declined from 121.8kg/person in 1965 to 102kg/person in 1996. Barley, formerly a food of considerable importance, which was strongly promoted by the government to avoid grain imports, has been abandoned by most people; declining from 36.8kg/person in 1965 to 1.5kg/person in 1996. The other big change is in wheat consumption, increasing from 13.8kg/person in 1965 to 33.4kg/person in 1996. The much greater consumption of breads and other baked goods as well as noodles is responsible for this increase. After animal feedstuffs, wheat is the largest food import. In 1996, 11,000 metric tons of wheat was produced in the country, compared to 3,177,000 metric tons of wheat which were imported. Because Korean homes do not have ovens, breads and other baked products are commercially produced foods. In general, commercially prepared foods have increased with Korean's economic development and urbanisation.

Increased Presence of Foreign Foods

Until the last decades, the presence of foreign foods in Korea was modest. There have been Chinese and some Japanese restaurants serving food modified for

Korean tastes, but few places served other foreign food except for the restaurants of international hotels. With the economic development, however, international fast food restaurants appeared on the scene.

Among the chain fast food restaurants present in Korea are Burger King, Kentucky Fried Chicken (KFC), McDonald's, and Pizza Hut. The first McDonald's opened in Korea in 1988 and by June 1998 there were 123 outlets (McDonald's 1998). This number of Korean stores compares to 2,594 outlets in Japan. Calculated on a population basis, McDonald's has almost eight times as many stores in Japan and seventeen times as many outlets in the USA (which opened the first store in 1955). Japan's economic development and globalisation happened almost twenty years earlier than Korea's. Japan's first McDonald's was opened in 1971, seventeen years earlier than Korea's first outlet. As of June 1998, there were 127 KFC and 143 Pizza Hut restaurants in Korea (Tricon Global Restaurants 1998). When calculated on a per capita basis, Japan has about three times the number of KFCs as Korea, and the US has seven times as many. But with 143 Pizza Huts, Korea has somewhat more (>40%) outlets per head of the population than Japan, but only about 1/10 the number of stores per capita compared with the US. One has to take into account, however, that there are also other chains or independent restaurants serving pizzas and other fast food. Fast food chain restaurants are mainly found in the big cities, but now are spreading beyond them (Foreign Agricultural Service 1997). Although common, these restaurants are, by and large, patronised by younger people.

The acceptance of foreign foods is increasing for a number of reasons, in addition to people having more money to purchase it. Until the late 1980s, Koreans were not permitted to travel overseas for pleasure. Since then, Koreans have travelled overseas like never before, and in doing so are being exposed to other cultures and cuisines. In addition, the large number of Koreans living in Japan and the USA, and the contacts they have with friends and relatives in Korea, introduces Japanese and American foods to Korea. The American military presence in South Korea, with its many bases with American style restaurants, exposes large numbers of Korean civilian employees and visitors of these bases to American food. These military bases have supermarkets for American military and civilian employees. The black markets associated with these bases sell American foods from these bases, and thus have become indirect routes for the introduction and consumption of American food products, many of which had no legal access to the Korean economy as long as import restrictions were maintained.

Countercurrents to Globalisation

Korea has had a tradition of isolation and xenophobia, due largely to the aggressive behaviour of neighbouring Japan and China. From 1400 until the 1870s, the only regular Korean contacts with the outside world consisted of missions bearing tribute to China and trade with the Japanese in Korean harbours. Contact with Western nations was not permitted until 1882 (Fairbanks et al. 1973). Japan's brutal colonial rule of Korea (1910–1945) and its attempts to Japanise Korea are strong cultural memories. Many Koreans see the division of Korea into North Korea and South Korea, which followed the colonial period at the end of WW II, as an act perpetuated by outside interests. The presence of the American military in Korea, while seen as necessary because of the North Korean military threat, is not liked. Considering these factors and the relatively short time that the country has been open, it is surprising that Korea has oriented to the outside world as much as it has.

Globalisation is also resisted by the fact that many Korean are anxious to preserve their own culture, which, because of systematic Japanese efforts in the colonial period to erase Korean ethnic consciousness and the extremely fast pace of social and economic development in more recent years, is felt to be under threat. From the 1970s onwards, moreover, the government promoted a re-awakening of national pride in an effort to boost morale. The result of all this is that among wide segments of the population there is a great interest in 'our things'. In this context, measures were taken by the authorities to limit the impact of foreign culture, for instance by making foreign language signs on shop fronts or foreign business names illegal and by protecting the Korean film industry. Many of the anti-foreign declarations and sentiments have this intention of preserving Korean culture against regional and global influences.

There is a strong duality with regard to attitudes about foreign trade. While Korea's economic miracle has been based on export driven industrialisation, imports of most foreign goods, other than raw materials, have been strongly resisted. Koreans have an emotional, and almost spiritual attachment to Korean rice. During the decade ending in 1996, imported rice was banned. Under the Uruguay Round Minimum Market Access commitments, Korea agreed to gradually increase rice imports to a level equivalent to 4% of the domestic rice production, which will occur in 2004 (Foreign Agricultural Service 1997).

Consumption of foreign products, although desirable for reasons such as the status they impart, their quality, novelty, etc., is considered to be unpatriotic, much more so than in the sentiment expressed by the occasional 'Buy American' campaigns in the USA. Consumption of imported goods is almost a moral issue. Even the consumption of products made in Korea under foreign licence may become a target of criticism. The makers of Ch'ilsung, a soft drink similar to Seven-Up, in advertisements list as its selling points: 'No caffeine, no colouring, no royalties.'

Shint'o Puri – Korean Foods are Better for Koreans

With regard to food, the resistance to globalisation is most succinctly expressed in the slogan *shint'o puri*. The characters that express shint'o puri translate literally as: 'body and soil are not separate'. In its current usage, shint'o puri means that food from Korean soil is best for Korean bodies. Originally, however, the phrase is derived from a Buddhist concept that expresses the inseparability of the karma of a person and that of his surroundings. In its new meaning, shint'o puri lacks a scientific basis; human beings are omnivores with great plasticity in diet. Natural selection has not, so far as we know, selected human bodies to function best with particular local food resources. Nonetheless, shint'o puri ideology is expressed in numerous television shows, and in newspaper and magazine articles. Housewives and other consumers are taught to distinguish foreign foods from Korean grown foods and in market stalls the place of origin of all products sold is indicated. Among the foods of concern are beef and Chinese grown vegetables such as chilli peppers, yellow onions, and garlic. Not only are Korean grown foods seen to be better for Korean bodies, but also foreign foods are often claimed to be dangerous because of insecticide contamination.[3] The use of insecticides in Korean agriculture is one of the heaviest, if not the heaviest, in Asia (Asian Development Bank 1987), but current volumes agricultural chemicals are not openly communicated (Foreign Agricultural Service 1997). Foreign food safety issues and increased scrutiny of food imports have occurred following stated Korean government concerns about the nation's rising trade deficit (Foreign Agricultural Service 1997). Foreign produce may or may not have more insecticide residues than Korean produce, but truth may be of secondary importance to the economic interest groups concerned.

Shint'o puri is a belief sincerely held by many Koreans, but it has been openly promoted by anti-trade activists. The Agricultural Cooperative Federation, the main Korean farmer's organisation, actively promotes shint'o puri (*Figure 5.1*). The organisation's book on its history (*Nonghyŏp Samsibonyŏn Sa* 1996), contains a chapter on its efforts to try to prevent the opening of Korean's markets to foreign agricultural products, as called for by the Uruguay Round Minimum Market Access agreements. They write that the promotion of shint'o puri was developed as a tactic to influence consumers not to buy imported products, after the Federation was unable to influence policy to block food imports.

One expression of shint'o puri produced by this organisation is a poster (*Figure 5.2*) showing a giant grain of Korean rice squashing the quintessential foreign food: a hamburger (Robert Macke, personal communication). The poster's text describes the nutritional superiority of rice. Most nutritionists would probably agree that neither hamburgers nor polished white rice are ideal foods for people. Foods produced in Korea are also often promoted to be, and are commonly believed to be, better tasting than their foreign counterparts. The irony of shint'o puri, with regard to Korean beef, is that cattle and all Korean farm animals are fed not with plants produced in Korean soil but with imported feedstuffs. Yet these animals are grown in Korea by Korean farmers, which is important. Shint'o puri is used selectively, targeting products that compete or might compete with Korean products, but ignoring essential imports such as animal feed.

Figure 5.1 Members of the Korean Agricultural Cooperative campaigning for *shint'o puri*, a concept derived by the Cooperative, which says that food grown on Korean soil is best for Korean bodies. Shint'o puri is used to resist the importation and consumption of foreign foods.

Wild-Gathered Foods

Another aspect of Korean preference for Korean foods is the interest in and continued use of wild-gathered foods, mainly food plants (*san namul*) and rice-field grasshoppers (*mettugi*).

South Korean food markets have, in addition to the abundant and diverse plant products of its agriculture, many wild food plants that are gathered from its fields and forests (see Pemberton and Lee 1996). This study documents the presence and abundance of wild-gathered food plants that are brought to markets. Part of the motivation to document this practice was the realisation that this use of wild food plants was an apparent continuation of ancient food culture in a rapidly changing modern industrial country.

Food markets were visited and samples of plants that appeared to be gathered from the wild (wild-gathered) were taken from 1989–1995. The most frequently visited markets were the largest wholesale-retail markets in Seoul, the Karak Shijang and the Kyŏngdong Shijang. These markets are comprised of many private sellers at both indoor stalls and outdoor spaces around the market buildings. Some large modern supermarkets (Lotte, downtown and Chang Hwa in Itaewon) were also frequently sampled. In addition, samples were obtained

Figure 5.2 Poster showing a giant grain of Korean rice squashing a foreign food hamburger. The caption reads: 'Eating Our Rice Creates a Healthy Diet'. The bar graph on the rice grain shows in declining order the percentage of starch, water, protein, fat, and minerals that the grain contains. The poster was produced by the Korean Agricultural Cooperative and the Korean Ministry of Agriculture, Forestry and Fisheries as a part of the shint'o puri campaign to promote Korean foods and to resist the importation and consumption of foreign food.

from sidewalk sellers in Seoul and vendors near the gates of parks and mountain temple areas outside of Seoul. Visits to the main markets were made periodically, but were most frequent (bimonthly) during the spring and autumn, when most wild food plants appeared. Marine algae were excluded from the samples, as were fungi which, with the exception of well-known cultivated species, were infrequently encountered.

(a) Market presence and food uses

One hundred and twelve species in 82 genera and 40 families were encountered among wild food plants sold at Korean markets. All are terrestrial flowering plants, except for two ferns (royal fern – *Osmunda japonica* Thunb. and bracken fern – *Pteridium aquilinum* L.). Herbaceous species comprise 79 of the total and woody species 33. The life forms of the 112 plants include nineteen trees (17%), seven shrubs (6.3%), 13 vines (11.6%) and 73 herbs (65.2%). With the exceptions of Chinese cedrela (*Cedrela sinensis* Juss.) and bush cherry (*Prunus tomentosa* Thunb.) from China, and *Pinus rigida* Mill. from the United States, the plants are probably Korean natives. At least three others, a wild amaranth (*Amaranthus mangostanus* L.), a wild lettuce (*Lactuca indica* Hara), and water dropwort (*Oenanthe javanica* (Bl.) DC), might be introduced as well. The 112 species and 40 families constitute 3.7% of the vascular plants and 23% of the vascular plant families occurring on the Korean peninsula.

Green leafy vegetables (new shoots, rosettes, whole young plants and leaves) were the major type of food plants found. This group comprised 82 species (73.2% of the total) in 62 genera and 27 families. The life forms of these plants include four trees, two shrubs, six vines, and 70 herbs. The foliage foods of the woody plants (species of *Actinidia, Aralia, Kalopanax, Celastrus, Euonymus,* and *Cedrela*) were all new spring shoots, whose leaves were not fully expanded. The two exceptions to this were the mature needles of pines, but these are eaten as flavourings and used in wine making and not consumed in quantity. Almost a third (29 species in eighteen genera) of the species yielding green foods belong to the sunflower family (Asteraceae). The lily family (Liliaceae), with ten species in eight genera, and the parsley family (Apiaceae), with seven species in six genera, were also numerous. Most of these plants were seen only during spring (April and May). Two species, a wild kiwi (*Actinidia arguta* (Sieb. et Zucc.) Miq.) and lamb's quarters (*Chenopodium album* L.) were seen only as dried leaves. Two others, Japanese trout lily (*Erythronium japonicum* Decne.) and ligularia (*Ligularia fisheri* (Ledeb.) Turcz.), were observed as both fresh and dried leaves; the remaining leafy foods were only seen as fresh produce. The new shoot vegetables of woody plants had the shortest periods of availability, often as little as to two weeks. Rosettes of shepherd's purse (*Capsella bursa-pastoris* (L.) Medikus) were common even in winter. A few wild vegetables, such as a wild stonecrop (*Sedum sarmentosum* Bunge), whose mature leaves are palatable, or others, such as the mugworts (*Artemisia* species) that produce new growth over long periods, were common from the spring through autumn. Pine needles were seen mostly in the autumn because of their use in autumn festival rice cakes and not because of seasonally related palatability.

These leafy vegetable foods are used mainly as *namul,* cooked side dishes that are important parts of meals. Usually namul are prepared by steaming or blanching leafy or root vegetables, placing them in small serving bowls with sesame oil seasoning. Namul are served at room temperature.

Fruits were the next most abundant type of wild food with 25 species (22.3% of the total) in eighteen genera and thirteen families. All of these fruits are borne on woody plants and include sixteen trees, five vines and four shrubs. The most numerous group of fruit producing plants was the rose family (Rosaceae) with seven species in five genera.

Fruits were most common during the autumn. Figure 5.3 shows a wild kiwi (*Actinidia arguta*) sold in Korean markets in autumn. The green cones of pines were spring products and the mulberry (*Morus bombycis* Koidz.) fruit was seen during July. Fleshy fruits tended to have short periods of availability, while most dry fruits were present much of the year. The most common uses of fleshy fruits were for direct consumption as fresh fruit and in wine making. These wines are not true wines but rather liquor-like products, made by placing the fruit in a large jar, adding sugar and allowing fermentation to occur. After a week to several weeks, *soju*, a Korean distilled spirit made from sweet potatoes, is added. These popular home and restaurant made wines use both sweet fleshy fruits and those that are not sweet such as dogwood (*Cornus officinalis*), green pinecones and chestnuts. Oak (*Quercus* spp.) acorns (*Figure 5.4*) are used to make a gelatine-like food called *tot'ori muk*. Tot'ori muk is made by removing and powdering the internal meat from acorns and soaking it in water to remove unpalatable compounds. Clean cold water is added to the leached material, which is boiled

Figure 5.3 Wild-collected kiwis offered for sale in a Korean market. There are several small, delicious (ca 1″) wild kiwis in the markets.

Figure 5.4 Traditional market showing acorns from several species of oaks for sale. They are used to make a cooling jelly (*dot'ori muk*) eaten in summer.

while stirring. This mixture is put into moulds (usually shallow rectangular pans) to cool and set to a brown opaque jelly. This is a very common cooling summer food eaten with chilli, green onions and soy sauce and served in restaurants as well as sold in markets. All of the acorns used for tot'ori muk are wild-gathered.

The roots of seven species in seven genera and four families were found. All are from herbaceous plants and three of the seven are from vines. The root foods have the longest periods of availability, being present much of the year, probably because they can be harvested and stored over much greater part of the year. *Ixeris japonicus* Nakai, a small rooted sunflower family species, is most common in the spring and is gathered before it flowers. With the exception of kudzu (*Pueraria thunbergiana* Benth.) roots, from which a tonic juice drink is expressed and a starchy tea-like drink is made, these vegetable roots are usually cooked to prepare a number of dishes including *namul*. The roots of a bellflower vine (*Codonopsis lanceolata* [Sieb. & Zucc.] Trautv.) are most frequently crushed and grilled with red pepper paste, but are also ground and mixed with milk and honey to make a drink.

Five flower foods or products in four genera and families were encountered. These were pine pollen (probably from two *Pinus spp.*) sold in the form of a country made cookie, dried flower buds from a day lily (*Hemerocallis fulva* L.), that are used as namul, and the flowers of a rhododendron used to decorate rice cakes and in wine making. In addition, stonecrop (*Sedum sarmentosum*) flowers,

85

as well as the leaves, are used as namul. The pines produce pollen and the rhododendron bloom in the spring. The day lily flower buds are collected in early summer and dried, so that they may be sold for much of the year. A few other plants, in addition to stonecrop (*S. sarmentosum*), provide more than one type of food resource. A wild kiwi (*Actinidia arguta*) provides young leafy shoots in the spring and fruit in the autumn. The new spring leaves of day lily are used as the flowers during the summer. Red pine (*Pinus densiflora*), one of the most common trees in South Korea, provides pollen, green cones and needles.

About half of the wild-gathered species in markets were uncommon. This frequency was due primarily to the large number of leafy vegetable species that were infrequently seen. Many of these, such as the wild violet (*Viola acuminata* Ledeb.), were seen only in mixtures of many plant species. About a quarter of the other species were of common occurrence and a fifth very common. Most fruits were common in their seasons in the large markets. Most root species were very common.

The 112 wild food plants constitute about 3.7% of Korea's flora (Lee 1979), including both North and South Korea. Since none of the collections were made in North Korea or, it seems, from the subtropical broad leaf vegetation of the southern coast of South Korea (no plants restricted to this area were seen), the actual food market use of the flora from which the collections were made is much higher. About 20% of the total number of wild edible plants listed in Lee 1969 for both North and South Korea were found in contemporary markets. This is a high percentage of marketing of the known edible plants in Korea's flora, especially when one considers the collection area, and the fact that Lee's list contains plants used as emergency foods as well as more palatable species.

(b) Recent cultivation of wild food plants

There are nineteen species of wild food plants in South Korea for which the Korean Rural Development Administration had evidence of cultivation as of 1992 (Lee 1989; Rural Development Administration 1993). Most (15/19) of these plants provide leafy vegetables. Two, balloon flower (*Platycodon grandiflorus* (Jacq.) A. DC.) and bellflower vine (*Codonopsis lanceolata*), are cultivated for their roots and another, a sunflower family plant (*Ixeris dentata* [Thunb.] Nakai) is grown for both its roots and whole young plants. Sichuan pepper (*Zanthoxylum piperitum* (L.) DC.) is grown for its fruit, which is used as an aromatic spice.

The areas of cultivation for these crops varied from less than a hectare for six of the least cultivated plants, to more than 700 ha for each of the three most cultivated plants; balloon flower (*Platycodon grandiflorus*), bellflower vine (*Codonopsis lanceolata*), and the leafy wild aster (*Aster scaber*). These recent crops are grown both in open fields and inside vinyl plastic covered houses. Most of these plant species were grown in both situations, except for the important root crops, which were almost entirely field grown, and wild aster and *Youngia sonchifolia* Maxim, which are vinyl house crops. Overall, there is more area of field culture than vinyl house culture for most of these new crops. The trend from 1989 to 1992 was one of increasing cultivation of wild type food plants. Five of the nineteen plants cultivated in 1992 were probably not cultivated in 1989. Of the fourteen species cultivated in both 1989 and 1992, twelve had increased areas of cultivation during these three years, and seven of these increased manifolds. Eight of the nine South Korean provinces each had more than 1,000 households involved in the cultivation of wild type food plants as of 1992, when almost 25,000 households country-wide grew these plants.

Although the area of cultivation of food plants traditionally wild-gathered doubled between 1989 and 1992, it is still small as compared to the area devoted to vegetables long under cultivation. The total area of wild food plant cultivation in 1992 was 3,525 ha., versus 5,579 ha. for lettuce, 6,403 ha. for spinach, and 44,440 ha. for cabbage (Ministry of Agriculture, Forestry and Fisheries, 1993).

The four most commonly cultivated of the new food crops (wild aster – *Aster scaber,* bellflower vine – *Codonopsis lanceolata*, balloon flower – *Platycodon grandiflorus* and *Youngia sonchifolia*) apparently have not been grown elsewhere as food. Many of the new crops are also some of the same species that were most commonly encountered in the markets. Cultivation certainly contributed to the market commonness of certain species such as wild aster (*Aster scaber*), which has a relatively large area of cultivation. Bracken fern (*Pteridium aquilinum*) and shepherd's purse (*Capsella bursa-pastoris*), two of the most common market species, do have larger areas of cultivation but not nearly enough to account for their market abundance. Market abundance probably relates to commonness in nature and buyer preference as well as to recent cultivation for some species.

(c) Rice-field grasshoppers

Grasshoppers have been a common food for people in many parts of the world (Bodenheimer 1951). Rice-field grasshoppers (*Oxya* spp.) are eaten in most East Asian countries. In Korea these grasshoppers are called mettugi and were a common food eaten as a side dish at meals, as a lunch box ingredient and as a drinking snack (*Figure 5.5*). The use of rice-field grasshoppers declined during the 1960s and 1970s with increased insecticide use. As I documented elsewhere, rice-field grasshoppers as human food experienced a revival in South Korea during the late 1980s and early 1990s (Pemberton 1994).

Some mettugi appeared in beer halls and upscale drinking places but were expensive. I did not see any mettugi during four years (1989–1992) of monitoring Seoul food markets, where they were once common, and where silk moth pupae (*Bombyx mori* L.), a human food that is by-product of the Korean silk industry, are almost always present. Limited numbers of mettugi were gathered in areas away from agricultural fields (and insecticides), such as in mountains and even in the outer DMZ military security zone, where agriculture is limited. The mettugi food culture of Korea had become rare and seemed to be disappearing.

Figure 5.5 Korean Rice-field Grasshoppers (*Oxya* spp.) Prepared for the Table.

Then on October 8, 1990, the Korean language newspaper *Chungang Ilbo* published an article titled 'The mettugi revival' (Mo and Hŏ 1990). It described the rebirth of mettugi gathering and selling in Kyŏngsang Namdo, a province in the southern part of the country. Shortly after the article appeared, I visited the centre of this revival, Ch'ahwang-myŏn (a district of Sanch'ŏng County), where I interviewed the Ch'ahwang-myŏn Agricultural Cooperative Manager Park Chung-ki, and two local farm women Im Pun-nam and Kim Ssang-sun, who were active mettugi collectors.

Ch'ahwang is small district with about 3,000 people, most of whom belong to 744 farm families that cultivate 642 ha of paddy rice (1990 figures). Before insecticide use intensified in the 1960s, mettugi were abundant in and around the rice fields and were collected for both home use and sale. The elevation of Ch'ahwang-myŏn is from 380 to 420 m, so it has cooler nights and consequently fewer problems with rice pests than areas at lower elevations. Despite this situation, the farmers could not avoid the government policy requiring at least three sprays per season. In 1981 the rules mandating insecticide use were relaxed and farmers started using less, which allowed the mettugi populations to begin to increase. In 1982 some mettugi began to be collected and were sold again in the local market at Sanch'ŏng.

The decline in insecticide use and the desire of some Koreans to eat pesticide-free rice led to the development of organic rice farming in Ch'ahwang-myŏn.

This was economically viable because the yields of rice were the same in unsprayed fields as in sprayed fields, and organic rice sold (and still sells) for higher prices. In 1989 the Ch'ahwang Agricultural Cooperative, which functions primarily to buy, mill and sell rice, began to buy dried mettugi from the farmer-collectors. In that year, more than 600 litres were purchased from more than 300 families. The farmers earned 4,000 wŏn (US $6.06) per litre. The Cooperative sold the mettugi in bulk for 4,250 wŏn per litre (US $6.44). The farmers probably sold another 600 litres at the traditional market that is held at intervals of five days and on the street. In 1990, more than 600 families (out of 744) sold 1,744 litres of mettugi to the Cooperative at 5,000 wŏn per litre (US $6.98). The Cooperative sold them for 6,500 per litre (US $9.08). Much of the 1990 sale went to a supermarket company in Pusan, which divided the mettugi into 0.2-liter packages and sold these for 3,000 wŏn (US $4.19). Mettugi were also sold by mail order and to out-of-town visitors to the Cooperative.

In 1990 the average collector sold two litres of mettugi to the Cooperative, but some collectors brought in as much as 40 litres, and one man, who had no rice field to tend, sold 160 litres to the Cooperative. Mettugi are usually collected by older women, usually from mid October to early November. They are collected by hand primarily from rice fields, until the rice is harvested; some are taken from other crops (such as dry beans) and from wild vegetation in the surrounding mountains. The average collection rate is about 0.25 litres per hour, while the best rate is one litre per hour. Both Mrs. Im and Mrs. Kim collect for fifteen days each year on a part time basis. Collected mettugi are steamed or boiled, then dried in the sun for one day and in a room for two more days. In 1990, Mrs. Im (age 58) collected 100 litres, with the help of her husband, and sold 40 litres to the Cooperative. She sold most of the remainder at the five-day market and gave some to relatives. She was pleased to say that her city-dwelling grandchildren get mettugi in their lunch boxes. She has been collecting and selling mettugi for five years. Mrs. Kim (age 37) has been collecting and selling mettugi for eight years. She collected 80 litres in 1990.

During 1990, the income per hour for collecting mettugi for these women ranged from 1,250–5,000 wŏn (US $1.75–6.98), excluding the time spent in processing and marketing the mettugi. The average 1990 income for farm households (3.8 people) was US$16,706 (Korean Ministry of Agriculture, Forestry and Fisheries 1992) and many families in hilly areas such as Ch'ahwang-myŏn earned less. The added income from mettugi collection and sale was, then, significant to these families. Mrs. Im said: 'Mettugi helps us live'.

In 1991 and 1992, large numbers of mettugi continued to be bought and sold by the Ch'ahwang-myŏn Cooperative and many people came to buy directly from the farmers (Min Pyŏng-hong personal communication). In 1992, the Cooperative bought mettugi for US $9.91 per litre and sold them at a bulk rate for US $12.03 per litre.

The food preparations of dried mettugi vary. Sometimes they are eaten dried without seasoning. They are usually pan-fried with or without oil after the wings and legs have been removed. During or after cooking, they are flavoured with sesame oil and salt, or sesame oil and sugar, or soy sauce with or without sugar. I have also seen live ones fried whole. These turn red like shrimp do as they cook. Many of these preparations produce a product with good snack food essence. They are bite-sized, crispy, crunchy, and salty and/or slightly sweet. Korean preparations of rice-field grasshoppers are, to my taste, much better than the sweet sticky Japanese preparations of *Oxya* (*inago*) that are sold in tins and restaurants in Japan.

Reasons for Wild Foods Consumption

The commercialisation and consumption of wild foods occurs because of the desire of many Korean people to eat wild foods, rather than the need for food from wild resources. South Korean agriculture and imports can adequately supply all the food needed by the country. The wild food plants also provide relatively few calories to the people who eat them. No cereals or pulses were encountered among the wild foods in this study, and the wild-gathered roots are not staple starches but occasionally consumed vegetables. The desire to eat wild plants is then not out of necessity, but primarily because many Koreans believe that wild plants are nutritionally superior to cultivated plants and freer of agricultural chemicals. Many of these wild food plants, of course, also have special tastes that are sought by some consumers. Some people believe that wild food plants taste better than cultivated species. Wild gathered food plants are more expensive than traditional crop plants, and a wild-gathered vegetable, such as balloon flower (*Platycodon grandiflorus*) roots, is often twice the cost of a conspecific that is cultivated.

There are few scientific data on the nutritional components of wild gathered food plants in South Korea. Since these plants are usually less succulent than cultivated species, they may have more minerals, vitamins, protein and other nutrients per unit of fresh weight than either recent or traditional cultivated food plants. However, the desirability of wild food plants probably relates more to the belief that they are imbued with a healthy wholesomeness, rather than a concern for specific chemical nutrients.

Food in Korean culture has more overt health connotations than it does in the West and wild animal foods are also thought to be very beneficial to one's health. Yet, there is no obvious marketing of non-marine wild animal foods, except for rice-field grasshoppers (mettugi) that many Koreans consider to be a health food. Indeed, mettugi (probably *Oxya* spp.) have high levels of iron (43mg/100g), vitamin B2 (5.6mg/100g) and protein (64.2g/100g) (Ch'ae et al 1962). In Ch'ahwang, mettugi is used to prevent and cure constipation and to treat heart problems. Mettugi (*Oxya velox*) is used as a drug in traditional Korean medicine, prescribed to treat the convulsions of children, coughs, tetanus and weakness (Kim 1984).

Interestingly, this wild food gathering, this apparent continuation of an ancient hunter-gatherer culture, exists in a modern industrial country. As of 1992, around the time when research for this chapter was done, Korea ranked fifth in the world for steel production and sixth in passenger car manufacture (Johnson 1995). Since Korea's economic development and urbanisation are recent, one might assume that this food gathering culture is a remnant of a more agrarian society, which will fade as people become more removed from their rural roots. It is also possible to think that the adoption of introduced foods such as international fast foods will eliminate many traditional food ways, including wild-gathered foods. Indeed, many young South Koreans are enamoured with the new fast foods and appear to know little about wild plant foods. However, the increased cultivation of these species and marketing of both the newly cultivated and gathered wild food plants in the most fashionable and prestigious markets in Seoul suggests that their use may persist. I do not have data on the amounts of wild gathered food plants sold over time, so I cannot assess the trend in marketing of wild plant foods. South Korea's cultural values relating to the superior healthfulness of wild-gathered food plants are strong enough, however, to promote their continued use, despite the country's continued economic growth and globalisation.

The recent cultivation of wild food plants in South Korea is also related to a reduction in rice cultivation. The government has reduced the land area devoted to rice culture in order to maintain higher market prices in the face of declining rice consumption in the country (Ministry of Agriculture, Forestry and Fisheries 1993). The reduction in land devoted to rice culture has created both the need and the opportunity for novel crops such as wild food plants and medicinal plants. The cultivation of wild food plants on these newly available lands appears to be taking place because of both the Government's encouragement and the initiative of individual farmers and villages.

During the spring, commercial wild vegetable gatherers, wearing large kangaroo pouch-like collecting bags, can be seen working the forests and fields. Many amateur gatherers are also at work (and play) to bring wild vegetables and a taste of spring to their families' tables (*Figure 5.6*). The Korean word for wild vegetable is san namul, which literally means mountain vegetable. Traditionally mountains are numinous places and even in the metropolis of Seoul many people almost daily go to draw water from natural springs in the surrounding mountains, which is supposed to be good for one's health and called *yaksu*, 'medicinal water.' South Korea's loved mountains are not only sources for many of the wild food plants, but perhaps also impart to these plants that special wholesomeness that makes them so desirable.

For older Koreans, much of the appeal of eating mettugi lies in the feelings of nostalgia that it brings. The mettugi revival gives people a chance to taste the past.

Hierarchy of Food Preference

Wild forms of new cultivated wild-gathered plants are more expensive than cultivated forms. Market sellers would often indicate whether the plant was wild

91

Figure 5.6 Korean Women Collecting *San Namul* to Eat as Vegetables.

or cultivated. Seller's indications of wildness were not always reliable, since wild forms are more valued, and claiming wildness for cultivated forms could bring the seller more profit. Imported vegetables and perhaps meats are at times claimed by sellers to be domestically produced because these are more valued. This is the basis of the shint'o puri related education efforts to enable people to distinguish Korean grown foods from imported foods.

The hierarchy of Korean food preference from the least to the most desirable is:

– foreign grown domesticated foods
– Korean grown domesticated foods
– Korean grown newly cultivated wild-type foods
– wild-gathered foods collected in Korea

Some newly cultivated wild-type foods may be grown outside Korea and some wild-gathered foods may be collected outside of Korea and sold in Korea. Presumably these would be less valued than their Korean counterparts.

As far as the vegetables are concerned, this hierarchy may be explained as the result of the application of two principles, one grounded in Korean tradition and the other – shint'o puri – a recent invention, or invented tradition, due to the pressures of globalisation. Although many san namul and most mettugi are not collected in the mountains, these wild-gathered products are, nevertheless, imbued with a kind of wild energy and wholesomeness that is often associated with the mountains.

A similar kind of hierarchy can be observed in drugs. Korean traditional medicine is widely consumed and exists side by side with modern science based medicine. While examining the current use of insects and other arthropods in traditional Korean medicine (Pemberton 1999), I found that the use of this drug material is increasing. In addition, most of the interviewed traditional medicine doctors indicated that they tried to prescribe arthropod drugs from Korea as opposed to imported ones. Figure 5.7 shows a traditional medicine doctor with medicinal centipedes, which, like most medicinal arthropods, are imported from China. In 1996, Korea imported 49,000 metric tons of herbal medicine materials worth $US 72,000,000 (Foreign Agricultural Service 1997). The expressed wish to try to sell Korean species probably is related to shint'o puri ideology and perhaps a desire to be politically correct.

Conclusion

Although Korean diets have been dramatically affected by globalisation, its food patterns are influenced by overt cultural values, as well as by preferences developed from growing up with a specific set of foodways. Despite the shifts

Figure 5.7 Traditional medicine doctor selling centipedes, used primarily to treat arthritis. Although traditional medical doctors prefer to prescribe drug materials from Korea, much or even most of it (like these centipedes) is now imported, mainly from China.

seen in modern Korea's food culture, the country's beliefs are likely to preserve its traditional, and in the case of san namul and mettugi, its ancient foodways.

Most Koreans still strongly prefer Korean food. A few years ago I spoke with some Korean college students (the group that most likes international fast food), who just returned from a trip to China. When I asked what the highlight of their trip had been, they responded rapidly and strongly that it had been eating Korean food in Beijing at the end of their tour after being deprived of Korean food for one week. Globalisation will continue to influence Korean food patterns, but there may be more resistance to food recognised as foreign than elsewhere.

Notes

1 The kind help of the following individuals and organisations has been indispensable for this study: Robert Macke, Foreign Agricultural Service, United States Department of Agriculture, Washington DC; Cho Yeon Hwang, Ft. Lauderdale, Florida; Jeanne Litterst and Laura Mallillo, Tricon International, Louisville, Kentucky; Carol Skinky, McDonald's Corporation, Oakbook, Illinois; Boudewijn Walraven, Leiden Univ., the Netherlands; Ban, Y. US Embassy, Seoul.

2 These and the following statistics are from the Foreign Agricultural Service, United States Department of Agriculture, 1997 Agricultural Situation Report for South Korea. This report draws on various Korean language statistical summaries, primarily from the Korean Ministry of Agriculture Forestry and Fisheries, the Korean Customs Service, and the National Livestock Cooperative Federation.

3 Similar claims of chemically contaminated imported produce are now commonly heard in the US, some of which is promoted by protectionist interests.

6

BARDOT SOUP AND CONFUCIANS' MEAT

Food and Korean identity in global context

Boudewijn Walraven

Introduction[1]

In 1919 the missionary Charles E. Sharp contributed an article to the periodical *The Korean Mission Field* under the title 'Shall We Eat Korean Food'. The 'we' he spoke of were the foreign missionaries active in Korea, and his answer to the question was affirmative, at least in principle. Both the example of Jesus Christ, whom Sharp quotes 'it behoved (...) in all things to be made like his brethren that He might become a merciful and faithful High Priest in things pertaining to God', and the experiences of the missionaries in the field should lead to the conclusion that it was desirable to act as a Korean to the Koreans. 'Eating food together is among all people a token and expression of fellowship and to few people does it mean so much as to the Koreans' (Sharp 1919:139–141). But Sharp continues:

> Over against this law of becoming a Korean to the Koreans, and antagonistic to it, stand two other laws, those of heredity and habit. We have received a certain inheritance from our forefathers, and certain courses of action have been decided for us before we were born. We cannot escape from this. We might as well try to change the color of our skin.

In other words, in Sharp's view the predilection or tolerance we have for certain types of food is to a large extent physically determined. Differences between various races or nationalities are grounded in the body, making total cultural assimilation physically impossible.

Although colleagues of Sharp who had eaten Korean food regularly for years, declared to have suffered no fatal consequences and even were convinced that it was quite healthy (Hall 1933:187), deeply-felt convictions of this kind are common and may exist even with regard to the food, not of different countries, but of different regions within one and the same country. In the early 1990s, a man in Chŏnju in Southwest Korea spoke to me about the impossibility for the inhabitants of that city to live in Kyŏngsang Province, an hour's drive away. 'We can go there, but we cannot stay for more than a day. The food there doesn't agree with us, that's why.'

One might think that in the present situation of pervasive globalisation such attitudes are on the wane, and to a certain extent they no doubt are. Yet the intimate connection between food and identity, which is a matter of cultural values and symbols rather than of physiological predispositions, ensures that strong local predilections and prejudices with regard to food remain. In this chapter, a brief survey of the ways in which Korean identity in the age of globalisation may be defined in terms of food will serve as a stepping stone to a discussion of an international clash of local values that for a large part takes place in the globalised arena of the Internet.

The tendency to regard certain foods as epitomising Koreanness will be examined by looking at three kinds of food, which together would constitute what the Dutch are wont to think of as the essentials of a regular meal: starch, vegetables and meat.[2]

Rice

For starch, the obvious choice is rice, which in Korean metonymically stands for food in general. Hence the phrase '*pap mŏgŏssŏyo?*', literally 'Have you eaten rice', may simply mean 'Have you eaten?' Another, even more general, derived meaning of *pap* (cooked rice) is 'livelihood/a living'. Rice has a long history on the Korean peninsula; its cultivation began in the Bronze or Iron Age and preceded the first formation of a unified Korean state by many centuries. Although rice has not always been the staple for everyone, it has still acquired a special symbolic value. This is well illustrated by the indignation still aroused by the fact that during the Japanese colonial period (1910–1945) Korean rice consumption per capita fell in spite of an increase in production, because substantial quantities of rice were sent to Japan, while the Koreans were forced to eat 'inferior' grains such as millet or barley imported from Manchuria. In fact, rice has generally been associated with wealth: the phrase 'white rice with meat soup' connotes the good life, while tacitly acknowledging that not everyone can afford rice (Kim 1994:24; also Hong 1995:91).

The Korean preference for rice somewhat puzzled early Westerners who came to Korea. Homer Hulbert wrote:

> The extreme difficulty of keeping paddy-fields in such a hilly country, the absolute necessity of having rains at a particular time and of not having it at others, the great labour of transplanting and constant cultivations, – all these things conspire to make the production of rice an incubus upon the Korean people.

(Hulbert 1969:16)

Yet, Hulbert notes, 'out of a hundred men who have saved up a little money ninety-nine will buy rice-fields as the safest investment'. In his *A Korean Village: Between Farm and Sea*, Vincent Brandt (1971:49–50) writes that in the village of Sŏkp'o 'attitudes and values focus primarily on rice, so that possession of paddy land, work connected with rice agriculture, and the grain itself are all far more prestigious than the equivalents for other crops'.

The vehemence with which farmers have resisted rice-imports from abroad (which the government under strong foreign pressure reluctantly had to concede in 1993), and even more the sympathy that they received from students and members of the general public, testify to the strong symbolic value attached to rice, and to an association with national identity. When the pressure rose to liberalise agricultural imports, a campaign launched by the farmers association to convince Koreans that Korean-grown farming products were intrinsically healthier for Koreans than imported products made use of the slogan *shint'o puri*, literally 'the body and the soil are not two'. (*Nonghyŏp Samshibonyŏn Sa* 1996:215–217[3]) This is a striking example of creative recycling, for originally this is a Buddhist phrase used in Tiantai philosophy, which means that an individual's karma and that of his environment are inseparable (cf. Pemberton in this volume; Kim 1994; Grinker 1955:206). The message that the farmers wanted to convey struck a cord in nationalist hearts, and shint'o puri became the title of popular song lambasting those who give in to foreign fashions (see *Figure 6.1*).

The symbolic value of rice in Korea is beyond doubt, and it might be argued that the concept of 'rice as self' (Ohnuki-Tierney 1993) is applicable to Korea as much as to Japan. Some foods are, however, more 'self' than others, and in Korea at present pride of place is given not to rice (which is perhaps too bland a food to represent Koreanness), but to a vegetable dish, *kimch'i*, which is also mentioned in the song 'Shint'o puri':

Rice and barley,
soy and azuki beans...
Our things for our bodies,
why look for other people's food?
Don't forget, don't forget
Red pepper paste and bean paste,
Kimch'i and kkaktugi [radish pickles].
For us Koreans,
for you and for me
body and soil are one,
body and soil are one![4]

Kimch'i

The pickles called kimch'i are widely considered to be quintessentially Korean by Koreans and foreigners alike. Hulbert called it 'the favourite sauerkraut, ...

Figure 6.1 Imported liquor offered to a shamanic deity prompted a discussion among shamans whether the principle of shint'o puri is valid for gods as well as humans.

whose proximity [because of its strong garlic smell] is detected without the aid of the eye' (1969:17). As an accompaniment to almost every meal, it has almost as great a claim to be called a staple as rice. During the twentieth-century Korean diaspora, wherever Koreans went (whether it was to Japan, California or Kazakhstan) kimch'i has followed as 'a persistent bond linking the Korean people' (Chu 1991:102). Young Korean-Canadians are on record as having expressed the conviction that kimch'i and respect for one's elders are the essentials of Korean culture they should absolutely preserve (Yu 1994:272) and Korean-Americans have named their own information web site 'Kimchinet' (http://www.kimchinet.com).[5] Kimch'i was considered such an indispensable part of Korean food that when Korean troops were sent to Vietnam in the 1960s, shipments of kimch'i had to be sent to them, which led to its first commercial mass production (http://kimchi.kfri.re.kr/2-2-1.htm). Before that time, all kimch'i was home-made.

This is not the place to discuss the manifold varieties of kimch'i (there are several hundreds of ways to prepare it, for different seasons, using completely different ingredients, and every region has its own variations). Instead, it should be noted, first of all, that in spite of its perceived 'Koreanness' it is not a kind of food that is totally unique to Korea, as it belongs to the 'fermented vegetable group' which, as Hulbert noted, also comprises sauerkraut, as well as Japanese *tsukemono* (pickles), and secondly that over the centuries kimch'i has changed considerably. In Korea, too, what one might call the 'Latin-American Revolution' – the far-reaching changes in diet occasioned by plants (peppers, potatoes, tomatoes, tobacco) introduced from the Americas – has triumphed. Only in the eighteenth century did Koreans begin to use the chilli pepper, which nowadays gives kimch'i its 'characteristic' red colour and pungent taste (Chu 1991:86–91). The addition of *chŏtkal*, pickled sea-food (oysters and other shellfish, anchovies etc.), too, is a relatively recent phenomenon, while the kind of cabbage that presently is used most commonly for kimch'i was only introduced about a hundred years ago. This does not, however, reflect the way most Koreans feel about kimch'i; to them it is as if the modern form of kimch'i always has been an integral part of Korean culture. They frequently assume, moreover, that to non-Koreans it is hardly possible to eat and really appreciate kimch'i, although in this respect, as we shall see, perceptions are changing.

It is not surprising, therefore, that in comparisons with other cultures kimch'i emerges as a symbol of Korea and Korean culture. In 1976, a Korean writer active in Japan, Kim Yang-ki (1987), entitled an essay in which he compared Korean and Japanese culture: 'Kimch'i and *oshinko*' (oshinko is another name for Japanese pickles). The anthropologist Han Kyŏng-ku (1994) in an article with the English title 'Some Foods are Good to Think: Kimchi and the Epitomization of National Character' argued that kimch'i is particularly suited to projections of national character. The aggressive red colour and the spiciness of kimch'i (both due to the adding of red pepper powder) stand for energy and masculinity. As a simple, unsophisticated and inexpensive vegetable food, kimch'i also fits the Korean self-image as underdogs who through hard work rise in a world where the lazy fat cats linger over big steaks.

Han Kyŏng-ku has also traced how Koreans' view of kimch'i changed and became more and more positive as the Korean economy developed and confidence in one's own capacities and pride in Korean culture grew. Due to its pungent smell, kimch'i is not a food that is easily accepted by all foreigners. Yet, by the time globalisation became the key word for the economy in the 1990s, the internationalisation of kimch'i, which thirty years earlier was unimaginable, came to seem a distinct possibility, even a necessity. It is typical of the Korean interpretation of globalisation that it means above all that Korean culture receives global recognition. Accordingly, the author of a book on the cultural anthropology of kimch'i wrote: 'If the self-respect of our nation is not to be damaged in global society, kimch'i should be propagated to people all over the world as our characteristic culture' (Chu 1991:116). Korean publications suggest that since he wrote these words some progress has been made towards that end. An editorial in the English-language *Korea Herald* noted with satisfaction that kimch'i had 'become a favorite of some of those international athletes who took part in the Atlanta Olympics' (eleven tons of kimch'i were supplied to the Athletes' Hostel) and that kimch'i also had been included 'on the official menu of the 1998 World Cup soccer games in France' (*Newsreview* 29 November 1997). Ironically, this editorial added that for export the less salty, less spiced and less garlicky Japanese version of this 'national food' stands a better chance of conquering international markets. Therefore local producers should not hesitate, the newspaper editors opined, to refine the dish somewhat, so that 'Korea, as the originator and home of this unique vegetable food', may receive the recognition for it to which it is entitled. The objection that in this way kimch'i would lose its truly Korean character was countered with the argument that the characteristics that stand in the way of propagation abroad are not essential (an argument with history on its side, as we have seen) and are disliked even by many Koreans; 'a growing number of Koreans no longer relish fermented foods prepared with overly hot and salty ingredients'. In this context, it may be noted that so far Japan, where kimch'i has become so popular that it is widely produced locally, is also by a wide margin the largest export market for Korean export kimch'i, the total value of which in 1997 amounted to $39,692,000 (http://kimchi.kfri.re.kr/2-2-2.htm).

Now that kimch'i has become an export product, it has to be marketed, too (see *Figure 6.2*).[6] For this purpose, it is emphasised that it has great qualities as a health food. In publications designed to impress the world with the excellence of kimch'i, the salutary effects of all fermented foods are pointed out and kimch'i itself is said to have anti-carcinogenic effects, to be low in calories and cholesterol, and to contain rich supplies of the vitamins A, C and B-complex (*Newsreview* 14 November 1998).

Kimch'i is not only seen as a symbol of national identity by researchers, journalists or the general public, but also by the government, which has given it official status. It has been designated as one of ten symbols of corporate identity (CI, defined as a 'systematic image management tool that has been widely used among business enterprises') selected by the Ministry of Culture and Sports (*Newsreview* 11 January 1999). 'The selected symbols', a newspaper report said, 'are expected to help spread positive images of the country and its people'. The only other food item selected as a CI symbol was *pulgogi*, broiled beef.

Thus with kimch'i one sees a chain of interlinked connections: to begin with a plain preference for the food as such, which is so strong that in some cases one is tempted to speak of an addiction; then various (and changing) concepts of

Figure 6.2 A Poster Propagating Consumption of Kimch'i in Japan.

identity and symbolic meanings based on the importance of this food in daily life, and finally conscious symbolic manipulation, which again is based on the more spontaneous symbolic connotations. For the second and third phase in this scheme, actual consumption is secondary. In fact, in recent years, the quantity of kimch'i eaten by Koreans has declined (as has that of rice).

Dog Meat

Whereas not everyone may like kimch'i and it has taken even the Koreans a while to convince themselves that the world outside Korea also should

101

appreciate its excellence (which seems undisputed by nutritionists), kimch'i is not a truly controversial food, in stark contrast to the last item on the menu: dog meat. It is precisely because of its controversial nature and the multicultural dimension of the controversy, which involves questions of national identity and intercultural stigmatisation, that the eating of dog meat deserves closer scrutiny. It is certainly not because dog is so important in the Korean diet, because it is not. In a recent survey, half of the respondents said never to have eaten it, and among those who had many had tasted it only once or twice (Orange 1995:373).

As the eating of dog meat has long been a fairly normal practice in most of East Asia (China, the Philippines, Vietnam, etc.; Chang 1977:56–58, 67; Elisseef 1995) the debate is to a large extent the result of the intensification of East-West contacts promoted by modern communication and the organisation of international mega-events, while changes in the food culture as a whole have been greatly affected by the mutually related processes of modernisation, industrialisation and globalisation. Against this background, the confrontation of local preferences with global pressures surrounding the consumption of dog meat furnishes an interesting case for the investigation of the changing food culture of twentieth-century Asia and East-West relations in this respect.

A few lines from the work of the American anthropologist Cornelius Osgood, who did field-work in a village on Kanghwa Island in 1950, supply without much ado the essentials of the traditional form of dog eating in Korea:

> Besides the two hunting dogs kept by one young man, four other households each have a scrawny-looking cur. These are kept to eat during three hot days of the year when the meat is regarded as having a special salutary effect. The dog is killed by strangling it with a rope thrown over the branch of a tree. The hair is then burned off and the carcass cut up and cooked.
>
> (Osgood 1951:77–78)

In short, it was seasonal and not very frequent: only four households out of a total of 27 in this particular village kept dogs to eat. The same picture emerges from a village study that was conducted about twenty years later (Sperl 1974:140). Other ethnographic evidence from the twentieth century, as well as nineteenth-century descriptions of Korean customs, also shows that dog meat was not a daily food, but mainly seasonal, eaten on the so-called 'dog days' (*pok nal/pok il*), three days ten days apart, of which the first (the main day to eat dog stew) is the third day designated with the cyclical character *kyŏng*[7] after the summer solstice. These days were supposed to be the hottest days of summer. The eating of dog was neatly mirrored by the eating of sparrows, wild boar or wild rabbit on a special day in winter: the third day designated with the character *mi* after the winter solstice (Shin 1991:667; Yi et al. 1974:115). In both cases, the eating of meat, which was not part of the daily fare, whatever its kind, was intended to strengthen physical resistance against extreme weather conditions. In fact, farmers – who constituted the majority of the Korean population until the second half of the twentieth century – rarely ate meat except upon these occasions. The quantity of livestock kept by farmers was generally small, and cows were above all valued as work animals for ploughing. (Hence the cow is symbolically associated with agriculture rather than with meat.) For the farmers, beef was not a normal food item. In passing it may be mentioned that probably early in the twentieth century – and I suspect in an urban context – a substitute was devised for the dog soup (*kaejang* or *kaejangguk*) eaten in the middle of summer to retain stamina, which was called *yuk-kaejang* (literally 'meat dog soup', 'meat' here referring to beef).

A report from the year 1929 of the Korean Society for the Prevention of Cruelty to Animals, an organisation with Korean, Japanese and Western members, also confirms the impression that the eating of dog meat was not widespread (Hobbs 1929:258–260). The Society showed concern for the plight of overloaded pack horses and the mistreating (referred to as 'torture') of animals by unlicensed doctors, but the traditional way of killing the dogs to be eaten, which in recent years has become the object of fierce attacks by animal-rights campaigners, was not mentioned at all, nor was the eating of dog meat itself.

In spite of this, however, there is some historical evidence that dog meat was also eaten, even if in moderate quantities, outside a rural or strictly seasonal context. The *Veritable Records* for the reign of King Chungjong refer for the year 1534 to roasted dog meat offered to a high official as a bribe (*Chungjong Shillok* vol. 78:1a). In 1649, the Governor of Kangwŏn Province is censured for eating dog meat in a period of national mourning (*Hyojong Shillok* vol. 1:39b). A record from the year 1777 refers to government officials who go to eat dog meat soup in 'a place where they slaughter dogs outside the palace gate', apparently a kind of restaurant specialising in dog stew (*Chŏngjo Shillok* vol. 4:20a). In a nineteenth-century poem, *Nongga wŏllyŏngga* ('The Farmer's Works and Days'), which describes the life of the peasants during the four seasons, the daughters-in-law bring dog meat and wine as a present when they go to visit their parents in the eighth lunar month (Yi Sŏk-rae 1974:140).

The fact that according to a late Chŏson description of Korean annual customs, *Tongguk Seshigi* (Im 1972:211), dog meat was sold on markets, also suggests consumption on a larger scale. In another source of roughly the same period, *Han'gyŏng Chiryak*, a nineteenth-century description of the capital, however, reference is made to specialised markets for beef, pheasants, poultry and pork, but not to dog butchers (Yu 1956:319–320). The evidence is somewhat ambiguous, but at least until the colonial period (1910–1945) the consumption of dog meat undoubtedly was mainly associated with farmers trying to keep up their stamina in the oppressive, humid heat of mid-summer.

A point that should not be overlooked is the fact that dog meat in Korea always has been medicine as well as food. Of course in East Asia, where there is a great general concern with the medical properties of daily foodstuffs, the distinction is to a certain extent artificial. Yet, it is possible to distinguish between cases in which dog meat (or any other part of the dog) is consumed for medical reasons only, and cases in which pleasure and physical benefit go together. By and large, dog can be taken by anyone as medicine, irrespective of age or sex, while (traditionally) as food it is predominantly eaten by men. Even in the latter case, though, the health aspect is usually present in the minds of the eaters.

The *Precious Mirror of Korean Medicine* (*Tongŭi Pogam*) of Hŏ Chun (1975:1134), first published in 1613 and still popular as a repository of traditional medicine, specifies the medical properties of parts of the body of the dog in detail. Its penis will cure male impotence, but is also effective against 'the twelve female complaints below the girdle'. Taken on the first dog day it reduces transpiration for a 100 days. Dog meat in general is said to be 'warming' (*yang*), and beneficial for the Five Vital Organs, the arteries, the stomach and intestines, bones and joints; the blood of a black dog is a remedy for difficult birth and footling breach birth, the teeth for epilepsy and obstinacy in children, the heart for depression and rage, and the kidneys for post-partum fatigue of the kidneys and 'kidney chills', while the gall removes discharge from the eyes and the stomach; the claws, when decocted, promote the flow of mother's milk.

Medicinal use of parts of the dog has a long history but it is not a thing of the past. The form this kind of medicine takes is not necessarily the common dog stew, but often the so-called *kae-soju*, literally 'dog liquor', which is actually an extract of parts of the dog and not an alcoholic drink. Nor are the beneficial effects of dog meat only expressed in the terminology of traditional Korean (i.e. Chinese) medicine. In summer, the Korean media often discuss the various methods of overcoming the fatigue caused by the sweltering heat, weighing the relative merits of *samgyet'ang* (a soup with ginseng and chicken), duck, black goat and dog meat, employing the phraseology of modern Western medicine. Dog meat is said to contain the vitamins A, B1 and B2, easily digestible proteins, and to be low in cholesterol and high in poly-unsaturated fat (e.g. *Han'guk Kyŏngje Ilbo* 4 August, 1997).

Although dog meat also seems to have been eaten by people for no other reason than they had a taste for it – at any time, irrespective of the season – apparently it always has been a kind of food with particularly strong symbolic associations and usually has been consumed within a rather circumscribed context. I am tempted to say that in this respect dog meat is to other meat/food what alcohol is to water or tea.[8] Apart from the fact that because of its seasonal associations dog meat symbolically stands for summer (as – in certain regions – pumpkin pie for November and plum pudding for Christmas), it also had religious connotations. Followers of different faiths related to it in different ways. Buddhists would avoid it entirely, while Confucians had such a taste for dog meat that, according to oral tradition, it was nick-named 'Confucians' meat' (*yuyuk*). To justify their predilection, Confucians could point to the canonical authorisation of the Book of Rites (*Liji*), where dogs are mentioned as (sacrificial) food (Legge 1885:289,372,470). Because in late Chŏson Korea

Buddhist belief was strongest among women and Confucianism to a large extent a men's affair (a contrast that was more pronounced in Korea than in China or Japan), the differences between Buddhist and Confucian attitudes toward the eating of dog meat also reinforced the associations of dog meat with male gender, which it already had because of its yang-stimulating properties.

Korean shaman rituals, too, are associated with women rather than with men. The shamans, who have borrowed a great deal from Buddhism, do not categorically reject the eating of meat. In fact, among their deities there is a division between the gods who bring affluence and good luck and who receive meat (albeit no dog meat) as sacrificial offering on the one hand, and gods who bestow life and offspring and are vegetarian on the other. However, when the shamans deal with the fate of the recently deceased, they may cite the eating of dog (referred to as *mongmongi*, 'Woof-woof') as particularly deleterious to one's karma, requiring special efforts to save the spirit of the deceased from suffering.

Dog stew (*kaejangguk*) is mentioned several times in the sacred writings of the influential New Religion called Chŭngsando ('The Way of Chŭngsan'; Chŭngsan is the name of its founder, who is venerated as Sangjenim, 'The Lord on High'). Sangjenim (1871–1909) apparently had a taste for kaejangguk, and on one of the occasions his followers prepared it for him he explained why dog meat is a superior meat.

> Why he liked to eat dog meat
> Because one day He ordered them to slaughter a dog for Him, they slaughtered a dog, made dog soup (*kut'ang*) and served it. Then Sangjenim spoke: 'This meat is the food of superior persons.' When the disciples asked why, He said: 'Farmers enjoy this meat and in this world farmers are none but the superior persons.'
> *(Chŭngsando Tojŏn* 1993: Book 4:89)[9]

In this passage, one recognises the connotation of dog meat as a source of animal protein for poor farmers, but this is given a new and potentially revolutionary meaning. On another occasion Sangjenim said (*Chŭngsando Tojŏn* 1993: Book 5:123): 'Kaejangguk is a food people eat, but students of the Way (*toga*) did not and thus they felt resentment (*han*). Now to eat this soup is to dissolve resentment and reform government (*kaejŏng*).' Thus in Chŭngsando dog stew acquires a religious as well as a political meaning. Apart from that, however, it is also clear from the scriptures that the believers served their leader with this dish as a token of respect.

The question now has to be addressed how the great changes that have taken place in Korea's society have affected the eating of dog meat. It is clear that if it had remained a purely rural phenomenon, by now it would have almost disappeared. At present, over 80% of all Koreans live in cities. Moreover, while large-scale urbanisation took place, the rural subsistence economy, in which dog meat was a rare source of protein, has made way for a consumer society with numerous alternatives. The question cannot be answered, however, without first considering the effects of certain pressures arising from Korea's increasingly frequent international contacts after liberation in 1945.

The International Uproar over Dog Meat

In the second half of the 1980s, many unsuspecting Dutch primary school children were made to watch a particularly gruesome video, which showed how Koreans beat to death a dog they were going to eat. This was part of an emerging international debate which still goes on at present, not least on the Internet.

The 1980s campaign to stop the cruel killing and eating of dogs in Korea cunningly made use – not unlike the Korean movement for political democracy – of the fact that the Korean government, due to the approaching Olympic Games, was particularly anxious to transmit a positive image to the world and extremely sensitive to pressure that seemed to jeopardise that purpose. The result was that some more or less cosmetic measures were taken: establishments that served dog meat were removed from places were foreign visitors might see them. *Poshint'ang* ('body-strengthening soup', at that time the usual name of dog stew) made way on the menu for such 'novelties' as *yŏngyangt'ang* ('nourishing soup'), *kyejŏlt'ang* ('seasonal soup') or *sagyet'ang* (which might be translated as 'soup for all seasons'). A law that was designed to curb the eating of dog meat, restricted the sale of 'repugnant foods', *hyŏmo-han shikp'um*, without clearly specifying what was meant by this. In this way, dog stew was to a certain extent driven from the public view, but already in the summer of 1988, before the Olympics had begun, a reverse movement was noticeable. When the democratisation process that began in 1987 gained momentum, there was a feeling that the government was no longer able to enforce policies that were unpopular with at least a sizeable portion of the population, and these included the measures taken against the poshint'ang restaurants.

As said, the international campaign against the eating of dog meat continues, with Brigitte Bardot as one of its champions (which has prompted Koreans to add yet another name to the many appellations for dog stew: Bardot soup; Orange 1995:374). At the moment, the next big international event in Korea, the Football World Championships, scheduled for 2002, is used by activists as a lever to draw international attention to Korea and exert extra pressure. There is no doubt that the campaign may reinforce existing perceptions of other races or nations as being fundamentally different and inferior. Worldwide, the stigma of being dog-eaters has been attached to Koreans and certain other Asians and complicated their relations with other nationalities. According to the British anthropologist John Knight (personal communication), in the 1950s hunters in the Japanese prefecture of Wakayama feared that Korean workers involved in road construction there would constitute a threat to the survival of their precious hunting dogs, even though there was no clear proof that these workers actually had a craving for dog meat. Similarly Koreans and other Asian immigrants to the USA may become the object of suspicions of this kind when the neighbour's pet goes astray. The stigmatising of all Koreans as eaters of dog meat is common (Hall 1997) and I found it expressed with particular venom on an Internet site that, although ostensibly for the benefit of singles looking for social contacts, in practice seems designed for the enjoyment of the editor of *Maledicta*. The Los Angeles author of a message so obscene that it is best left unquoted hid behind the 'signature': 'Gooks are dog-eating barbaric monkeys' (http://www.korealink.com/singles/asia/messages/784.html). In Britain, in supposedly more polite company, Jeremy Clarkson opined in October 1998 at the Motor Show that the Koreans were too busy eating dogs to design a decent car (Smith 1998).

Animal-protection activists usually express themselves in a less offensive manner. In fact, sometimes the arguments pro and con are summed up with admirable detachment and even-handedness. Yet, it is inevitable that their campaigns strengthen stigmatisation and occasionally there is more than a trace of condescension in their own pronouncements, as the following quotations (all from the Internet) attest: 'South Korea Legalizes The Slaughter of Dogs for Meat. *The Civilized World* [emphasis added] is disgusted at the thought of people eating "Man's Best Friend. There can be no forgiving this inexcusable act of cruelty' (http://www.dogbiz.com/dont-eat-dog-meat.htm). After Korea's economic crisis the editors of this site added: 'After lunch [dog meat, of course] it's back to the office to figure out another way to beg more money (again) from the International Monetary Fund (your tax dollars) and to ship more Korean products to those gullible Ignorant Westerners.' Gory detail is not shunned: 'To see a dog's bloody head on a table with flies buzzing around it eyes beading out, and all the skin ripped off, for sale is ... *the sign of a barbaric nation* [emphasis added]' (http://www.paws.org/korea/korea09.htm). 'Cruel Korea tortures pets,' appeared as the subject of a discussion in the Newsgroup 'soc.culture.korean'. Letters sent to English-language newspapers published in Korea presented similar views: 'We [Westerners] think that only most backward and desperate societies will stoop to eating dog' (Letter to the Editor, *Korea Herald*, 6 December 1996). Obviously in these passages it is not just those South Koreans who eat dog meat but the whole nation that is in the dock. Consequently it is sufficient to be Korean to become a target for protest actions. The Progressive Animal Welfare Society (PAWS) on its homepage urges sympathisers to write to Korean representations abroad and to Korean multinational companies such as Samsung, Hyundai, LG and Daewoo (http://www.paws.org/korea/ucando.htm). To see this in perspective, one would have to imagine that international animal protection organisations would ask Chinese, Koreans and Philippinos to protest against the mass slaughter of millions of pigs in The Netherlands in 1997 in order to contain an epidemic of swine fever, – the ultimate purpose of this being not so much to protect people's health as to safeguard the highly lucrative export of Dutch pork – by writing to Philips or Royal Dutch Shell.

Bias may also be detected in criticism of the medicinal use of dog meat for its supposed aphrodisiac properties, which is singled out by Western critics as particularly unforgivable. This betrays not only a puritanical view of human sexuality, but also suggests inspiration by the stereotype of the 'Lustful Oriental' whose overheated sensuality knows no bounds (Said 1995:187–188). Again a selection from the Internet: 'It was pointed out to me that the association of a prostitution area with the dog meat area is usual throughout the country' (http://www.earth.org.hk/Seoul.html). 'I cannot help thinking that dogs are only used here as an aphrodisiac' (http:\www.paws.org/korea/korea08.html). Elsewhere, under the caption: 'Abusers' Paradise – take your pick of the flesh on offer,' photographs are displayed of 1. 'A Hooker,' 2. 'Pigs,' 3. 'A Dog Corpse' and 4. 'Cats' (http://www.earth.org.hk/Seoul.html).

If one thinks of the passage from the *Precious Mirror of Korean Medicine* quoted above, it is obvious that the medicinal use of dogs does not only serve the purposes of lechery. Although not all applications of parts of the dog enumerated in the *Precious Mirror* are of equal importance, a substantial part of its total consumption for medical reasons is not to stimulate sexual prowess. A young man of my acquaintance, who normally would never eat meat of any description, started eating dog meat when he was diagnosed as suffering from tuberculosis. Women and elderly people, too, eat dog for health reasons. Of course, many Koreans and not a few Westerners in Korea eat dog in summer in order to suffer less from the oppressively humid heat, among the foreigners many Catholic fathers and nuns. Korean doctors prescribe it for this purpose and I have been assured that it does have some effect. Thus, without convincing scientific evidence, I would hesitate to call it 'superstition', as both non-Korean and Korean opponents of eating dog meat do (Editorial, *Korea Herald*, 30 November 1996). In any case, to the degree that dog meat is medicine, it is not quite clear why Westerners should single out Korea for criticism, considering the extensive and often cruel use the Western pharmaceutical (and cosmetic) industry makes of animals.

Finally – should it be mentioned? – one should not discount consumption for culinary rather than libidinous pleasure. One of Korea's most prominent literary historians, a great lover and connoisseur of dog meat, once told me that if one would like to get acquainted with all the regional differences in Korean cooking, there would be no better way than to try all the local variations of dog meat, which he thought reflected the characteristics of regional cooking better than any other dish.

Korean Reactions

How have Koreans reacted to this massive, often ferocious and sometimes vicious assault? A minority does not feel personally attacked, wholeheartedly sympathises with the campaign and even contributes to it. Thus, in fact, the debate is not between Koreans (or Asians in general) on the one hand and non-Asians (Westerners) on the other. The Korean Animal Protection Society actively opposes the eating of dog meat and looks for support overseas in order to achieve its aim. In practice, however, considerations of national pride and national culture constantly crop up. Even Koreans who fundamentally agree with the campaign in favour of the dogs are often anxious to take away something of the opprobrium the eating of dogs excites in the West. The arguments they use vary in quality: 'The custom of dog eating did not originate in Korea but in Vietnam. People nowadays do not eat dogs as much as they used to. Mostly elderly people eat dogs because they believe that it increases their life span and it's good for their health' (from a message to the Newsgroup 'alt.talk.Korean'). Another 'explanation' furnished by a Korean supporter of the anti dog-meat campaign ran: 'The habit of eating dog meat goes back to the Korean War when all food was in short supply (. . .) Of course, dogs were slaughtered and eaten by starving people' (http://www.paws.org/korea/korea02.htm).

Other Koreans, however, resist the campaign more radically, seeing in it an attempt to destroy Korean culture. A particularly striking example of radical rejection based on nationalistic feeling is found in an article written by a professor of the Seoul College of Education, An Ch'ŏn (1991:31–56), entitled: 'Dog Meat and International Political Culture'. The author regards food culture as that part of culture that is most resistant to foreign influences, and thus in a sense its most essential part. Remains of dog bones suggest that the palaeolithic inhabitants of the Korean peninsula (who are without problem assumed to belong to 'our people', *uri minjok*) already ate dog meat. The first foreign attack against this ancient custom was in a sense domestic, as it was led by Francesca, the Austrian-born wife of South Korea's first president, Syngman Rhee. The lack of popular support for top-down instructions to abandon the custom of dog eating resulted in a cosmetic change of name: from this time dog stew was sold not as kaejangguk, but as poshint'ang, 'invigorating soup'. According to An Ch'ŏn, policemen went around with buckets of paint to force owners of dog meat establishments who were slow in changing the name on their signboards to paint them over.

The second attack was the one already mentioned in connection with the Seoul Olympics, which led to the disappearance of dog meat from the view of foreign tourists and to another change of name. Discussing these attacks, An Ch'ŏn expresses sympathy for those who campaign against the suffering inflicted on animals worldwide, but questions their right to single Korea out as worse in this respect than other nations. 'We have to be resolute in our attitude towards the pressures of western cultural imperialism with regard to the food culture of dog meat, and have to maintain a spirit of independence.' 'The desperate struggle for the eating of dog, [a custom] which has survived the struggle with foreign cultural invasions, is a praiseworthy act of heroism.' Pointing out that it is a object lesson to learn how to withstand foreign political pressure, An Ch'ŏn compares the resistance of the Korean people in this case with the patriotic movement started by concerned citizens in the first decade of this century to collect funds to pay off Korea's national debt and safeguard independence. Future generations, An concludes, in hindsight will recognise the importance of the fight for dog meat, and say: 'Our ancestors were magnificent: enthusiastically they ate dog meat in spite of the cultural inroads made by foreign powers, resolutely sticking together, as with one mind, to save the culture of eating dog meat. The desperate struggle to protect the culture of eating dog meat has ended in a brilliant victory for our people.'

It remains to be noted that the 'future ancestor', An Ch'ŏn in a footnote confesses, 'as an individual' never to eat dog meat, because he loves dogs too much. The actual consumption of food in his case entirely makes way for its symbolic value.

Feelings such as those expressed by An Ch'ŏn are not confined to a small circle of nationalist intellectuals (Kim 1994:24–25), but crop up in every discussion about the eating of dogs. Similar reasoning is found in a large, almost quarter-page advertisement for an alcoholic drink, *Paekseju* (*Figure 6.3*), that appeared in the daily *Chosŏn Ilbo* of 15 July, 1997 (in the middle of summer and after a Korean court had condoned the eating of dog meat). The first two lines, set in very large type, declare: 'Let's openly eat poshint'ang now!', and are followed by a paean to dog meat stew: 'poshint'ang, from antiquity always loved by our people, [is] a good dish we are proud of.' The advertisement explains in some detail the nutritional virtues for which 'our ancestors' ate dog meat and quotes old historical and medical sources for authoritative backing. Praise of Paekseju only occupies about one quarter of the total space, at the very bottom. The one but last line reads: 'Together with our own healthy food our own expertly brewed alcohol is best.' For the purposes of this advertisement, which reflects both the shint'o puri ideology and the changed legal situation after November 1996 (also note the re-emergence of the appellation poshint'ang), it is entirely irrelevant whether the readers actually eat dog meat stew or not, as long as they drink Paekseju. What is important is the nationalistic concept represented by poshint'ang.

Outside Korea, there is an ethnic – rather than a nationalistic – variation on this theme. One of the battlefields where the discussion for and against the eating of dogs rages most fiercely is the State of California, where the East-West encounter is part of daily life. There attempts by Asian immigrants to pursue their old life style have led to the stipulations of California Penal Code, article 598b (passed in 1989), which says that every person who possesses, imports into California, sells, buys, gives or accepts animals traditionally and legally kept as a pet or companion with the intent to use them for food is guilty of a misdemeanour punishable by up to six months imprisonment or a $1000 fine. This has prompted a young American-Asian, Donna Wong, to counter-attack an in an internet magazine called *Yolk* (http://www.yolk.com/magazine/iss2/dog.html): 'American society, founded on Eurocentric principles, roars again in triumph as it alienates another of its many peoples who may seem different to the dominant culture.' Why is it permitted to eat rabbits, but not dogs? Provocatively she gives a recipe for Dog with Black Beans ('serve with white rice'). At the end there is a brief description of the author: 'Donna Wong is a political science major at UCLA. She has yet to taste her first bowl of dog stew.'

Figure 6.3 A newspaper ad for a brand of liquor praises the age-old Korean custom of eating dog meat.

In spite of both international and national pressure, the actual consumption of dog meat has remained at a considerable level, as may be inferred from the fact that in the years following the Olympics dog meat was imported from South-America. Kim Kwang-ŏk (1994:25), who proffers this information, has noted the irony that, although a 'health food' was concerned, in this case the principle of shint'o puri apparently did not apply. In 1998, the total consumption of dogs as food and as medicine was estimated to be about 100,000 tons per annum and the number of specialised restaurants roughly 6,500 (*Han'guk Kyŏngje Shinmun* 27 October 1998).[10] Although many Koreans never touch dog meat and it is often claimed that it is not popular among young people, those who like it are able to afford it more often thanks to the growing affluence of the past decades.

After a Korean court of appeal on 20 November 1996 decided that dog meat in principle could be eaten as food, in spite of the legislation against the sale of 'repugnant foods' (*Korea Herald* 22 November 1997),[11] some of the restrictions to its consumption that had been the consequence of its semi-legal status fell away, leading to new developments. Dog slaughterhouses were opened, which may put an end to criticism directed at the cruel ways of killing the dogs, rather than at the eating of dog meat itself. Nevertheless, the sale and consumption of dog meat still take place in a kind of legal no-man's land. One of the consequences of this is that inspections of sanitary conditions applying to other foodstuffs have been lacking. Therefore, in May 1999, a Member of Parliament for the opposition Grand National Party proposed legislation to solve this problem by regularising the sale of dog meat. He quickly put this plans on hold because it was feared that it would adversely affect a by-election, but the mere fact that the issue was openly discussed by a parliamentarian demonstrates that there is more support for a public defence of Korean customs than in the past. The proposal sparked a new round of debate, in which the various positions were once more stated. Those in favour said that it was time to stop deferring to the opinions of foreigners. Opponents and the government feared international protests, as well as damage to Korean trade and major international events to be held in Korea, and talked of a new cosmetic law, forbidding the display of dog carcasses. As a compromise it was suggested that a distinction should be made between pets and dogs for consumption. A poll taken found that 56% out of 4158 respondents were in favour of this (implying that they did not absolutely opposed the eating of dog meat), with 36.6% against (*Han'gyŏre Shinmun* 31 May 1999).

In the meantime, there have been new trends in the way dog meat is eaten. In April 1997, a newspaper reported the opening of a restaurant specialising in dog meat in Pundang, a recently built area of high-rise apartments in Sŏngnam, one of Seoul's satellite cities, a distinctly 'modern' and rather affluent area (*Chungang Ilbo* 24 April 1997). This restaurant offered dishes that were much cheaper than usual (4500 wŏn or less) and more variety in the methods of preparation (dog *teppanyaki*,[12] for instance). The owner announced his intention to open a chain of similar restaurants elsewhere. This may have the effect of changing the association of dog meat with old-fashioned, unsanitary and out-of-the-way places where groups of men gather to eat (and drink), and 'normalising' dog meat as just an alternative to beef, pork or chicken. The new restaurants seem to be places where a busy office worker could casually pop in for lunch. There are also some indications that the consumption of dog meat among women is increasing. No less than 23% of the women from a limited sample questioned by Hyundai Department Store said they enjoyed poshint'ang, while 72% said they did not object to the eating of dog meat (Choe Young-min 1998).

Figure 6.4 A restaurant advertises cheaper dog-meat soup because of the economic crisis (the 'IMF-crisis').

Conclusion

Seen from a certain distance, the dog meat debate is interesting because in many ways it is a replay of colonial debates and reproduces the colonial dilemmas, the confusing push and pull of opposing forces that do not neatly coincide with ethnic or national boundaries. The defence of cultural identity still clashes with demands made in the name of 'civilisation', even though there is no longer a coercive colonial overlord.

It also shows that although many Koreans are highly sensitive to foreign criticism, in this case for the foreseeable future local custom is not likely to be wiped out by global pressures (just as the eating of horse meat – to certain Americans no less repugnant than that of dog meat – survives in many places, among which Japan and the Netherlands). The question is in what form the eating of dog meat will be preserved. Will it keep the mystique its rich traditional symbolic connotations have lent it? Or will it change its image and become one consumer product among many? The attempt to create a chain of relatively cheap dog-meat restaurants with new types of dishes, which in Western media was reported under the headline '"McDog" Restaurant Chain Challenges McDonald's' (http://www/mcsspotlight.org/media/press/reuters_8jun97.html) points towards the latter, as does the increasing number of women who eat dog stew. Sophisticated restaurants serving French red wine with dog meat (Choe Young-min 1998) confirm this trend.[13] Eating dog has also become less seasonal, even though summer undoubtedly still is the period of maximum consumption. Yet, in all this the older associations retain a certain force, which may be harnessed to promote new developments. In the transition towards the further commodification of dog meat, the identification with Koreanness serves as an effective marketing concept, in the same way shint'o puri helps Korean farmers to hold on to their share of the market in agricultural products. Thus a poshint'ang restaurant advertising on the Internet claims to maintain 'pride in our food', offering 'local meat exclusively from inland regions'.

Notes

1 I am indebted to Antonetta Bruno, who kindly sent me source material from Korea.
2 While I developed the theme of this chapter, choosing this trinity as its focus, I was not yet aware of the fact that Kim Kwang-ŏk, from whose work I have considerably benefited, had dealt with exactly the same three foods in an article in the journal of the Korean Society for Cultural Anthropology (Kim 1994).
3 I thank Robert Pemberton for sending me this source.
4 This song, with lyrics by Kim Tong-ch'an, is sung by Pae Il-ho on a cd with the same name: Seoul Records 1993, no. STRCD-10002.
5 All internet addresses are given as they were at the time of writing. Meanwhile, however, they may have disappeared, or their contents my have changed.
6 Marketing is also increasingly relevant within Korea itself, as modern life styles make the preparation of kimch'i at home more difficult.
7 The character kyŏng is the seventh in a row of ten (called the 'stems') used in East Asia to designate hours, days, months and years. The character mi, which also occurs in the main text, is one of twelve terms (called the 'branches') used in conjunction with the row of ten to refer to moments in time.
8 In China, too, dog meat seems to have had particular connotations. Frederick Mote has remarked: 'Whenever it [i.e. dog meat] is specified, however, it carries a special significance.' Because it is, for instance, the favourite food of the irascible counterfeit monk Lu Zhishen in the Water Margin Novel and in Ming drama a Mongol general is represented as eating dog meat for each meal, Mote is led to the conclusion that 'The association with fierce and wild behaviour is clear.' Frederick W. Mote, 'Yüan and Ming', in Chang 1977:242.

9 My translation. This passage is omitted in the English version of the scriptures Chŭngsando has published.
10 The Korean Animal Protection Society estimates, on what grounds is unclear, that about two million dogs are killed annually (http://www.paws.org/korea/korea04.htm).
11 Some of the details mentioned are of interest for the quantitative information they provide: a man had been given a 3 million wŏn fine, in itself a considerable sum, but small when compared with the 500 million wŏn of dog meat he allegedly had sold.
12 Slices of meat and vegetables grilled on an iron hot plate and served with a dip.
13 In recent years red wine has enjoyed great popularity in Korea because of its assumed beneficial effects on health.

7

FAMILY HOSPITALITY AND ETHNIC TRADITION AMONG SOUTH ASIAN WOMEN IN THE WEST OF SCOTLAND

Helen Bush and Rory Williams

Introduction

This chapter conforms to the theme of the volume in that its primary focus is the exploration of an Asian cuisine in a European city.[1] It differs, however, in that this exploration is facilitated by a comparison with a second, non-Asian cuisine, that of Italy. Specifically, we describe the food choice of South Asian (i.e. with a direct line of descent from the Indian sub-continent) and Italian women living in Glasgow (West of Scotland). In the course of investigating factors which shaped their food choice in hospitality, we found the most important factors to be closely related to the construction of ethnic identity.

Comparison of these two ethnic groups, and of women from the general Glasgow population, was originally made because in Britain, South Asian migrants have high levels of heart disease compared with the general population, and migrants from Italy have low levels. This is despite the fact that both groups of migrants come predominantly from rural areas where levels of heart disease are low. Recent studies suggest that patterns of diet and exercise have led to an excess energy intake in South Asians in Britain, and also that total fat forms a high proportion of intake among South Asians abroad, though there are exceptions. Yet in rural India total fat intake forms a small proportion of energy intake, even smaller than in Italy, which still has the quite low proportions of fat associated with the Mediterranean diet.

Why should this turnabout have happened among South Asians, but not Italians? A number of possible factors need consideration, including patterns of preferred body size in conditions of economic insecurity, responses to income constraints, patterns of reduced energy expenditure and restriction of exercise due to changes in work or experience of hostility, and the extent to which food sharing and food exchange follow obligatory patterns of high energy intake in which health is not a major consideration. Our study has measured all these factors, and we have explored how considerations of health compare with the social and symbolic importance attached to family hospitality in the reports of food choice by South Asian, Italian and general population women in Glasgow (Bush et al 1998). Here, however, we focus on the extent to which obligatory patterns of food choice exist in these groups of women, and are reflected in conventions of hospitality.

Family hospitality of any kind has great social significance, and can be expected to cast light on the wider sociology of the meal. In an important series of papers in the early 1980s, Anne Murcott described the traditional cooked dinner of South Wales, consisting typically of roast meat, potatoes, at least one additional vegetable, and gravy, forming a plateful. She analysed its social significance as time-consuming, as evidence of women's labour, and as served in accordance with the preferences of others who eat the meal. She found it to be a repetitive expression of family communality, even when members eat it at different times and places, and a token in a gift exchange between husband and wife, the skills for which are passed on from mother to daughter.

It is surprising that these marital and family features of traditional Welsh meals have not provoked more comparison with English or Scottish meals, and with the culinary traditions of other cultures. At the same time observers of Italian and Greek families have noted similarly that a woman's mode of cooking could be used to estimate her domestic virtue, with the reputation of her family depending on her behaviour (Hirschon 1989; Colpi 1991). Among Asia Minor refugees in Greece, easily prepared foods are 'prostitutes' food', suggesting even more rigorous marriage obligations than in South Wales. And studies of Muslim families in the Indian subcontinent and in Britain have commented on similar themes in the construction of wifely virtue (Saifullah Khan 1976; Jeffery 1979).

These observations on the internal family symbolism of a cooked meal are paralleled by other references to the meal's impact on external status and reputation. This is already implied by assessments of the cook's domestic virtue, but hospitality adds a further dimension. Until the time of wartime rationing in Britain, the impact of which minimised the differences in the diet of the social classes, the recipe books of the middle classes 'appeared to put a high value on effort' so that Avery suggests 'to be seen to take short cuts was to lose caste. The preservation of your caste, in the elaborate middle class structure of pre-war England, was a highly important matter' (1984: xii). In their more recent study of women in York, Charles and Kerr found that some gave up formal entertaining because of the pressure it exerted upon them: 'Cooking a meal for visitors is, in some way, a presentation of status and skills to the outside world and women and their families are judged on the basis of what they provide' (1988:217).

Again, cross-cultural comparison would raise important issues. As industrialisation proceeded in the last century, economists noted the diminishing proportion of expenditure on food as income rose – an observation which continues to be exemplified in income comparisons today. To the extent that it is an indicator of income and status, therefore, food, and especially food given in hospitality, would be expected to hold much greater significance in pre-industrial or peasant cultures, and religious values add to its significance (Pitt-Rivers 1977). This tends to give a collective, obligatory quality to local food cultures in peasant economies, and to their locally-specific culinary traditions. The migrants from South Asia and Italy which are of interest here originate in what may be called a peasant-based economy which still preserves many of these culinary features. The South Asians are primarily from the East (Indian) and West (Pakistani) Punjab, and the Italians from hill country near Frosinone, to the East of the Roman Campagna, or the area of Barga in Tuscany. Most migrants had been born in farming villages or agricultural market towns, and their parents had generally worked on their own land or in their own small businesses. At the same time these food patterns are disappearing in the western cities to which they have come. There is a global expansion of the western food industry, a post-modern ethnic consumerism in the food hall, and an internationalisation of food tastes (Holm 1996), which may be reflected in idiosyncratic patterns of hospitality. How far migrants adopt these patterns is a question of great interest.

The questions we address here are, first, in comparison with general British patterns, do migrant groups from both peasant-based economies represented here show evidence of stronger commitment to hospitality than the general population, of more elaborate forms of cookery when presenting hospitality or a cooked family meal, or of status and reputation being at stake, and are there differences in these respects between Britons of South Asian and Italian origin? For example, do they differ in the symbolic importance accorded to meat and animal products? Second, do British-born generations of these minorities show evidence of change in these respects?

Our sample consists of 259 women, aged 20–40, divided into five sub-groups depending upon place of birth (*Table 7.1*). Migrant women were born in Italy or on the Indian sub-continent, while second and subsequent generations were born in Britain. British-born Italians divide more or less equally into those whose parents or grandparents were born in Italy. A general population group consists of non-Asian/non-Italian women living in Glasgow. We focused on women for two reasons. First, the coronary mortality of South Asian women is even higher compared with the general population than that of men (Balarajan and Bulusu 1990), and the gain in weight is marked in those longer resident in Britain

Table 7.1 The Sample

	Number	Mean Age
Italian (first generation)	39	34 years
Italian (second and subsequent generations)	51	32 years
South Asian (first generation)	63	31 years
South Asian (second generation)	56	27 years
General population	50	29 years

(Williams 1993a). Second, women are generally responsible for food preparation. Nevertheless, our work has relevance for men since other studies in Glasgow have shown that the diets of men and women have similar ethnic patterning. Details of methodology and analysis are reported elsewhere (Bush et al 1998).

Our approach in this instance was to ask respondents what sort of meal they would arrange for relatives whom they had not seen for some time, since we hypothesised that a meal of this kind is more likely than most to be bound by certain long-standing conventions in the choice and presentation of food. We describe cross-generational continuities and changes in the content and structure of the meals and we make broad comparisons on these bases to show inter-ethnic similarities and differences. In addition, we explore reasons offered by respondents themselves for their menu choice.

Frequency of Family Hospitality Meals

There are important differences between the ethnic groups in the extent to which such meals are part of the ordinary currency of life (*Table 7.2*). In the general population women, such meals are special in that the median frequency is less than once a month, and only 11% have such a meal every week. British-born Italians partake in these meals to a similar degree. However for migrants in both minorities the median frequency is at least monthly, and a quarter or more have such a meal every week. For British-born South Asians this overall frequency is sustained, with slight tendencies towards both increased and reduced occurrence of family hospitality meals. For migrant Italians, this polarising tendency is even more marked. A greater proportion of women in each of the ethnic minorities find such special occasion cooking 'enjoyable' or 'okay' than general population women, though there are no differences with regard to day-to-day family cooking (*Tables 7.3 and 7.4*). With the exception of migrant Italians, the

Table 7.2 Frequency of Special Meals

	Migrant South Asian	British-born South Asian	Migrant Italian	British-born Italian	General population
once a week or more	15 (25%)	13 (24%)	11 (29%)	6 (13%)	5 (11%)
less than once a week	9 (15%)	12 (22%)	3 (8%)	5 (11%)	2 (4%)
once a month	28 (47%)	17 (32%)	7 (18%)	11 (24%)	12 (27%)
less than once a month/rarely/never	8 (13%)	12 (22%)	17 (45%)	24 (52%)	26 (58%)
Total responding	60	54	38	46	45

p = .00003

Table 7.3 Attitudes to Special Occasion Cooking

	Migrant South Asian	British-born South Asian	Migrant Italian	British-born Italian	General population
It's enjoyable	29 (46%)	25 (45%)	24 (62%)	34 (67%)	28 (57%)
It's okay	27 (44%)	21 (38%)	10 (26%)	9 (18%)	6 (12%)
It's boring	1 (2%)	1 (2%)	1 (3%)	–	2 (4%)
I dread it	5 (8%)	9 (16%)	4 (10%)	7 (14%)	10 (20%)
Respondent does not do	–	–	–	1 (2%)	3 (6%)
Total:	63	56	39	51	50

p = 0.01

Table 7.4 Attitudes to Day-to-Day Family Cooking

	Migrant South Asian	British-born South Asian	Migrant Italian	British-born Italian	General population
It's enjoyable	18 (29%)	10 (18%)	11 (28%)	16 (31%)	7 (14%)
It's okay	34 (54%)	36 (64%)	22 (56%)	18 (35%)	31 (62%)
It's boring	9 (14%)	7 (13%)	3 (8%)	13 (26%)	8 (16%)
I dread it	2 (3%)	3 (5%)	3 (8%)	2 (4%)	4 (8%)
Respondent does not do	–	–	–	2 (4%)	–
Total:	63	56	39	51	50

p = n.s.

majority of women, notably migrant South Asians, consider the consumption of foods associated with their culture to be very important. British-born Italians are least likely to hold this view with more than a quarter stating such foods to be of little or no importance to them, but polarisation of attitudes are also evident here, with 40% stating that 'traditional' foods are very important to them (*Table 7.5*).

The emphasis on food in the life of South Asian women is maintained by the amount of time spent cooking day-to-day meals. The collected data indicated

Table 7.5 Importance of Foods Associated with South Asian and Italian Culture

	Migrant South Asian	British-born South Asian	Migrant Italian	British-born Italian
Very important	42 (66%)	29 (52%)	16 (41%)	20 (40%)
Fairly important	20 (32%)	23 (41%)	17 (44%)	17 (34%)
Slightly/not at all important	1 (2%)	4 (7%)	6 (15%)	13 (26%)
Total	63	56	39	50

p = .001

that on weekdays and Saturdays, migrant and British-born South Asian women spend more time than the other three groups preparing and cooking food, and it is only on Sunday that the ethnic groups do not differ in the amount of time thus spent. Respondents in all groups are primarily responsible for their household cooking, with a slightly greater proportion of migrant South Asians having this responsibility than women in the other groups (*Table 7.6*).

The Structure and Content of the Meal

Women from the General Glasgow Population

A brief description of the menus of these women will set the other groups in context. A modal meal (in the statistical sense of the most frequent single type), corresponding to the traditional British roast 'Sunday lunch', was described by half of the women in this group. Meat was emphasised in this meal to the extent that in some cases it was the only food mentioned as, for example, duck or roast pork or roast lamb. Reference to 'all the trimmings' by two women indicates the familiarity of this type of meal in Britain, such that the interviewer is presumed

Table 7.6 Responsibility for Cooking in Respondents' Households

	Migrant South Asian	British-born South Asian	Migrant Italian	British-born Italian	General population
Respondent	55 (87%)	41 (74%)	28 (72%)	41 (80%)	39 (78%)
Others	8 (13%)	14 (26%)	11 (28%)	10 (20%)	11 (22%)
Total responding	63	55	39	51	50

p = .33137 (n.s.)

to know in what 'all the trimmings' consists without need of further elaboration. In the modal menus there are no references to such trimmings as gravy or stuffing; accompaniments are potatoes (roast or unspecified) and vegetables, specific types being given in two cases. Some respondents who offered a modal menu did indicate a first course or a dessert, but the general lack of desserts in particular throws into relief the central role of the main course, particularly its meat component.

Close variants of the modal meal used alternatives to roasting: grilling, baking or boiling meat, or presenting the results cold. Three women would offer steak pie. The respondents' own explanation was that a pie is easy to produce and, significantly, two said they dreaded special occasion cooking while the other found it boring. The choice could be a cheaper way of retaining meat's central position; at interview the partners of two of these women were unemployed and the third was a single mother. This interpretation is supported by Wood's suggestion that 'close substitution' (1995:69) occurs when money for food purchase is restricted. The stew, hotpot or casserole which two women in this group would offer provides a further hot, and cheaper, alternative. Another variant suggested steak rather than a roast. A traditional Scottish variant was present, though not prominent: two women said they would produce a meal of mince and potatoes, one adding cabbage and doughballs (i.e. suet dumplings).

It is in the proliferation of alternatives to this British meal of cooked meat and vegetables that the general population women differ very significantly from most of the four minority groups. Approximately one quarter of general population women offered menus from an alternative (i.e. non-British) cuisine, mainly those of the ethnic minorities featured here, for example, spaghetti bolognese, another pasta dish e.g. lasagne, or a vegetarian meal or curry.

South Asians

The diet of the Indian subcontinent is based on cereals, with meat, vegetables and pulses forming side dishes in a meal, the number depending upon income (Abraham 1989). Thus meat is not a major dietary component, but the most striking feature of the meals reported here, apart from their marked similarity, is the prominence it is accorded by both generations. The modal meal includes meat as a main dish and rice, with only one woman, British-born, mentioning neither food. Like the general population women, some South Asian women described the special meal more or less completely in terms of the meat which would be presented:

Biryani,[2] korma,[3] tikka (chicken) (British-born)
Shish kebab,[4] chicken, roast meat (British-born)
Rice, biryani, kebab, kofte,[5] roast chicken ... (we) consume more meat (migrant).

Other more comprehensive menus are also heavily meat-oriented, for example:

pilao,[6] *chapatti*,[7] kebabs, chicken curry, meat curry, yoghurt, salad, sweet rice (migrant)

salty rice, chapatti, kebabs, fried chicken, meat curry, chicken curry, yoghurt, sweet dish (migrant)

brown rice, chapatti, kebabs, fried chicken, meat curry, chicken curry, yoghurt, sweet dish (British-born).

pilao rice, *naan*,[8] kebabs, roast chicken, chicken and lamb curries, salad and yoghurt, *kheer*[9] (British-born).

Rural diets of the north of the Indian sub-continent have tended to include little meat, as we noted above, although it is a prestigious food. Among Indian Muslims, for example, greater prestige is attached to the meal which includes more dishes and high status types of meat (Rizvi 1981). Chicken is particularly prestigious and figured extensively in our respondents' menus, sometimes in an unspecified form, but also roasted or curried. By contrast, fish was offered only twice as a component of the South Asian family hospitality meal. It is not an important food in the Punjab, despite the abundance of rivers which give the region its name.

Of 63 migrant women, only two did not mention meat at all; one is Sikh, the other Hindu. They may both, therefore, be vegetarian and the reference of this Hindu respondent to pilao rice may mean that it includes vegetables rather than meat. Of 57 British-born South Asian women, two did not mention meat (one is Hindu) and two others referred to 'curry' but since the type is unspecified these may be meat-based. Half the migrant women mentioned two or more meat items in their menu, while only 25 British-born women did, a difference which is statistically significant ($p=<0.05$). If this is not an artefact of reporting, the reduction in number of meat items may indicate a shift in the attitude of British-born women toward meat as a symbol of prestige, which in itself might indicate changing attitudes to their culture.

Rice has special significance for Muslims in particular, but also for Sikhs, because it is not grown in the Punjab and so has to be imported, adding to its cost which may explain its status in family hospitality. Bread, the native Punjabi staple, appears as chappatis or, very occasionally, as naan in roughly half the South Asian menus, but its omission from others may, like 'all the trimmings' in the general population menus, simply reflect an assumption that its nature as an integral part of a meal obviates the need to list it.

Close variants of the modal meal of meat and rice occurred in seven migrant and eleven British-born women's menus and consisted mainly in the omission of rice or a main meat dish, although three British-born women included one or two foods of other cuisines. The menus of respondents who did not include meat correspond to the modal meal in all other ways.

Turning from these central elements to more peripheral dishes, we note that *pakoras*[10] and *samosas*[11] are included in the menus of almost a quarter of

British-born South Asians, but appear less frequently in those of women born on the Indian sub-continent. One British-born woman remarked that more fried foods are a feature of special meals. A recent ethnographic study of young Asian women in Glasgow confirms that 'fried foods' equate with pakoras and samosas (Bradby 1996).

Foods from other cuisines are uncommon in South Asian menus. Two women include tea and biscuits which according to South Asian conventions of hospitality are offered separately and prior to the main meal. Cakes were included in one migrant menu and possibly have celebratory significance. Lasagne and spaghetti are included in the menus of two British-born women; Bradby (1996) reports South Asian women in Glasgow making lasagne but including ingredients such as garlic, chillies and ginger to render the flavour more like that of a South Asian dish.

Italians

It has been said that 'there is no such thing as Italian cooking, only Sicilian, Piedmontese, Neapolitan, Venetian, Florentine, Genoese and so on' (Roden 1989:1). Despite this historical variation in regional cuisines, there is a formal Italian meal structure which comprises a 'succession of courses with no main course' (Roden 1989:198). Regional variations have declined with the transformation of Italy into an industrialised society in the fifties and sixties, and the associated population movements from the South to the richer North so that 'now the culinary borders have been confused and there is no longer a precise geography of food' (Roden 1989:3).

A meal closely resembling the classic Italian meal structure and consisting typically of three or four courses was described by four fifths of the Italian-born, though by less than half of British-born Italians ($p = <.001$). The structure and 'traditional' nature of the meal was emphasised by some women.

Pasta forms the first course of migrant women's menus. Very few in this group did not include pasta in their descriptions, compared to over one third of British-born Italians. This is a significant difference ($p < .01$) and reflects a more general use of non-Italian cuisine (see below) which is ironic given the current popularity of pasta and Italian cooking generally in Britain, its widespread availability and its promotion in the media, not least as a 'healthy' food. A range of different meats are described by migrant Italian women, including beef, steak and chicken and usually specified as roast. However, the central emphasis on meat, which is obvious in South Asian and general population meals, is generally lacking in Italian menus.

Close variations on the modal meal were suggested by a further quarter of migrant women, and only three described menus which differed markedly from the modal. Of these three, one had lived in Britain for over thirty years and offered a meal more closely resembling the modal meal of the general population women than of the other migrant Italians. The second grew up in

France and said she cooked in a French manner rather than Scottish, and the third was a Sicilian who had lived in Scotland for a little over two years but who was married to a Scot. A fifth of British-born women described meals which resembled the modal but varied slightly in structure, or in content, or sometimes through the inclusion of majority culture foods.

Nearly one third of British-born Italian women described menus which bore little or no resemblance to the modal Italian meal, a statistically significant difference from migrant women. Some in this group had clearly been influenced by cuisines other than their own, saying that they would choose Indian or Scottish foods, while others incorporated items from more than one cuisine.

It appears, then, that foods of the majority culture and of other minorities have been adopted to varying degrees by British-born Italian women, to the extent that they can be considered as suitable for inclusion in their family hospitality meals.

To summarise, most variation in terms of ethnically-specific menu content and structure occurred in the menus of general population women and British-born Italians, although a modal meal corresponding to the British roast 'Sunday lunch' was described by two fifths of general population women, and a classic Italian meal by just under half the British-born Italians. The frequent use of alternative cuisines in both groups contrasts with both South Asian groups and with migrant Italians.

Reasons for Choice

At the outset it was hypothesised that a meal to be offered to relatives not seen for some time would be subject to established conventions regarding the type of food offered and the manner in which it would be presented. The foregoing has shown that some conformity of choice is apparent, not only for South Asians and Italians, but also for general population women. The following section describes the range of explanations for choosing these meals.

Some initial responses to a question on reasons are non-informative. A small proportion of respondents (about a fifth) did not supply anything further than 'Because I like it', despite probing by interviewers. Leaving these aside, a wide variety of reasons emerged. That food is 'traditional' is a common explanation but much more so for South Asians than for Italians. Some respondents did not use 'traditional', but obviously had a similar notion in mind:

> It's our culture to eat and serve these foods to visitors, and it's tasty food (migrant South Asian)
> It's Asian culture to serve these foods (British-born South Asian)
> [It's a] normal Italian meal (migrant Italian)
> [It's a] standard Italian family thing (British-born Italian)
> ... it is a fairly easy, typical menu that Italians would eat (migrant Italian).

Habit is a related reason given:

> Because of the people – that's part of their diet (general population)
> Sort of foods I've been eating for years (migrant Italian)
> It's the kind of food they're used to and expect (British-born South Asian)

and many of these habitual choices are connected to rules governing hospitality:

> Because we have to offer them good things and from our own point of view these are good (migrant South Asian)
> Because guests are in the house (British-born South Asian)
> He is our special guest – coming after performing a religious ceremony (migrant South Asian).

That guests are due respect simply because they are guests is stated explicitly by some South Asian respondents, but it is apparent that an underlying motive may be present in that failure to show respect could have serious consequences. One migrant South Asian women said particular foods are chosen to respect guests so that they couldn't say anything bad about the family; her interviewer reported the respondent's intimation that to offer otherwise could have a negative effect upon the marriage prospects of family members since the wrong choice of food could call their suitability into question. Respect for guests is not an issue made explicit by Italian or general population women, but something analogous can be recognised in the responses of those who made their choice to please their parents. The wish to please, or perhaps to avoid friction, is suggested by the migrant South Asian woman who said '...you have to serve what they like', implying not only the need to respect guests but also perhaps that her preference was of no account. The frequent explanation that foods are selected because they are well liked by visiting relatives or guests can also be interpreted as a demonstration of respect.

Also akin to these explanations is the concept, already referred to as important in South Asian hospitality of the prestige which number and content of dishes in a meal confers upon the host:

> I like these foods and visitors expect this food. It's very tasty and respectable to serve these foods (migrant South Asian)
> ... it looks good if we cook special (migrant South Asian).

The notion is not peculiar to South Asian respondents; witness the general population woman who said she chose her menu to impress her family. Another from this group, by explaining her choice as something decent, demonstrates respect for her guests and perhaps also for herself.

All these ideas (culture, tradition, habit, rules of hospitality and respect for guests, observance of guests' preferences, and care for reputation) make up a coherent constellation of explanations, and form by far the dominant specific formulae used in accounting for the meal chosen. This confirms that our choice of question did indeed elicit a meal of symbolic importance. Other specific formulae were much less frequent, though often interesting. A small number of Italian and general population women said they would chose particular foods specifically because of their health-promoting qualities or for reasons relating to nutrition. For other women, considerations of health or nutrition only partly explained their choice:

It's healthy, traditional food so everyone is pleased (migrant Italian).
I think they're healthy and they present themselves well (British-born Italian).

A number of British-born Italians (seven cases) and general population women (thirteen cases) made their choice on the basis of ease of preparation, a reason scarcely considered by migrant Italians (two cases) and British-born South Asians (one case), and never by migrant South Asians. For Asian women, on the contrary, the effort required to make a meal for guests is a visible sign of the respect which they aim to show:

The visitors will enjoy it and see that I went to a lot of trouble (migrant)
If I cook vegetables they might say what am I feeding them? Vegetables will be simple and rice and meat is a little bit harder to cook (British-born).

For some women, a degree of effort is required beyond that normally expended in food preparation in that, as one British-born Italian observed, it 'forces you to do it when somebody else is coming'. The explanation that particular foods are chosen because they are 'special' or, to a lesser extent, 'good' is peculiar to South Asian respondents; it may be that the effort required to prepare them contributes to their singularity:

These are special foods – they take a long time to make so we make them on special occasions (migrant).
It takes time so we don't make it every day (British-born).

Thus the amount of time required for preparation appears to be a feature of family hospitality meals. By contrast, speed and ease of preparation are frequently stated reasons for the choice of general population women and, to a lesser extent, of British-born Italians. There is no suggestion in these groups that stigma attaches to the easily prepared meal. Ease of preparation is a more frequently stated reason for choice than cost, to which only four respondents made explicit reference and then, with one exception, in conjunction with other reasons. The only South Asian respondent who referred to cost would make her choice *because* it is costly, again apparently because of the messages of appearance and status which such food will convey.

Novelty is a surprisingly rare reason for the menu chosen, and is wholly absent in South Asian accounts. When asked the reason for her choice, one migrant South Asian woman began 'I don't know really' but went on 'I can't make fish or pizza for them'. How inappropriate some British foods can be is revealed by one British-born South Asian respondent: 'Just imagine if relatives are here and you make fish and chips'. The unsuitability of such foods may be due to their novelty, or to the ease with which they can be prepared (Bradby 1996).

Health, ease and novelty, therefore, on the one hand, are occasional considerations, and culture, tradition, habit or respect for guests' preferences on the other hand are common considerations, in choosing meals for family hospitality.

We can consider now the relationship between these contrasting sets of reasons for choice and the structure of the meal. The great majority of all the women who said they would offer the modal meal which we have identified would do so for the reasons which we have connected with tradition. Most of the others in this category chose a modal meal because the foods involved are 'special', 'good' or meet the demands of hospitality or they formed part of the family's culinary tradition. Variants of the modal meal, described earlier, were also chosen on similar grounds. Meals from alternative cuisines, on the other hand, and other meals clearly differing from the group's modal meal but hard to classify, were generally chosen for reasons of ease, speed or time pressure, for novelty, or for health reasons phrased in biomedical language.

Conclusion

We have described 'traditional' Punjabi, Italian and British meals considered by our respondents to be appropriate for family hospitality. By using the term 'traditional' we do not mean to ignore history, and we have drawn attention to the way in which regional, post-war and émigré variations have occurred in Italy and among British Italians. Similar caveats would apply to South Asian groups other than Punjabi. But all these groups can outline a stable modal family hospitality meal pattern to which they ascribe the qualities of tradition, culture, custom, familiarity, reputation or acceptability, and it is this 'insider' ascription that we identify as traditional.

In our introduction we posed two questions about hospitality patterns. First, whether migrant groups from the peasant-based economies represented here show evidence of stronger commitment to hospitality than the general population, of more elaborate forms of cookery when presenting hospitality or a cooked family meal, or of status and reputation being at stake, and whether there are differences in these respects between Britons of South Asian and Italian origin. Our data confirm the greater importance of the hospitable meal among the migrants, who cook it far more frequently than the general population women. The data also confirm the greater conformity to the traditional meal among migrants than the general population women, and the greater elaboration of cookery among the two minorities, in terms of recipes for such meals. However, South Asians were more attached to their traditional foods than Italians, it was only the South Asians who spent longer hours in cooking generally, and it was only they who made explicit mention of considerations of reputation, status, and rules of respect for guests.

We also included in this question issues of the content of the meal, in particular whether these minorities differ in the symbolic importance accorded to meat and animal products. Our data confirm the greater salience of meat in the special family meals of Punjabi migrants, here mainly Muslims, compared both with Italian migrants and with the relatively high proportion of general population women who used alternative cuisines. Meat is prestigious in the Punjab, and considerations of hospitality have therefore accentuated the use of meat in Britain where it is easily available. If this is a valid indicator of tastes in fat consumption, it is consistent with the greater overall and saturated fat intake among the South Asian migrants (Anderson et al 1995) found in this study. This trend may be reaching a limit, however, for our data also point to a reduction in the amount of meat used among the British-born.

Why should hospitality, and an elaborate traditional meal, have been more important to the two migrant groups? This needs to be the subject of a separate analysis, but a sketch can be given of the possibilities.

One possibility is that the question we asked had a different familial context in the situation of migrant groups, precisely because they might have left many relatives behind, thus making the chance to see these relatives more of a formal occasion. Certainly migrant South Asian women in Glasgow are less likely than general population women to have parents or siblings nearby, though because of the patrilineal bias this does not apply to migrant South Asian men (Williams et al 1994). But while this meal context might have given added weight to issues of status, reputation and respect when entertaining relatives, the longer hours South Asians spent in cooking, and their greater attachment to traditional foods, applied to meals of any kind. Again, the question about frequency of hospitality meals applied to any meal with the sort of menu described, and the frequencies given by the migrant groups in response make it highly unlikely that they were given only to relatives seldom seen.

A broader context than the familial one is thus needed to account for these findings. In the introduction we pointed to a coherent complex of economic, religious and cultural considerations which help to promote hospitality in peasant culture. In a largely subsistence economy, food is the main product of labour. In the religion and reciprocity of many of these cultures the guest is sacred and the gift a fundamental basis of trust and alliance (Pitt-Rivers 1977; Du Boulay 1986; Mauss 1990). Hence there is frequently an elaboration of food in the culture, a multiplying of occasions for hospitality and religious feasts, and an obligation to serve particular customary foods. Even coming from more broadly peasant-based economies, the migrants of this study reflected similar emphases. The highest proportion of income was spent on food among South Asian migrants, and while the proportion spent by Italian migrants was not high, because their income was high anyway, in absolute terms they spent most of all the groups on food (Bush and Williams 1995). Adult retention of religious identity, and subjective importance of religion among Muslim, Sikh, Hindu and Catholic groups in Glasgow (all still drawing migrant members from former peasant communities) is much higher than among the largely indigenous Protestants (Williams 1993b), and informal patterns of reciprocity and patronage have been noted as major features of South Asian communities in Britain (Shaw 1988; Werbner 1990). While these are fragmentary indications, and the whole topic is neglected and needs more development than is possible here, it is consistent with this picture that the hospitality of these migrant groups was more elaborate and frequent.

Why then were South Asian migrants more attached than Italian migrants to their traditional foods, and why did they spend longer hours in cooking, and show more concern with reputation, status, and rules of respect for guests? This again needs to be the subject of a separate analysis, but the answers we anticipate would point to differences in the extent of their encapsulation (Mayer 1971; Anwar 1985) and of their enclosure within a domestic setting. Among Italians, 61% of migrants and 94% of British-born spoke English at home, against 5% and 40% respectively among South Asians. Among Italians likewise, 100% of migrants and 88% of British-born were baptised Catholic, but only 82% and 70% were married to Catholics, whereas among South Asians all were Muslim, Sikh or Hindu and only one marriage had taken place outside these religious boundaries. These indications suggest that South Asians are likely to have retained features of their culture of origin with less attenuation.

In the case of the Punjabi emphasis on meat, however, and the relative absence of such an emphasis among Italians, it seems to be the cultures of origin themselves which differ. The difference is one of aspiration rather than practice, for meat is only available to a limited extent in peasant cultures and tends to be associated with feasts. Once a taste of this kind is formed, and in addition meat becomes easily available, as in British cities, it can be expected to become a necessary festal accompaniment. Why Italians do not have this taste so strongly, on the other hand, is unclear. Our data suggest that in Glasgow Italian migrants are more weight-conscious than South Asian migrants (Bush et al 1996), and individualistic values connected with this may have been influencing the development of their everyday cuisine for a longer time (Camporesi 1993:Chap. 12), to the extent that hospitality is also affected.

In addition we asked whether British-born generations of these minorities show evidence of change in these patterns. For British-born South Asians we find that frequency of hospitality, and the importance of a traditional meal on such occasions, are undiminished; but the reduction in meat items may well be an indication that the tradition is being reinterpreted to reduce fat consumption. For British-born Italians, on the other hand, the trend in choice of hospitality is definitely assimilative. A number of British-born Italians are not merely adjusting the externals of their hospitality to suit the British context (accommodation), but are beginning to think of the British roast as their traditional meal (assimilation).

Again, the reasons why there are opposing trends among the British-born in these two minorities may be related to differences in the extent of their encapsulation. The weaker indications of encapsulation among Italians in Britain suggest that British-born Italians would indeed be more inclined to follow British traditions of hospitality.

Patterns of hospitality thus correspond with patterns of encapsulation, and are referred by hosts to concepts of tradition. Encapsulation includes structural differentiation of the minority group through religious affiliation, language, in-marriage or racism, and more fluid processes of network formation and communal moral judgement (Mayer 1971; Anwar 1985), which are essential to the way people construct their identity. That sense of identity, in turn, is explicitly linked with the concepts of tradition which have been described. It is the social construction of identity, therefore, which is at the heart of the patterns of hospitality discussed here.

The special attachment of migrant and British-born South Asian women in our study to foods and forms of hospitality which they report as traditional indicates the importance for them and their households of the assertion of their ethnic identity. This relates, amongst other things, to their Indian and Islamic religious traditions and to their recent history as former colonial subjects of the United Kingdom. For Italians, who share a medieval Christian tradition with the British, and who do not carry a legacy of British imperialism, the reassertion of identity is less of an issue. In matters of religion, the medieval history of hostility between Christianity and Islam has left barriers of fear and suspicion on both sides. And in the history of empire, the structuring of colonial societies by concepts of race has shaped the experience of British ethnic minorities also, so that while Italians in Britain have been the subject of xenophobic hostility (Colpi 1991), they have not been subject to the process of racialisation which has assigned to South Asians a special position identified by the concept of 'race relations' (Miles 1982). The response to all this, particularly by Muslim Pakistanis and their British-born families, has been an increased self-reliance and autonomy (Werbner 1990) which has sometimes made adapting to aspects of British society more difficult (Anwar 1985). There has been a re-emphasis of South Asian, particularly Muslim, cultural and religious traits, and where inter-ethnic relationships do lead to a re-emphasis on cultural and religious traits, it is no surprise to find that the collective symbolic values attached to food are reinforced at the expense of individual preferences (Williams et al 1998).

Notes

1 This chapter is derived from the study 'Dietary Change in South Asian and Italian Women in the West of Scotland', funded by the ESRC from 1992–1995 as part of the research program 'The Nation's Diet: The Social Science of Food Choice'. The research team was Hannah Bradby, Helen Bush and Rory Williams (MRC Medical Sociology Unit, Glasgow), Annie Anderson and Mike Lean (Dept. of Human Nutrition, University of Glasgow). We acknowledge with thanks all our respondents,

and our team of interviewers and dieticians. We thank Marilena Ireland for explanations of some foods described by Italian respondents. This chapter is modified from an article published in *Sociology of Health and Illness* 1998, 20 (3):351–380.

2 A sauce, often meat-based.

3 A mild, creamy sauce, frequently eaten with chicken.

4 Cooked meat served between pieces of bread.

5 Pounded meat or grated and boiled vegetable made into balls and cooked in soup.

6 Dry, separate grains of rice which may incorporate small pieces of meat or vegetables, and served with a separate sauce which may also contain meat.

7 Flat, unleavened bread.

8 A type of bread, cooked in a tandoor oven.

9 Milky pudding with rice.

10 Pieces of meat or vegetables coated in batter, deep-fried.

11 Small, triangular pastries filled with meat or vegetables, deep-fried.

EATING THE HOMELAND

Japanese expatriates in The Netherlands

Katarzyna J. Cwiertka

Introduction

Although the role of remembering *places* in the creation of the concept of 'homeland' is often emphasised, the objects that belong to those places are just as important (Gupta 1992, Malkki 1992).[1] They are the representations of homeland inserted into the interstices of day-to-day life expatriates once lived. Expressing identity in terms of food is both the widespread and long-standing (Murcott 1996). Food is often seen as the epitome of everything the expatriate misses about home. This feeling is especially strong in the case of immigrants and refugees, for whom food may remain the only link with the life left behind, as Helen Bush and Rory Williams have demonstrated in the previous chapter. A similar issue will be dealt with here, although I shall focus on a different category of displaced people.

In recent decades, we have borne witness to the movements of people on a global scale in a variety of frequencies and forms; 'diplomats, businessmen, bureaucrats, academics, tourists, veterans of foreign wards, overseas volunteers, artists, refugees, youths on an intercontinental walkabout', (Hannerz 1992:246) and many more. In this chapter I will concentrate on one of these categories – the globally mobile employees of transnational companies.

As a consequence of the globalisation of markets and labour, an increasing number of people of various nationalities live ever-changing lives, as the result of relocation by their employers from one country to another. A characteristic feature of these employees and their families is the fact that they make little effort to assimilate in the local culture where they happen to reside, but rather encapsulate themselves in their home culture as they travel. Contrary to immigrants and refugees, these displaced people are affluent. This enables them to maintain their original habits and create a surrogate home without too much difficulty. They have their own schools for their children, special shops selling their food, and special clubs providing the kind of entertainment that they like. They usually socialise with their own compatriots, rarely establishing friendships with local people. The knowledge of the fact that they will be transferred to another country within a relatively short period of time diminishes their eagerness to engage in dialogue with the local culture.

This chapter is a case study of such 'globally mobile employees'. It deals with the Japanese community in the Netherlands, with a particular focus on their foodways. The point of departure for my investigation is a presumption that the diet of the Japanese abroad may serve as a window to revealing their attitude towards their homeland and the degree of integration with the country of residence.

According to the data available at the Japanese Embassy in The Hague, almost six thousand Japanese were residing in the Netherlands as of October 1996, at the time when the material for this study was collected.[2] Approximately five-sixths of them were temporary residents and the rest were permanent residents. In principle, temporary residency implies a stay in the Netherlands of no longer than five years. However, in some cases, it may last for as long as ten years. As far as the temporary residents are concerned, the employees of Japanese companies and their families constitute more than 70% of the total number. They are followed by students, teachers, and researchers with their families, almost 12%, the category of 'others' accounting for about 10%, and government employees (diplomats, employees of Japanese schools etc.) with families constituting 4%. Freelancers and reporters end the list, at about 1%.

Information concerning permanent Japanese residents in the Netherlands available at the embassy is practically non-existent. The majority of them are spouses of Dutch citizens and, generally speaking, they do not participate as wholeheartedly in the activities of the Japanese community as the temporary residents do.

The highest concentration of Japanese residents in the Netherlands, almost 60%, is the Amsterdam area. 80% of all Japanese nationals are accommodated in the area referred to as 'Randstad', i.e. the conglomeration of cities including Amsterdam, Rotterdam, Utrecht, and The Hague, covering approximately 250 square kilometres.

The data for this project was acquired mainly through a questionnaire distributed among Japanese women living in Amsterdam and its surrounding area in the fall of 1996. Women, generally, seem to pay more attention to consumed food, and in most cases are the ones who cook family meals. Therefore, statistical and anthropological studies concerning food usually rely on female informants.[3] This was also the main reason for concentrating on female Japanese in this project. Moreover, as my main concern was to investigate home cooking, I focused on married women.[4] Single people are believed to be less involved in cooking activities at home, and dine out more frequently.

75 questionnaires and 37 food diaries containing a weekly record of the family menus are the core source of this study. Supplementary interviews were also conducted. Although it is evident that this randomly collected data covers only a small fraction of the Japanese community in the Netherlands, its analysis

leads to conclusions that are representative for the majority and provide a useful basis for comparative research.

I divided the 75 respondents to the questionnaire into three groups, as there were indications that the lifestyles of the members of each group, and their diet, differed *(Figure 8.1)*. The first group was formed by temporary residents – 44 women married to Japanese men sent to the Netherlands by their employers. The second group consisted of permanent residents, nine women married to Japanese men who came to the Netherlands of their own initiative.[5] The third group of respondents was formed by 22 women with Dutch partners. For convenience, I will refer to the families from the first and second group as 'Japanese families', and those from the third group, as 'mixed families' throughout this chapter. Moreover, I will use the working name of the 'employees' for group I, and the 'adventurers' for group II.

Group I, which constitutes the greatest share of the Japanese community in the Netherlands and represents the category of the displaced people that this study concentrates on, will constitute the main focus of my analysis.

Dutch Reality

It goes without saying that food prepared and consumed in the Netherlands can never be exactly the same as in Japan. Even if we do not consider the fact that some kinds of food cannot be obtained outside Japan, the taste and/or shape and/or texture of exactly the same kinds of foodstuffs may be different in different parts of the world. Fresh vegetables and fruit, meat, fish, or even water can determine the taste of Japanese dishes prepared abroad. However, given that this issue lies outside the scope of our inquiry, this chapter will focus more

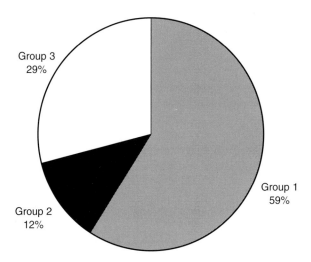

Figure 8.1 The Three Groups of Respondents.

generally on Japanese patterns of consumption in the Netherlands, and the extent to which these patterns undergo changes as a result of the confrontation with Dutch circumstances. In other words, I will attempt to assess how the Japanese outside of Japan are counterpoised between acculturating with the new food culture and retaining their own, and will investigate what determines their choices.

Information acquired through the questionnaire indicated that the majority of the Japanese residing in the Netherlands changed their consumption habits to a certain degree and adapted to the new circumstances. 64% of respondents to the questionnaire answered positively to the question: 'Did your diet change since your arrival in the Netherlands?'. 21 out of 27 respondents, who answered negative or did not answer this question at all, indicated, in answers to other questions, that residing in the Netherlands did influence their diet.[6] This means that 92% of respondents agreed that their diet had altered since they left Japan. In this chapter, I will try to uncover the character of the culinary change, which these Japanese claimed to have undergone, and to find out how the remaining 8% managed to resist this change.

The main factor that led to changes in the foodways of the Japanese living in the Netherlands seems to have been the difficulty in acquiring certain ingredients, their high price, and bad quality. The difficulty in purchasing good quality seafood cheaply on the one hand, and relative inexpensiveness of meat, on the other, resulted in the increased consumption of meat dishes. Moreover, the increased application of cookery techniques that required the use of fat, such as frying and deep-frying, consequently led to the increased consumption of fat among my respondents.

The collected data clearly indicates that certain kinds of food, fresh as well as processed ones, were less frequently consumed since their arrival in the Netherlands due to the difficulties in purchasing them or the inconvenience of using the Dutch versions. For example, dishes that required the use of meat cut into small pieces or thinly sliced – widely available in this form in Japan – were prepared less frequently in Holland, because meat is usually sold in big chunks there.

Certain dishes were prepared more frequently and others less often, since arrival in the Netherlands. The fact that respondents mentioned the same dishes on both occasions indicates that subjective factors, such as economical resources and taste preferences, are to a large extent responsible for the content of the Japanese diet outside of Japan. Nevertheless, the fact that foreign dishes that entered the Japanese diet in the beginning of this century and were since domesticated, such as *nikujaga* (meat-and-potato stew flavoured with soy), British-style chicken or beef curry, and *gyōza* (Chinese dumplings, usually shallow-fried), are mentioned as dishes prepared more often, and dishes that require the use of seaweed, various sorts of Japanese mushrooms, and vegetables not easily available outside of Japan are mentioned as those prepared less often, is obviously related to the objective fact of the availability of ingredients.

As a consequence of the limitations described above, Japanese home menus in the Netherlands lack variety in comparison to Japan. The ingredients that are cheaper and easier to acquire get priority, and this, in turn, determines the kind of dishes that are prepared in the majority of households. Respondents repeatedly complained of the lack of variety in their diet, and the increase in the use of fat as a consequence of the repetitive use of frying instead of other cooking methods. The lack of seasonal change in ingredients was also expressed. One respondent sounded extremely negative: 'I feel as if I have been eating the same food all year long' (Mrs. D. from group I).

Nevertheless, it should be stressed that the structure of the majority of the Japanese home dinners, as revealed in the food diaries, was based on the pattern: soup, rice, *tsukemono* (Japanese pickles) and side dishes, which reflects the typical structure of a Japanese meal.[7] In other words, a meal would still be classified as 'Japanese-style', even if the side dishes were non-Japanese, because it adhered to the 'rice-soup-side-dishes' structure. On the basis of the questionnaire, I was able to estimate that the women from the Japanese families (group II and I) prepared Japanese-style dinners approximately four to five times a week.

A general impression gained from the collected data is that cooking Japanese style in Dutch circumstances requires much time, effort, and inventiveness (*Figure 8.2*). The women tried to experiment with Dutch ingredients, to arrange the menus to suit the Dutch food market, and had to perform tasks they did not need to do in Japan, such as filleting fish.

Nowadays, there are several Japanese grocery stores in the Amsterdam area, and each big city has at least one shop that sells Japanese soy sauce, California-grown Japonica rice, and the other ingredients that are essential for Japanese-style cooking. Recent developments within the Japanese food industry have allowed more products to be delivered to consumers overseas. Only three out of all 75 respondents to my questionnaire stated that they never shopped at Japanese food stores. Japanese ingredients and processed foods have become more easily available recently than they were a few decades ago (*Figure 8.3*). The items most frequently purchased in Japanese food stores, apart from soy sauce and rice, were various soybean products (*miso, tōfu, nattō,* and *abura-age*), frozen, salted, dried, and fresh fish, instant noodles (*rāmen*) and dried noodles (*udon* and *soba*), frozen and fresh vegetables (giant radish, yam, burdock, pod soybeans, Chinese chives, lotus root, winter squash), Japanese flavourings and ready-made sauces, and pickles.

Shopping is not the only way to get the necessary ingredients for the preparation of a Japanese style meal abroad. Three-fourths of the respondents received food parcels from Japan with a frequency ranging from once a year to once a month. However, families belonging to group I, that is the 'employees', clearly received packages more frequently than the other two groups. Some women also grew Japanese vegetables and herbs at home, for example garland chrysanthemum (*shungiku*), beefsteak plant (*shiso*), pod soybeans, Japanese wild

Figure 8.2 *Nishin Donburi* (Herring Donburi) – a result of playful inventiveness of Japanese expatriates' wives in Holland. Donburi is the name of a Japanese dish that derived from the name of the vessel it is served in – a big-size bowl. The bowl is filled with boiled rice and a topping, for example seafood deep-fried in batter, pieces of chicken pan-fried with vegetables in soy sauce, or slices of raw fish. In Nishin Donburi, pieces of salted herring – a Dutch speciality – are used as topping (Photo: J. van der Kooi).

chervil (*mitsuba*), and giant white radish sprouts. Producing homemade pickles also seemed to be a far more popular activity abroad than in Japan. Half of the respondents who stated that they made tsukemono at home (mostly using an instant pickling medium) have only began this practice since they left Japan.

Returning to the question asked at the beginning of this section, it seems that the main dietary change among the respondents to the questionnaire concerned the content of the meals rather than their structure. As far as home cookery is concerned, the majority of warm meals served by Japanese families in the Netherlands were reported to be Japanese-style.

Dining Out

It also seems that residing in the Netherlands has had a greater influence on the dining-out habits of the Japanese families than on their home menus. Despite the global spread of cuisines and catering chains, the range of restaurants that offer their services in the Netherlands differs from those in Japan. This difference is

Figure 8.3 Japanese housewives buying seafood from a specialised dealer during the Japanese festival in Amstelveen.

relatively larger than for Japanese people residing in the US, because many well-known American caterers, such as Denny's, Red Lobster and others from the genre of the middle-range type restaurant chains referred to in Japan as 'family restaurants' (*famirii resutoran*), do not operate in Europe. Moreover, the variety of dishes offered by Japanese restaurants in the Netherlands is not comparable with the variety offered by the great number of small restaurants that specialise in one specific type of food, such as noodles or deep-fried pork cutlets (*tonkatsu*), one can find in Japan. Moreover, as far as the internationally diffused cuisines such as Italian, French, and Chinese are concerned, different menus are offered within the range of these cuisines depending on country where they are served. All these factors create specific dining circumstances for the Japanese residing in the Netherlands.

It is difficult to estimate whether the Japanese dine out in the Netherlands more or less frequently than they did in the homeland. I would be inclined to say that this depends on individual circumstances, and thus no generalisations can be made.

Nevertheless, a change in dining out habits was obvious, arising both positive and negative reactions among the respondents. The lack of specific kinds of restaurants, and the lack of variety, appeared as the main complaints. High prices were also mentioned. At the same time, some respondents were happy to explore new types of restaurant food.

The most popular eating-out facilities among the Japanese in Holland turned out to be Chinese, Japanese, Italian, and French restaurants (*Figure 8.4*). Low prices and familiar ingredients and taste were the greatest advantages of Chinese restaurants. The possibility of eating sushi or other Japanese dishes that cannot easily be prepared at home was the main reason for the popularity of Japanese restaurants, despite their relatively high prices. Italian and French cuisine, are the most well known western-style restaurants in Japan, and it is not surprising that they are also popular among Japanese people residing outside Japan.

It should also be mentioned at this point that French cuisine is the foreign cuisine with the longest tradition in the Netherlands, but is rather expensive. Chinese-Indonesian cuisine is the most popular among the Dutch, and enjoys a good reputation as far as quality and prices are concerned. These aspects must also have some impact on the dining-out choices of the Japanese community.

'Westernisation' and 'Japanisation'

As observed earlier, the major change in the diet of the majority of my respondents was the westernisation of their menus as far as the used foodstuffs and applied cooking techniques are concerned. However, we should be aware of the fact that not all of these changes were the result of their migration to Europe. We should also take into account the fact that some of my respondents who were in their thirties lived with their parents before leaving Japan. Thus, for many of them moving abroad meant a switch from their mothers' cooking to their own. This is particularly relevant for the second and third group of respondents.

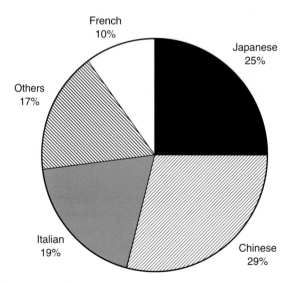

Figure 8.4 The Most Popular Restaurants Among Japanese Expatriates in The Netherlands.

In Japan I lived with my parents, and my mother did most of the cooking. I ate out quite a lot too. Generally, I did not pay much attention to nutritional balance. I really only started to cook once I came to the Netherlands after I got married; my child was born soon after. My lifestyle changed and I became very conscious about cooking as healthy as possible.

(Mrs. T. from group II)

In Japan I mostly ate Japanese-style food prepared by my mother. Since I have to do the cooking myself in Holland, the Japanese-style breakfast is too time- and energy-consuming and I cannot manage.

(Mrs. N. from group II)

When I lived with my parents, I had a western-style or a Japanese-style breakfast; whatever I felt like. Now, when I have to cook myself, I somehow end up eating a bread-based breakfast every morning.

(Mrs. S. from group II)

In Japan I never had bread for breakfast (like the rest of my family, I had a rice breakfast). In Holland, bread is much more convenient.

(Mrs. I from group III)

The above statements concern breakfast, which has by now become the most westernised meal in Japan. Generally speaking, two types of breakfasts can be distinguished in contemporary Japan. The first type is a traditional Japanese-style breakfast, also called a rice breakfast, which is based on rice, or rice gruel, miso soup, tsukemono and sometimes side dishes. The second type is the so-called western-style breakfast, or a bread breakfast, consisting mainly of toast, butter, marmalade and a fruit or vegetable salad.

For many young women, beginning a life of their own by getting married or moving out from the family house results in the shift to eating a less labour- and time-consuming western-style breakfast. A similar change could be observed among Japanese women when they moved to the Netherlands. However, residing outside Japan also created more favourable circumstances for this decision.

The preparation of Japanese-style breakfast takes five times more time and energy than the western-style breakfast. And in Holland the Japanese-style breakfast is also more expensive, and it is hard to find varied ingredients.

(Mrs. N. from group II)

In Japan, there are many more delicious kinds of miso and rice, so we used to have a Japanese-style breakfast every day. In the Netherlands the opposite is the case – there are so many delicious kinds of cheese and ham – so we decided to have western-style breakfasts instead.

(Mrs. W. from group I)

Relatively few of the many families, who already consumed bread breakfast in Japan, were affected by moving abroad. A little less than half of the respondents actually changed their breakfast habits. Nonetheless, a different quality of dairy products, bread etc. and different kinds of fruit are available in both countries and, therefore, it can be concluded that residing in the Netherlands affected the breakfasts of the majority of the Japanese.

Cheese is very good here, so we eat it quite often now.

(Mrs. G. from group I)

We eat much more fruit and more kinds of it. We also eat more cheese.

(Mrs. O. from group I)

In Japan I only ate white bread, but since I came here I often have brown bread.

(Mrs. H. from group III)

Dutch dairy products are very tasty, so I often eat yoghurt with cereals and fruit for breakfast. I don't think that I would do that in Japan, because Japanese dairy products are not so tasty.

(Mrs. E. from group III)

In Japan I only ate buttered toast for breakfast, but here I also have ham, roast beef and other kinds of meat.

(Mrs. M. from group III)

In Japan I was not so fond of cheese, but now I eat bread with cheese for breakfast quite often.[8]

(Mrs. A. from group I)

Now I also eat baguettes and croissants for breakfast.

(Mrs. K. from group III)

Some of the statements suggest that the Dutch circumstances have influenced the tastes of the Japanese. The collected data pointed in two directions. Firstly, acquiring a taste for foods that the respondents did not have the opportunity to try at all before coming to the Netherlands, or consumed them very rarely. Cheese, Dutch salted herring, white asparagus, potatoes, courgette, sweet peppers, various kinds of soups, steaks, chicory, yoghurt, and French, Thai and Italian cooking are the most frequently mentioned items. Similarly to broadening culinary possibilities of dining out, trying new food at home also made life in the Netherlands more enjoyable for some respondents.

Wine is good and inexpensive here, so I acquired quite a taste for it. I often drink it with cheese as a snack.

(Mrs. G. from group I)

There are so many kinds of vegetables here that I have never seen in Japan. We often travel to other European countries that are close by, too. I learned how to prepare western-style dishes from ingredients that cannot be obtained in Japan.

(Mrs. F. from group I)

Now I have the opportunity to eat foods that are unobtainable or expensive in Japan, such as various kinds of berries, cheese, beef etc.

(Mrs. Y. from group I)

The second tendency of changing taste preferences was acquiring a taste for Japanese foods which respondents had had little opportunity to eat since they left Japan. In fact, a process that one may call a dietary 'Japanisation' could be observed in the data of Japanese families residing in the Netherlands. In several cases from group II and I, though, Western elements were consciously removed from the diet since the family had moved overseas. Consequently, these Japanese families consumed less western-style foods outside Japan than they did in their homeland. For example, Mrs. B. has lived in the Netherlands since 1985, but still cooks mainly Japanese style. The family changed their style of breakfast from bread-based to a choice between bread-based or rice-based breakfast, and a Japanese style dinner was consumed almost seven days a week, which is more often than when the family lived in Japan. Mrs. B. claims that she learned to appreciate rice dishes more since she left Japan. In the case of a few other respondents, 'Japanisation' was clearly manifested in their dining out preferences.

When eating out, we now often choose a Japanese restaurant.

(Four respondents from group I)

In Japan, we dined out much more frequently western-style.

(Mrs. U. from group I and Mrs. N. from group II)

In other cases, domestic cookery became less westernised than in Japan.

My children eat a bread-based lunch, and therefore want to have rice for breakfast. In general, I think that we used to have Japanese-style meals when dining out in Japan, and at home we ate more western-style. Now, in the Netherlands, it seems the opposite.

(Mrs. R. from group III)

In Japan, I used to cook western-style sometimes. Now, I never do.

(Mrs. Z. from group I)

In Japan, we had bread for breakfast during the weekend, now we prefer rice.

(Mrs. D. from group I)

We eat Japanese-style at home most of the time.

(Mrs. L. from group I)

Basically, I don't see any difference in the way we ate in Japan and here. As I try to be careful about not maintaining a diet with too much fat and salt intake, it might be true that I cook more Japanese-style than I used to. We also consume more rice as a family than we did in Japan, because now I have to prepare four lunch boxes every day [probably all members of the family dined at canteens in Japan].

(Mrs. J. from group I)

Six respondents (8%) strongly claimed that they managed to retain exactly the same consumption patterns as when they lived in Japan. They should not be classified under the 'Japanising' phenomenon, but rather represent a small group of conservative consumers who limit the influence of outside circumstances on their home diet to the minimum.

All of them were young housewives with one or two children, and belonged to group I, which I called 'the employees'. None of them answered positively to the following questions:

(1) Is there any dish you have prepared less since you left Japan?
(2) Is there any dish you came to prepare more often since you left Japan?
(3) Is there any kind of food you came to like or dislike more since you left Japan?

Half of them stated that they never ate Dutch food, although the other three mentioned they did once or twice a month. Nonetheless, it seemed clear that residing in the Netherlands did not have much impact on their diet. These women made the utmost efforts to retain home cooking the way it used to be in Japan. They apparently possessed the necessary cooking skills, and only one of them stated that she did not like to cook. Almost all of them made tsukemono at home, using Chinese cabbage, cucumber and daikon, and two of them grew Japanese vegetables and herbs. They shopped at Japanese food stores approximately twice a week, regularly dined at Japanese restaurants, and received food packages from Japan approximately every two months. The items most often shipped from Japan were seasonings, tea, dried seaweed, dried vegetables, dried seafood, rice crackers and sweets.

Mixed Families

The interaction between the Japanese and Dutch food culture within Japanese families residing in the Netherlands generally occurred in two ways: 1. by incorporating Dutch dishes and processed food into Japanese menus; and 2. by preparing Japanese dishes from ingredients available in Holland.

As observed earlier, an increased consumption of meat and fat and a decrease in the consumption of seafood and vegetables was typical for the families from group II and I. However, none of the respondents from group I, and only a few from group II, indicated that their consumption of rice had diminished. For the

Japanese couples, a dinner consisting of rice, soup and side dishes formed the basis for the majority of evening meals. This type of culinary change can be classified as incorporating Dutch ingredients, or Dutch and other western dishes, into a basically Japanese-style menu.

The change of consumption habits of the women from mixed families (group III) was more radical than in the Japanese families (group II and I). They did not incorporate Dutch ingredients into Japanese-style meals, but rather switched from a Japanese- to a western-type of diet. Japanese-style dinners, as defined earlier, appeared on the tables of group III less often than the western-style meals consisting of a serving of meat, potatoes or rice and boiled vegetables, or a pasta dish with salad. Women from mixed families shopped at Japanese food stores approximately once a month and often even less frequently, while women from Japanese families did so around three to four times a month.

In addition to this, Japanese style dinners prepared by women from group III were less elaborate than those prepared by the women from group II and I. Their Japanese-style dinners could often be compared with the rice breakfasts of respondents from group I. On the basis of the collected data, it became clear that the Japanese women from mixed families adapted their foodways to Dutch norms and circumstances. The following statements reflect this culinary change in two respects: 1. the westernisation of the meal structure; and 2. the 'decapitation' of Japanese-style meals.

I hardly ever prepare only Japanese-style dishes.

The number of occasions when I can eat seafood has diminished. I find myself cooking some kind of meat dish almost everyday. I do try to eat more fresh vegetables, but in general I end up cooking mainly with oil. We also eat rice as a staple less often, and substitute it with potatoes and bread.

The main change has been a shift from a rice-based diet to bread-based one, and toward meat dishes.

I don't cook real Japanese dinners any more, and they lack in variety. Moreover, our breakfasts and lunches are all western.

In Japan I used to eat rice even with western-style dishes, such as stew. Here, there are so many kinds of bread that it has become my main staple.

I used to make a Japanese breakfast on weekends, but I never do it here. For lunch I usually have sandwiches, and generally the frequency of eating bread has increased.

Rice has been replaced by potatoes in my diet.

I hardly ever eat seafood. Meat and bread have become the core of my meals, and I feel that I do not eat enough vegetables.

The ingredients have changed, of course, but I have also incorporated Dutch recipes into my cooking. Maybe the climate is to blame for this, but I am using much more butter than I used to.

I have stopped eating rice, and also my culinary repertoire has become rather limited.

I hardly ever eat Japanese food at home. It is so troublesome to prepare that I practically never make it. We eat very internationally.

Similar phenomena were also observed among the respondents from group II.

I was surprised to find out that fruit is so cheap here, and that dairy products (milk, yoghurt and so forth), and potatoes are so delicious. My meals have naturally become western.

(Mrs. N.)

In Japan, I cooked Japanese style most of the time. In the Netherlands, I usually cook potatoes- and pasta-based meals at home.

(Mrs. P.)

Not only was the content of the served food adapted to the Dutch circumstances in the case of group III and some of the respondents from group II, but the way it was consumed had changed too. The respondents mentioned that they serve their food differently, be it only because of the fact that they do not even own a proper set of Japanese-style tableware.

Some women married to Dutch men complained about the lack of possibility to eat the foods they really wanted. In consequence, they acquired a taste for Japanese food, although they were not so enthusiastic about it before leaving Japan. In some cases, Japanese women with non-Japanese partners ended up eating different foods from the rest of their family.

Alex McIntosh and Mary Zey, in their inquiry into the role of women as gatekeepers of food consumption (1989), have noted that the man is an important force in the shaping of the dietary picture of each family. It seems reasonable to draw a similar conclusion on the basis of the data collected here. For example, women from group I prepared simpler menus when the husbands did not dine at home. The degree of westernisation of Japanese families permanently residing in the Netherlands has also been greatly determined by the taste preference of the husbands. For example, the husband of one respondent from group II still retained a taste for Japanese food after living in the Netherlands for more than twenty years, and as result of this the family dined Japanese style most of the time. The husband of another respondent, however, had resided in Holland as long as the other one, but he and his family now dine almost exclusively western-style. Having a non-Japanese partner was the crucial factor for their women from group III in changing from a basically Japanese-style to a western-style diet. Having a non-Japanese partner did not only result in a decreasing number of home dinners cooked Japanese-style, but also had an impact on the eating-out choices of the family, as well as an effect on their consumption habits in general.

The lack of refinement and anti-hedonism of Dutch foodways are established facts.[9] Dutch dietary culture presents many similarities with that of Germany and England, especially in relation to the lack of any sort of national *grande cuisine* (Mennell 1989). In these three countries, elites mainly copied the French model, which was the main obstacle for developing a highly refined cuisine of their own. The phenomenon known nowadays as Dutch 'national cooking' is a romanticised version of the folk kitchen elevated to a 'national' level during the twentieth century. The role of religion in the development of a negative attitude towards food consumption in Holland was also important. The relentless encroachment of French manners that colonised the elite from the eighteenth century onwards, had the rest of society recreate the Calvinistic ideal of frugality and sobriety, and it has only been since the 1970s that this dark picture of Dutch consumption habits began to change.

We should, however, not hold the nature of Dutch cookery alone responsible for the simplification of the diet of the Japanese-Dutch families. There are other aspects involved as well, such as the time devoted to cooking activities. All women from group I, for example, were professional housewives, while more than half of the women from group II and III worked outside the household. This, with no doubt, indicates that women from group I could devote far more attention and time to the preparation of meals. This aspect must also have played a role in the extensive westernisation of evening meals within group II and III, as Japanese-style meals are generally more labour intensive. As, moreover, the women from group I were professional housewives married to Japanese men, it is possible that they had limited contact with the local community and learned less about Dutch cookery and the use of Dutch ingredients.

Discussion

In this chapter, I have focused on the food habits of the Japanese community in the Netherlands, based on an investigation conducted among a group of 75 female respondents. Considerable differences in diet could be observed among the three groups distinguished in the beginning of the project on the basis of the family situation of each woman.

The 'employees' (group I) made relatively little effort to broaden their culinary horizons during their stay abroad. They had difficulties of fitting their culinary habits into the new circumstances. As we have observed earlier, some of them even made various efforts in order to maintain a more 'Japanised' diet than before they moved to the Netherlands. The 'adventurers' (group II) grew accustomed to the Dutch foodways with the years and made some of them their own. They were more inclined to abandon Japanese dietary customs, although at times tried to recreate them.[10] Among mixed families (group III), on the other hand, only traces of Japanese foodways could be found, and these were often limited to the nostalgic longings of the Japanese spouse. The major reasons behind this behaviour were the influence of non-Japanese husbands, and the external incentives to discontinue Japanese-style food habits, such as the difficulty in obtaining the necessary ingredients or their high price.

A comparison of the food habits maintained by the three groups provides an interesting backdrop for discussion. When analysing the social contexts of these different dietary patterns, we need to take four aspects into account: the duration of stay, the attitude towards the Netherlands, the intensity of contact with the local population, and the advantages of the dietary change.

The 'employees' reside in the Netherlands temporarily, while for 'adventurers' and the women from mixed families Holland was to become a new home. This fact may already encourage the latter to invest in cultural assimilation. Moreover, the fact that they come to the Netherlands more or less by their own choice most likely plays an important role in the formation of a more positive attitude towards the new place of residence and ignites their curiosity toward the new culture.

To the contrary, the 'employees' follow the logistic decisions of their employers with little individual influence on their destinations. This, along with the temporary character of their residence, is the most important factor responsible for the formation of suspicious feelings towards foreign culture and a tendency to recreate a Japanese lifestyle outside Japan in order to leave their identity as untouched as possible.

Another aspect that needs to be taken into consideration is the fact that as Japanese-style cooking in the Netherlands requires more effort than western-style cooking, maintaining the Japanese-style diet may serve as a sign of devotion to one's family and a source of pride for the Japanese housewives. Likewise, the health dangers that might be caused by a western-style diet with superfluous fat, sugar, and salt intake, as has been emphasised by dieticians in recent years, has certainly had some impact on the awareness of Japanese women of the health advantages of traditional Japanese cuisine. Moreover, as mentioned earlier, the availability of time and money for cooking Japanese-style is also responsible for the differences in the dietary acculturation of the Japanese in the Netherlands.

There seems to be another reason, however, for the 'employees' to cling to their Japaneseness, even more than the transnational employees from other countries do – the terrifying prospect of returning some day and all the problems that they will then encounter. Although in many respects the life of Japanese expatriates in the Netherlands is similar to that of American, German, French and other nationalities representing their companies, the Japanese do not just use their food as means of strengthening their identity while living abroad, or a remedy for homesickness (*Figure 8.5*). They, in fact, employ food to demonstrate their loyalty towards Japanese culture and society, which will eventually condition their safe re-entrance to Japan.[11] The 'crisis of

Figure 8.5 Food stands in the centre of entertainment during a Japanese festival. Here, frying noodles.

return' is a highly publicised problem that is experienced by all members of the family – children at school, mothers in the community and fathers in the workplace.[12]

> When Japanese leave Japan, their membership [social boundary] is suspended. Every year they are away, reentry as members of the group – reestablishment of relationships to the satisfaction of those at home –

becomes more difficult. It is particularly difficult if after reentry they betray their exposure to foreign ways, which reminds others of the severing of bonds. Reentry raises questions of identity that can be silenced only by strict conformity and virtual denial of the foreign experience.

(White 1992:106)

One of the strategies to ease the pain of return would be to continue to live as 'Japanese' as possible while abroad. The problem of adjusting to the circumstances at home after being away for a long time might be comparable to people from other cultures, but the social pressure and difficulties the Japanese returnees experience seem to be of a particular calibre (White 1992:105–122).

The social pressure that the 'employees' group experiences as members of the Japanese expatriate community, combined with the fear of return, no doubt enhances their devotion to Japanese-style cooking. Moreover, the objective possibility of contact with the local population is minimal. Being sent from one country to another during their husbands' careers,[13] the wives remain basically homemakers, so that, with a few exceptions, fellow Japanese end up forming their circle of friends. Meanwhile, the 'adventurers' working outside the household are able to make local friends and adjust to local circumstances. In the case of mixed families, the local husband and his relatives fulfil this role.

An obvious conclusion that can be drawn from this study is the fact that the Japanese community outside Japan is by no means uniform. We should be careful not to treat them as a homogenous mass of employees of Japanese companies, although we must admit that it is they who represent the majority of Japanese people residing abroad.

A question that comes to mind next is to what extent the case of the Netherlands described here is representative for the Japanese community worldwide. Many similarities as well as differences can certainly be observed in the lifestyles of Japanese expatriates residing in different parts of the world. As far as their diet is concerned, we may surmise that fewer problems appear in acquiring good quality seafood in Mediterranean countries, or in different regions of Asia, due to the frequent use of seafood in the local diet. We may also presume that more elements would have been adopted from local cuisines less sober in character than the Dutch. More research on the life of the Japanese abroad is the only way to find out to what extent these assumptions can be justified. However, as the existing accounts suggest, the 'employee' type of Japanese expatriate tends to recreate a Japanese lifestyle wherever s/he goes.

Sanda Ionescu, for example, points out that Japanese communities in Germany are so successful in recreating a sense of the homeland that some Japanese housewives living in Frankfurt and Düsseldorf complain that they hardly notice they are living abroad (Ionescu forthcoming). Gordon Mathews indicates that the Japanese who live in Hong Kong have also tended to live in a bubble.

Japanese tend to associate among themselves, Japan remaining more real than the Hong Kong world they temporarily happen to live in. . . . Japanese tourists in Hong Kong, this implies, want to be seen as cosmopolitan global citizens by their fellow Japanese because they are securely nestled in Japaneseness in their non-touristic lives. Long-term Japanese residents of Hong Kong, on the other hand, seem concerned less with being global citizens than with wanting to preserve their 'Japaneseness,' a Japaneseness threatened by the fact that they are in some sense global citizens, at least in living outside Japan's shores.

(Mathews forthcoming)

One might assume that as globalisation expands and more people are deterritorialised from their local settings, global-local relationships diversify and lead towards a direction far from uniformity and homogenisation. The case of the Japanese in the Netherlands that has been described in this chapter indicates that this process is not so straightforward as globalisation theorists might imagine. Nevertheless, despite all the efforts that the Japanese expatriates make in order to escape the impact that living abroad brings, it is hardly plausible that this experience does not affect them at all. Further research is needed in order to prove this assumption, but it seems quite possible that once returned home, the Japanese housewives recall with pleasure, and maybe even miss, the experiences and tastes of the foreign lands they visited.

Notes

1 This study could have never been completed without the help of Ikeno Sachiko who kindly offered me her time and advice during the collecting and interpreting of the data. During the preparation of the questionnaire, I received helpful remarks from Anneke van Otterloo and Kumasaka Keiko. I would also like to express my gratitude to the Japanese Women's Club in the Netherlands for all the support I received for this project.

2 Personal Communication, Japanese Embassy in The Hague, June 5, 1997. Since, the number hasn't altered much.

3 During the Fourth International Conference on Food Choice held in April 1995, the great majority of research was based on the information gathered from women, such as 'What are vegetarian women eating?', 'Food choices of three generations of women', and 'The diet of low-income women: the role of culinary knowledge' (University of Birmingham 1995). Japanese scholars also prefer female informants when food related matters are involved. For example, the project of the National Museum of Ethnology concerning the transformation of the table setting in modern Japan was based mainly on interviews with women (Ishige and Inoue 1991).

4 The majority of respondents also had children.

5 In some cases, the women left Japan alone. For example, two of my respondents left Japan to study music and anthropology respectively, and another one worked in the Netherlands for a Japanese firm. The men whom these women met and married in the Netherlands, similarly, left Japan to start their own careers abroad, respectively as a Japanese language teacher, a French cook, and as a hairstylist.

6 These respondents indicated that their dinners or breakfasts at home have altered and observed changes as far as dining out was concerned. They were also able to list dishes that started to appear more or less often on their menus since they left Japan.

7 For the details on the historical development of the Japanese meal pattern see Ōtsuka 1986.

8 Despite this relative flexibility as far as acquiring new culinary experiences is concerned, at the same time the difficulties in maintaining a Japanese style diet lead to frustration in the case of Mrs. A.:

> Vegetables here are of worse quality, or maybe I just prepare them wrong, anyway their taste doesn't agree with me. Water also tastes different, so every dish I cook turns out differently than it used to in Japan. Rice is also horrible, and somehow the taste of raw fish here makes me sick, so I never make sushi at home as I used to. ... Beef is awful and spinach has no taste.

9 For more details about Dutch culinary culture see the contribution of Anneke Van Otterloo in this volume, and also Van Otterloo 1987.

10 For example, one respondent still organises *mochi*-pounding tournaments at home after living in the Netherlands for more than twenty years. Mochi is a cake made by pounding steamed, glutinous rice.

11 In this respect, the Japanese are comparable to the colonial elites that resided in India, Indonesia, and other parts of the world in the late nineteenth and early twentieth centuries. See Burton 1993.

12 For details concerning this issue see, for example, White 1992 and Goodman 1990.

13 Many of my respondents already had the experience of living outside Japan before coming to the Netherlands, for example, a year in Ireland, two years in Thailand and three years in Australia, five years in Turkey, one-and-a-half years in the US, six years in Canada, four years in the US, three years in England, twelve years in the US, two years in Spain, one year in the US, five years in the US, three years in Canada, one year in Germany, five years in Switzerland, three years in the US, five years in Belgium, one-and-a-half year in Italy.

9

CHINESE AND INDONESIAN RESTAURANTS AND THE TASTE FOR EXOTIC FOOD IN THE NETHERLANDS

A global-local trend

Anneke H. Van Otterloo

Introduction

Culinary culture is a complex human achievement, often having a long history. Cooking and eating habits take root in groups of people who are exposed to certain established foods and ways of preparation from infancy. These practices become contagious to other groups of people. In this respect, culinary cultures resemble plagues, for they often affect people living far from the locus of infection. Ideas, habits and artefacts in the production and consumption of food, once invented, tend to spread widely throughout time and space. Thus they may flourish far from the point of origin, even globally. There are, however, important differences between the diffusion of culinary cultures and disease. One distinction is the apparent rule that people adopt culinary cultural elements only if they experience them as being palatable. In the case of plagues, one has to speak of involuntary victims of germs, rather than active adapters inclined to new experiences.

In this chapter, I will focus on an aspect of the socio-genesis of international cuisine in the Netherlands, more specifically the role of Chinese and Indonesian restaurants in the development of Dutch taste for the exotic. This refers to the table, or the area of food consumption, 'where the identity and differentiation of the group is brought out in the practice of eating together or separately, as well as in the content of what is eaten by different collectivities' (Goody 1982:38). Dutch taste can broadly be described as having been formed by natives and immigrants. More specifically it may be viewed as one of the unforeseen consequences of the colonial era. In section 2, therefore, I will devote some attention to the development of cultural patterns of travel and contact prior to the dawn of the twentieth century. At that time already, a complicated set of interdependencies between Asian and European countries had long been established. I shall return briefly to the historical relationship between Holland and the Dutch East Indies (now Indonesia) that has existed since the sixteenth century. The 'high' colonial period, which lasted from about 1800 until 1949 is of particular importance. During this era, the mutual relationships of interdependency greatly intensified and many cultural elements travelled back and forth between the two countries. My assumption is that this colonial relationship was a precondition for the genesis of the taste for exotic food in the Netherlands, as well as in Indonesia.[1]

In section 3, a much briefer period is discussed, dealing with the diffusion of the taste for exotic food, which initially was virtually monopolised by Chinese and Indonesian dishes served in restaurants owned by Asian immigrants. This epoch lasted about two decades – from 1945 to 1965. In subsequent years, described in section 4, the Dutch taste for exotic food has continued to expand and became more differentiated. It will be considered whether the widening circle of social groups sitting down at 'non-native tables' bears any relation to a change in the relationships between them. Perhaps the acceptance of foreign foods means a step towards more social equality between formerly hierarchically ordered collectivities. A short conclusion in section 5 will bring this chapter to a close.

Dutch-East Indian Trade and Colonial Relationships of Dependency: 1550–1950

The shift of the commercial and industrial centre of gravity in Europe from the South to the Northwest is an important marker for the start of the modern age.[2] The Low Countries played an important role in these changes; they were indeed at the heart of this process. The flourishing economic position of the Republic of the Seven United Provinces (1588–1795) during the seventeenth century must be seen in the context of a long-term phase of European economic growth, starting as early as the end of the fifteenth century.[3] At that time, the Low Countries were under the rule of the Habsburg monarchs, who through marriage succeeded in enlarging their domain to include the Austrian, Burgundian and Spanish territories. Situated at the estuaries of the rivers Scheldt, Maas and Rhine, the inhabitants of these lowlands knew how to take advantage of the new economic opportunities, with the port city of Antwerp taking a leading position. The developments of new technologies for flood control and land reclamation, and the construction of an improved infrastructure that included navigable canals and windmills, were an early Dutch contribution to the first round of modern economic growth. Not only were advances made in commerce and shipping, but also in agriculture, fisheries (especially herring), and industries, such as textile and timber.

The main diet in this formative period of the Dutch nation consisted of grains, tubers, meat or lard and fish, cheese and butter – just as before. The international importance of the grain-market in Amsterdam at that time led to the increasing abundance of wheat in the country. Wheaten bread became the most popular farinaceous food among the well-to-do citizens and the patricians in their country houses. Many wheat-based delicacies such as '*zoete melk met brokken*' (wheat bread soaked in milk) and gingerbread with sugar, confits and exotic spices became popular. From 1602 onwards spices became increasingly available due to the trading of the Dutch East Indian Company trade.

Initially, beer accompanied meals, but it was increasingly replaced by milk, buttermilk, or whey. The poor usually drank water. During the course of the eighteenth century, coffee became a popular beverage, to be enjoyed in the coffeehouses that had mushroomed in cities and towns. Tea – called 'women's tobacco' – remained a high status beverage for a long time, partly because of the costly tea-set required to drink it. It was drunk by the wives of patricians and bourgeois regents, diffusing very slowly down to the lower social strata during the eighteenth and nineteenth centuries (Jobse-van Putten 1995:151–226).

The pattern of increasing poverty and recurrent hunger crises after the sixteenth century was less marked in the Low Countries than the rest of Europe. Their famines came later – from 1750 to 1850 – and took place less frequently. This fact may be explained by the affluence of the Dutch Republic, mainly attained by its commercial prominence. By 1800, the administration by regents and merchants had come to an end, the trade-monopoly had shifted to England and the territory had been absorbed by Napoleonic France in 1795. This situation compounded the general impoverishment of the population, which had already set in with the economic deterioration of the late eighteenth century. After the French Period, the Low Countries became a kingdom in 1813, ruled by the Prince of Orange. In particular, William I (1813–1840), the king-merchant, tried to restore former Dutch commercial glory and give the country a new economic impetus by founding trading companies, constructing roads and canals, reclaiming land and introducing other modernising measures. His objective, however, was not immediately attained. Under his administration, the separation of Flanders and the Walloon provinces in the South, which came to constitute the monarchy of Belgium, took place in 1830. His successor had to surrender part of his sovereign rights to the rising social group of liberal bourgeois entrepreneurs, demanding political power in 1848. In contrast to England and Belgium, however, industrialisation had not yet begun. The country remained economically unstable throughout virtually the whole of the nineteenth century; a situation that enlarged the existing gulf between the poor masses and the rich few with every new crisis.

It was during this economically unstable period that the colonial regime in the Dutch East Indies was greatly intensified. The overseas farmers were ordered to cultivate agricultural export products like coffee and sugar, and direct rule was imposed on the population, especially on the island of Java. The establishment of the Netherlands Trading Society (*Nederlandse Handel Maatschappij*) and the so-called 'system of cultivation' (*cultuurstelsel*) by the Dutch government are cases in point (Brugmans 1983:103–117).

As mentioned above, Asian products had slowly begun to play a part in Dutch culinary culture, especially during the centuries after the establishment of the United East-Indian Company (*Verenigde Oost-Indische Compagnie*, or VOC) in

Amsterdam in 1602. This trading company boosted the export of exotic eastern products to European countries, among which stimulants took an important position (Schama 1987:180–183). Drinks, such as coffee and tea, became popular first in Dutch high society, and then trickled down to the lower social strata during the eighteenth and nineteenth centuries.

The availability of these new beverages was one of the factors that, in the long run, fundamentally changed the Dutch meal-pattern. Some specific examples are the institution of a cold breakfast, accompanied by coffee or tea, a coffee break in the morning and a cold lunch, again with coffee or tea. Sugar and cacao – foodstuffs that were cultivated in the colonies especially for export – became indispensable ingredients in all kinds of sweet snacks like biscuits, cakes and tarts. Gradually, the habit of serving confectioneries at tea parties by upper-class ladies of the eighteenth century transformed into the sweets that are enjoyed by all today.

The Arrival of Chinese and Indonesian Restaurants in the Netherlands: 1945–1965

World War II accelerated many aspects of the modernisation and democratisation processes that were already underway. Several West-East colonial regimes were not able to keep afloat and, as a consequence, the independent states of India, as well as Indonesia, came into being within a few years after 1945. Peace in the West did not necessarily mean peace in the East, and Dutch military forces were sent oversees to fight the riots and restore the old order, while defending their 'colonial possessions'. Finally, at the end of 1949, the Dutch transferred sovereignty of the East Indies to the Republic of Indonesia.[4]

In this part I will shift my attention from the relationships of dependency between (colonising and colonised) countries on different sides of the globe to the changing relationships between groups of people in the Netherlands. In this way, some light will be shed on the sociogenesis of Chinese and Indonesian restaurants in the Netherlands and the taste for exotic food in general. These two groups, the natives and immigrants, will, for reasons of some theoretical significance, be referred to here as the *established* and the *outsiders*.[5] The established Dutch natives, and the different flows of immigrants arriving after World War II and holding outsider positions, initially had a social relationship of hierarchy with accompanying feelings of *superiority* and *inferiority*. This kind of unequal relationship may be seen as bearing some similarity to the afore-mentioned situation of the dependencies between the Netherlands and the Dutch East Indies, two countries entwined by trade and colonialism. Both types of relationship are, of course, not independent of each other. Thus the immigrants, pioneering the path for the exotic taste of the Dutch, came from Asia, especially Indonesia and China. In this context it is important to keep in mind that, considered sociologically, relationships between people may be mirrored, symbolised and ritualised in their meals and eating habits.

Following the arrival of more than two hundred thousand Dutch people from Indonesia in the post-war years, the Dutch were increasingly confronted with Asian, mixed Dutch-Indonesian and Chinese, eating habits. Most of these people were 'Indo-Dutch' of Indonesian blood, born in the former Dutch East Indies. The origins, education, profession, income and outward appearance of the members of this group were not homogeneous. Although there was a widespread uncertainty as to what defined Indo-Dutch identity, it was clear that the common eating habits were indisputably their own. Even now these habits are still (or perhaps again) experienced as binding. Thus, in this respect, among others, these people differed fundamentally from those who had long been established in the Netherlands. Initially, therefore, they were considered and treated as outsiders.

The contrasts at the table between the established and the outsiders were sharp. At that time, little social appreciation was attributed to the delicacies of the hot meal and the possibilities of its refinement and variation in the Netherlands. After the severest post-war scarcities were over, the Dutch returned to their former rather dull and monomorphous eating habits. Housewives were still thrifty, possessed little culinary imagination, and preferred to spend their time cleaning rather than cooking. The daily warm meal consisted of potatoes, boiled vegetables and gravy, sometimes accompanied by a small serving of meat or lard. The whole affair was austere, frugally spiced and repetitive. The ritual of eating represented something viewed more as a necessity than as a pleasure. Foreigners describing Dutch eating habits have repeatedly presented a similar picture. The Dutch have never had a 'Rembrandt in the kitchen'. The pleasures of palatability were not held in very high esteem and it was not the custom to sit at the table together or share food with people from outside the family circle. Every 'stranger' was expected to leave the house by six o'clock, and 'eating out' was not generally done, except for by a small elite. In short, for the Dutch, eating fulfilled only a few social functions, of which the strengthening of the bonds among family members was the most important.

On the other hand, however, Indonesian immigrants (many of whom had Dutch nationality) had been accustomed to other ways. They habitually consumed several hot meals a day, which were richly varied and expertly prepared. Eating well was held in high esteem by all sections of the population, especially in Java. Most women, even if poor, were outstanding cooks. The *kokki* (native cook) was certainly the last part of the budget that an Indo-Dutch person would cut, as dinner guests were always expected. The native villagers' daily meal was simple and consisted of rice and several side dishes, but during the sacrificial repasts the women were busy the whole day, preparing festive dishes. The art of cooking had its origin in many traditions: Chinese, Indonesian and also Dutch, at least to some extent. These traditions had influenced each other thoroughly in the long pre-colonial and colonial periods, during which cultural cross-fertilisation had produced a great variety of refined dishes (Vuyk 1973). The now well-known Rice-Table (*Rijsttafel*), consisting of a variety of dishes served together with rice, is an example that is typical of the Indo-Dutch groups. The cultural emphasis on eating and culinary culture in Indonesia manifested itself in other ways as well; for instance, in the extensive street sale of prepared foods. Dishes, which much later became very well-known in the Netherlands, such as *sateh*[6] and *nasi goreng* (fried rice) from Indonesia and *loempia* (spring rolls) and *bami* (fried noodles) of Chinese origin, were prepared and sold in small portable kitchens on the streets of Batavia and other large colonial cities.

Due to the cultural contrasts in eating habits and the different social functions that meals fulfilled (in which climatic influences also played their part), it is comprehensible that the meagre Dutch stew, which the newly arrived Indo-Dutch were obliged to eat in their new home country, was little appreciated. Moreover, the degree of familiarity with Dutch food upon arrival was strongly dependent on the social stratum to which one had belonged in the Dutch East Indies. The higher classes were much better acquainted with Dutch habits (among which meals had their place) than the lower echelons. Because of the shortage of housing, a large number of the Indo-Dutch, were initially housed in so-called 'contract boarding houses' rented by the State. In these 'guest houses' they were only given rice once or twice a week and they had to be content with potatoes for the rest of the time. The landlords believed this to be 'for their own good'. That is to say that they were of the opinion that the newcomers had to assimilate themselves thoroughly. This situation sometimes led to conflicts, but was often accepted with resignation.

It must be noted that the people who managed the boarding houses actually had neither the expertise nor the ingredients to satisfy the longings of the Indo-Dutch people. Nevertheless, the assumption that their own living and eating habits were superior and the indifference to the plight of the immigrants is intrinsic of the figuration of the established and the outsiders. When, later on, the outsiders were able to prepare their own meals, the smell of garlic and other unknown spices was used to stigmatise them. The phenomenon of profound rejection of the favourite dishes of allochthonous people by autochthonous people has often been recorded by social scientists. Tolksdorff is of the opinion that this often leads to social discrimination and he records a number of swear-words used in this context (Tolksdorff 1978:349). Theodoratus writes about the treatment of Greek immigrants in the United States: 'Those eating garlic were considered offenders against public decency and morality' (Theodoratus 1983:90).[7]

In the contract boarding houses, housekeeping courses for Indonesian women, who had not previously been in the Netherlands, some of whom were illiterate, were organised at the initiative of church and private organisations. Washing and 'spring cleaning' were given the most emphasis there, not cooking. This was experienced as patronising, being directed toward teaching the attitudes and behaviour that the Dutch considered normal and correct, and also superior. Schooling and teaching methods were directly more toward conforming with middle-class traditions than stigmatisation, but they stemmed from the same group charisma, or the feeling of superiority of the established. This type of attitude is thus reminiscent of the attempts made around 1900 at 'civilising' working class women through cookery classes and housekeeping courses. Another parallel can be found in the United States, where, at the end of the last century philanthropists and reformers attempted to teach housekeeping to Italian migrants. Indeed these initiatives concerned the destitute inhabitants of slums, but the lessons were similar. They were aimed at discouraging the Italians from their own eating customs and promoting American methods of food preparation based on a more thrifty spending policy (Levenstein 1985).

The social pressure to conform the behaviour of the immigrants to Dutch standards has been heavy, both from the established and the outsiders themselves. The new inhabitants with their Indonesian past wanted employment, a home, and a good education for their children. In this process, they adopted Dutch norms and values in all respects. As far as the daily meal was concerned, this might have meant a complete surrender to potatoes, meat, and vegetables, resulting in a potentially gloomy future for ethnic eating. However, history turned out quite differently, because eating habits are tough to break. Notwithstanding their general assimilation into Dutch society, the Indo-Dutch stuck to their old customs in one respect, namely their meals. As soon as possible, many of them began to eat rice with side dishes and – most surprisingly – the established Dutch natives began to join them and hesitantly tried their dishes at their tables. How did this revolution come about and which social groups were involved?

This change occurred in several phases. Firstly, a network was built, ensuring food provisions of their own, which may be considered a process of ethnic emancipation. The trade in tropical products and spices, conducted by small businessmen and employees on ships, was intensified. Already before the war, a few exotic grocery shops (*toko*) were operating in Rotterdam and The Hague; after the war ethnic businesses became more numerous. In her book Bep Vuyk draws attention to the significant role played by Indo-Dutch women of the lower income groups (Vuyk 1973). To earn extra money (as they were no longer hampered by colonial taboos), these women provided meals to order, which were delivered all over the country by their husbands. Whenever possible they opened a little shop in their small rooms or, preferably, an eatery in their homes.

Here, as elsewhere, the ethnic catering business soon transgressed these borders and became available to a wider public. Auntie Mia's eating house, for instance, situated in the centre of Amsterdam became famous. Shortly after the war, students and artists with little money could choose between a plate of bami or of nasi, that could be eaten in every vacant corner of the house, even on or under the staircase. Her guests apparently thought that having plenty to eat for a low price amply compensated for the fear of bad breath that might offend the established. In this way the traditional Indonesian street trade in the Netherlands acquired a new image. A decade later this type of enterprise had multiplied and Indo-Dutch people could even buy the necessary ingredients at ordinary markets. At the same time, Indonesian women cooks lost their monopoly on the preparation and sale of Indonesian dishes, at least with respect to the rising Indonesian and Chinese restaurants. They continued to cook at home to serve their own ethnic clientele.

Thus, the numbers of people wanting to eat something other than potatoes increased because the cost was low and the atmosphere was very informal. The military now also joined the ranks of the students and artists of the earlier period. Some hundred thousand military personnel returned from Indonesia after the handover of sovereignty in 1949. During their stay there, many of Dutch soldiers had become acquainted with foreign dishes and come to like them. They also wanted to eat this food back home and began to introduce others to Asian delicacies.

Another group of immigrants now seized their chance – the Chinese. They did not come from Indonesia, but from continental China, and they had already established themselves for decades in the port cities as sailors. It was a small group, which just before the war did not exceed a thousand people; a situation that changed quickly after 1950. Attracted by the increasing interest of the Dutch in dining out, ever more Chinese people came to try their luck in the restaurant business, largely through chain migration. In the 1930s, there were already a few Chinese restaurants, such as Kong Hing in Amsterdam, which targeted a clientele outside the Chinese community. The newly arrived Chinese in the catering trades were exclusively here with this goal in mind. Thus, they adjusted their ethnic product to the local demand. They therefore advertised their eating-houses as Chinese-Indonesian, which implied that they served Indonesian dishes as well as their own Chinese fare.

In Indonesia itself, the combination of these methods of cooking, which came from distinct cultural traditions, had lead to refinement. In the Netherlands, with a completely different culinary culture, however, the opposite was true. Adaptation to Dutch taste, ingredients and economy led to a cuisine of little sophistication. The public, unused to delicate flavours, but keen on filling meals, hardly noticed this. 'Let's eat Chinese' was cheap and it had become fashionable, even among people who had no relationship whatsoever to Indonesia.

Those Dutch women who were most enterprising in the kitchen carefully began to experiment at home with loempia and nasi, carefully instructed by popular women's magazines such as *Margriet* (Daisy). Support was also given by the food industry, which was developing aggressively, recognising attractive possibilities in the sector of exotic food products. *Margriet* published the first recipes for Chinese and Indonesian dishes in 1950, and advertisements for canned nasi and bami appeared some years later (Salzman 1985). In presenting such different dishes, the inventive and progressive cook could now even gain praise and a new expert status. What a big difference from earlier times! Furthermore, with increasing prosperity, some aspects of the Dutch menu gradually began to take on a more exotic form, although this was not equally true for all social categories. The stage for the subsequent spectacular growth of exotic 'immigrant cuisines' had definitively been set. One could argue that traditional dishes from

Figure 9.1 A Chinese Restaurant at Zeedijk Street, Amsterdam, 1955 (Photo: Amsterdam Archives).

the Asian continent, prepared and served in many Dutch varieties, had played an essential part in this process. The Chinese-Indonesian restaurants were at the heart of this fundamental evolution of the taste of the Dutch.

The Expansion and Differentiation of the Dutch Taste for Exotic Food since the 1960s

Since about 1965, there has been an increase in public interest in cooking in general and foreign or 'ethnic' cooking in particular. Many cookbooks on exotic

Figure 9.2 and 9.3 The Interiors of a Chinese Restaurant in Amsterdam, 1957 (Photos: Amsterdam Archives).

cuisines appeared and foreign recipes were more frequently published in newspapers and magazines. The phenomenon of culinary journalism has since arisen. Leading newspapers informed their readers now not only about the preparation of loempia, but also of pizza and stuffed green peppers. Journalists collected recipes from all over the world, while Wina Born, their most famous Dutch exponent at that time, devoted one of her first cookbooks to 'aromatic dishes from the Mediterranean countries'. In her *Camping and Caravan Cookbook* she discussed the problems of the purchase and preparation of food for the traveller, 'with an index of the main foods in German, French, Italian, Spanish and Servo-Croatian'. By then, large numbers of Dutch people began to take holidays abroad on a regular basis, a trend made possible by increasing prosperity. Some Dutch took their food supply with them in cans and packages, but more people allowed themselves to now be guests in the newly discovered countries and to treat themselves to local dishes and specialities. At the same time, the new hosts in the, by then well-known tourist spots, learned that the Dutch were fond of green peas, steak and applesauce.

Simultaneously, a shift took place in the opposite direction. New groups of outsiders came to live in the Netherlands, now not only from the Far East, but also from the same Mediterranean countries that the established had recently discovered as destinations for their summer holidays. The Italians, Spanish, Greeks and Yugoslavians coming to the Netherlands often had very different regional backgrounds, but their place in the Dutch social ladder was the same – at the bottom. They came to perform unskilled work and were planning to return to their home countries immediately after they had earned money. In these respects they differed fundamentally from the Indo-Dutch, who came to settle in a new home country due to political forces. In the same period more people of Dutch nationality continued to arrive from the former colonial territories in the East and the West like Surinam. The Chinese were also flooding in to establish restaurants even in the farthest corners of the Netherlands. Dutch natives were therefore confronted with an increasing variety of peoples and groups with their own cultures and culinary aromas. The better off and the young went on to taste the foreign cuisines; the old and less affluent were irritated by the arrival of these strangers and did not try new food.

Now the history of the established and the outsiders at the table began to repeat itself, with all the accompanying initial rejection and disgust towards unknown tastes and smells. However, the Mediterranean immigrants also proved quick in establishing their own provisions for the preparation of their own familiar dishes. The Dutch food that was provided in the boarding houses did not go down well, and ethnic cafes rapidly became restaurants. A new type of stall appeared in the market place, where the necessary vegetables and spices were available, although sometimes at high prices. Ethnic groups also discovered each other's cuisines, for instance, the Italians and the Chinese. However, in the end most of them much preferred to prepare food at home, because the Italian restaurants in the Netherlands had adjusted themselves to

Dutch tastes and offered adapted dishes. Although Italian vegetables were sometimes replaced by Dutch ones, for the most part traditional preparation methods were preserved at Italian homes. Typical of this tradition are the diverse forms of pasta-based meals with a mixture of vegetables, meat and raw salad. The Dutch meal pattern, in which potatoes, vegetables and meat are served separately, was scarcely heeded. An exception was stews, a heavy winter fare that the Italian immigrants greatly appreciated in the Dutch climate. The well-known attachment to one's own eating habits, even over a long period, was even more notable in the case of the Italians, because many of them were married to Dutch women and naturalised. Although food preparation is also traditionally a female task in Italy, frequent role reversals took place in the mixed Italian-Dutch marriages; the husband regularly prepared food for his wife and children, who usually enjoyed his meals very much. In these families, culinary culture was held in as much esteem as in the (mixed) Dutch-Indonesian families. Italian food as a restaurant meal, take-away, or prepared at home has eventually become as popular in the Netherlands as Chinese and Indonesian food.

Of course, Italian dishes were not as well known in the Netherlands as French food had always been, at least in elite circles. However, they were not completely new, either. In the same way Indonesian food was known to some groups of people long before World War II, the Dutch were acquainted with ingredients like rice and pasta prior to the sixties. However, these materials were usually cooked in a different way than in the Netherlands. Macaroni, spaghetti and rice, as may be gleaned from pre-war cookery books, were at that time mainly used as deserts ingredients, usually made into a kind of porridge. In the mid-sixties, different ways of preparing rice and pasta, and even how to fill and bake a pizza, were explained in household literature. These dishes were, however, initially recommended for lunch, and not for dinner. However, eventually, just like in the United States, pizza has evolved into the most popular fast food in the Netherlands, especially among the young.

Ethnic businesses became so successful that large-scale Dutch and international food companies responded to the increasing demand for foreign and ethnic products. Market gardening increasingly produced mushrooms, green peppers, aubergines, courgettes, bean sprouts other vegetables that formerly were used very little. By the seventies, most availability problems for the ingredients needed to prepare formerly unusual foreign dishes had been solved for natives and immigrants alike. Facilities for the preparation of Indonesian, Chinese, Mediterranean foods (or whatever other types of ethnic food came after the initiators), even increased substantially, when the food industry succeeded in producing a large variety of dry and wet sauces and seasonings for every conceivable dish.

In this way, the origination and expansion of the taste for exotic food commenced in the Netherlands during the 1940s, 1950s and 1960s. Asian food without a doubt was a forerunner in this development, which has expanded

Figure 9.4 Next to Chinese and Indonesian restaurants, culinary influences from the United States are amongst the most visible on Dutch streets.

rapidly ever since. Most importantly, this trend did not remain limited to the circles of the elite, but diffused throughout all layers of the population. At present, one may speak of the Netherlands as being a multicultural society. This can be observed most clearly at the daily markets in the big cities, where fish, meat, vegetables and spices are sold. The Indonesian toko has now become only one among many other kinds of ethnic stalls and shops.

Conclusion

In this chapter I have focused on the development of the globalisation of Dutch culinary culture during the twentieth century. In particular I have examined the part that has been played by the expansion of Chinese and Indonesian restaurants in the Netherlands since World War II. The study of these early exotic restaurants, and the different groups of people who were involved in them, may have shed some light on the import and diffusion of foreign cuisines in the Netherlands. During the final quarter of the century, processes of acceleration took place through the arrival of new groups of immigrants bringing their own tastes. The Dutch, in turn, started travelling much longer distances, not only to other countries, but even to other continents. Thus the variations on the theme of 'foreign cuisine' has increased and differentiated, and new combinations have become innumerable. A whole series of ethnic food supplies and restaurants is now simultaneously available to the critical Dutch and the foreign consumer. One may well ask whether the sharp contrasts between the established and the outsiders at the table in some respects have today become more blurred. It might give some insight to Dutch social relationships to study the more and the less successful ethnic culinary varieties in the context of the groups involved. Whatever the case, the dominant attitude of narrow-mindedness in culinary matters and the fear of bad breath seem to have faded. This applies not only to the Dutch situation, but also holds true for other western countries. The manifestation of a sizeable taste for Chinese and Indonesian food among the Dutch about half a century ago, which was described in this chapter, may be seen as the *local* beginning of this obviously *global* trend.[8]

General processes ought to be shown in specific times and places. This story of the Dutch-Indonesian relationship and its aftermath is one of the innumerable varieties of the same general process of what Jack Goody called the development of a *world cuisine* (1982:154–74). In the socio-genesis of this world cuisine, Asian food has had a fundamental impact on the culinary cultures of the world as appetiser and initiator of a taste for the exotic.

Notes

1 See the chapter by Adel Den Hartog in this volume.
2 Part of this section is derived from Van Otterloo 2000.
3 See De Vries and Van der Woude 1995 for the Dutch history of the first round of modern economic growth since the sixteenth century.
4 Part of this section has been translated from Van Otterloo 1990:212–224.
5 For these sociological concepts, see Elias and Scotson 1965.
6 Pieces of meat or seafood grilled on skewers and served with peanut sauce or soy sauce.
7 See also Cottaar and Willems 1985:265.
8 It may also be seen as an example of 'the East in the West' (Goody 1996).

WARM MUSHROOM SUSHI?

An afterword

Boudewijn Walraven

... warm mushroom sushi roll with asparagus spears hanging out like dreadlocks, and a soft sweet Jerusalem artichoke enveloped in flaky pastry offset by caramelised cauliflower, leeks and feta.

(From the menu of a recommended restaurant in the category 'Global' of the 2000 edition of *Time Out: Eating and Drinking*)

This book is about the entanglement of two pervasive phenomena, food and globalisation. It is built on the premise that the central importance of the former makes it an appropriate and convenient focus to study the latter. The biological need for food, the pain of hunger and the joys of satisfying this want belong to the universal experience of humanity. This physiological immediacy of food serves as the unshakeable foundation for incredibly diverse and astonishingly complex cultural elaborations. Food is a fundamental key component of social relations from the very beginning of our lives. Caring for a newly born baby is above all the act of feeding it (and disposing of the resulting waste matter). Affection and respect are expressed through food and the eating of particular foods is part of major moments in life, from births to funerals. Our experience of time is to a large extent structured by culturally determined patterns designed to manage the physiological need of our bodies to have meals at certain moments. As a source of metaphor food is probably unsurpassed. It suffices, by way of experiment, to try to describe emotions and experiences without using the words bitter, sour and sweet. Food is a mundane, daily matter, but it also expresses what is sacred and sublime. Medieval Christians thought of Christ as a mother who nurses the Church (Bynum 1992:93, 159) and worshipers of Krishna at Mount Govardhan feast on vast quantities of food that is considered to be a transformation of Krishna's body (Toomey 1992:120). Food is life, literally and metonymically. It is also love, health, happiness, entertainment, business and industry. Politics, identity, status, gender, age and class – food is relevant to all of them.

The manifold meanings and universal significance of food, and also its concrete presence in human life afford a vantage point to explore globalisation, which is pervasive by its very nature, yet at the same time abstract and elusive. Wherever globalisation spreads its tentacles, food and foodways are major local concerns, providing a basis for the comparative study of globalisation. However, food is also linked to globalisation in a much more direct and specific manner. Commercial interests have always been the driving force behind globalisation (as they were behind early Western expansion) and foodstuffs, 'sugar and spice,' have played a crucial role in this. Because of the universal daily need for food, food producers are in principle able to market their products all over the world. Hence the attempts by Kikkoman to sell soy sauce in The Netherlands, and of the Dutch confectioner Verkade to make Japanese buy their cookies, not to mention McDonald's and KFC. Food is a promising target for commercial ventures wherever one goes, not only because it is a daily necessity, but also because of the common human desire for variation and the general proclivity to shape one's own life through the medium of food.

As the Introduction and the different chapters of this book attest, the commercial interests of food-producing companies are related to local food cultures in various and sometimes complex ways. Food producers have to respect local customs, but they may also actively help to promote certain trends. In recent years, several newly developed canned drinks have appeared on the Korean market that make use of 'native' or 'traditional' ingredients. Several of these appeal to the emotional value rice has to Koreans (cf. the chapters by Pemberton and Walraven). One is called Paegŭi minjok, 'White-clothed People', a metonymical appellation for the Korean people, who used to prefer white clothes in the not too distant past. Another rice-based drink is *shikhye*. People used to make it at home, but nowadays it is available in cans, which state with disarming candour: 'Nostalgia Drink, Shikhye: Since 1994'. The most interesting fact is that Yakult, the maker of this drink, which appeals to nationalistic feelings, is not Korean but Japanese (*Figures 10.1 and 10.2*). Pemberton's chapter, about local producers who market local products, at first glance shows the limitations of globalisation, but in fact the preference for san namul and mettugi is part of the same nostalgia discourse the rice-based drinks appeal to, and this derives its meaning from just these processes of modernisation and globalisation. In other words, local farmers in Korea, the Korean Agricultural Cooperative Federation and the transnational company Yakult all are confronted with the consequences of globalisation and economic liberalisation (which is an important component of globalisation) and attempt to benefit from the new conditions created by globalisation.

The food-related activities of large companies contribute to the commercialisation of aspects of daily life that in the past were unconnected to the market, or only indirectly. Traditionally, Korean housewives would make soybean sauce, soybean paste, red pepper paste, bean curd and even alcoholic drinks at home, often using ingredients they had cultivated themselves. In the twentieth century this began to change, but to a large extent this situation prevailed until the

Figure 10.1 'White-clothed People' – A New Korean Drink Made from Rice.

1980s, when commercial products increasingly pushed out their home-made equivalents. Around the same time, the supermarket and the convenience store made their appearance with their assortment of processed food, taking the place of markets where the bulk of sales consisted of primary products, which in many cases were sold by their actual producers.

169

Figure 10.2 A Traditional Korean Drink Manufactured by the Japanese Company Yakult.

The advance of the processed food industry and its outlets, the supermarkets, was part of a global trend which, as several chapters of this book suggest, has contributed to making the lives of women radically different and has significantly changed gender configurations. Women, almost universally the traditional preparers of food, have been liberated from time-consuming chores and enabled – to a certain degree – to look for work and pastimes outside the home. Men, at least in principle, have become less dependent on them. On the other hand, women have increasingly turned from producers into consumers of processed food. Rather than preparing the basic ingredients of their own cuisine themselves they are now 'free' to engage in exotic culinary adventures with the aid of ready-made spice mixes (which in many cases will offer recipes on the packaging as well, encouraging further changes in food culture).

What all the chapters in this book show is that local changes in foodways cannot be fully understood without taking globalisation into account. White's 'ladies who lunch' and Cwiertka's Japanese expatriates, for instance, live in an environment that has been shaped by globalisation, and they adjust their patterns of consumption in an attempt to manipulate the opportunities globalisation offers to their own advantage. The global village is actually highly urbanised, and it is only in this urban context that the ladies who lunch find the infrastructure that allows them their culinary diversions. The expatriates, who belong to the vast numbers of people who for a shorter or longer period are uprooted to serve the global interests of their companies, are able to satisfy their craving for Japanese food thanks to globalised commercial activities, which almost everywhere offer urban consumers a cosmopolitan choice of foods. During the workshop on changes in Asian food culture, which was the cradle of this volume, a paper by Ted Bestor (not included here) presented a striking example of what globalisation may lead to in such attempts to serve expatriates with 'their own food'. Diners in Japanese restaurants in New York are proudly served tuna bought at Tsukiji, the fish market of Tōkyō, which the day before was caught off the coast of Maine and from Kennedy Airport flown straightaway to Narita.

One implication of the importance of food-related issues for the most diverse aspects of human life is that these issues can and should be studied from the viewpoint of different academic disciplines. If there is one area in which the borderlines between disciplines may be profitably ignored, it is the study of food. The scholars from different disciplines who were invited to Leiden in 1998 to take part in our food workshop found that their disciplinary diversity was an advantage rather than a drawback. It takes a biologist like Pemberton, for instance, with his awareness of the amazing variety of wild-gathered foods sold in Korean markets, to realise how significant is this countercurrent to globalisation. Nutritional science reminds us of the physiological aspects of foodways and the – in the most literal sense of the word – vital issues that are at stake (cf. the 'milk and murder' issue of the danger condensed milk posed to children's health mentioned by Den Hartog), while anthropologists are particularly sensitive to the symbolical associations of food, which are so important in the definition of ethnic identity in a world where rapid changes and an abundance of international contacts constantly make us question who we are. The perspective of the historian is of particular value for the study of globalisation, which has a longer pre-history than one might assume. It is easy to forget how wide-reaching and deeply penetrating were the trade networks of the past. The first Japanese soy sauce was exported to the Netherlands in 1737 by the Dutch East India Company, and already in 1886 Kikkoman sent an employee to Europe to explore new opportunities to market its products (Tanaka 2000:6,7). The displacement of large groups of people for reasons of work is not a modern phenomenon either. For hundreds of years emigrants, slaves and contract coolies, forced or voluntarily, have been on the move, over enormous distances and in massive numbers. In the Dutch colony of Surinam, for instance, white settlers, African slaves and contract labourers from the Indian subcontinent and Java joined (and overwhelmed) the Native Americans (with notable consequences for local food culture). One may admit that present globalisation is different because of its scale and intensity, but its true nature cannot be understood as long as one is unaware of this pre-history. In accordance with this realisation, most chapters in this volume pay attention to the historical dimension. Den Hartog, for instance, presents us with one of the first examples of the marketing of an industrially processed food – a type of food that now has become dominant – by Western transnational companies. (He also made me understand why my Indo-Dutch mother, in a country full of fresh milk, insisted on feeding her children little spoonfuls of excessively sweet condensed milk, which she fondly remembered as a treat from her youth).

The focus of this book is Asia, but if it had limited itself to examining Asian food in Asia alone, it might be criticised for an Orientalistic bias. It is one of the defining characteristics of the present situation that Asian food has become a part of life elsewhere, sometimes as the food of the many Asians who have dispersed over the globe, and sometimes becoming part of local fare. Tracing how the Dutch acquired a taste for Indonesian food, Van Otterloo shows how these two channels of diffusion of Asian food may be connected. Because of the ready acceptance of Indonesian food in Holland and the almost complete disappearance of distinctively Dutch food – except for the priceless herring – at present Rijsttafel is about the nearest thing to typically Dutch food one might offer a foreign visitor.[1] The relationship between a colonial past and the diffusion of Asian food is, of course, very similar in Great Britain, where Indian food in many ways occupies the same niche as Indonesian food in the Netherlands. Bush and Williams do alert us to the fact, however, that for immigrants from the Indian subcontinent living in the UK Indian food still retains a very particular meaning (even though in fact it has substantially changed because of the health-endangering overabundance of meat), which makes their foodways quite different from those of both the autochthonous population and other migrants.

Varied as the approaches and subjects may be, each chapter of this book makes its own contribution to an understanding of what globalisation actually means in the late twentieth and early twenty-first century. The quotation from *Time Out*, in its recognition of a special category of food labelled 'global', suggests that globalisation is a process that divorces the local from its origins and creates a new culture that is no longer regionally definable. At first sight, it seems as if an argument can be made for this. Pizza and sushi have been appropriated by the world at large and are no longer exclusively Italian and Japanese. Yet, such cases are quite rare, and on further investigation adaptations to the local can almost always be detected. To realise how important the local remains, one only has to think what welcome 'global' hot mushroom sushi, or the mango sushi sold by the British Sainsbury supermarkets, would receive in Japan, or for that matter, pizzas with pineapple ('Pizza Hawaii,' a standard item on the menu of pizzerias in the Netherlands) in Italy. In fact, the phenomenon of globalisation would be of dubious significance if its meaning was confined to a process leading to the loss of all local affiliations and connotations. Taken in a wider sense, however, as the total sum of increasingly frequent global connections, globalisation is a process that stimulates a surprising richness of local responses. These responses, documented and analysed by the contributors to this volume, may be regarded as testimony to the ingenuity with which humans adapt and shape their lives to make them satisfactory and meaningful.

Note

1 The manner of presentation of the different dishes was from the outset hybrid Dutch-Indonesian rather than Indonesian.

REFERENCES

Abbott, Dina 1995 'Who feeds the urban poor? The Indian food-processing industry: an alienated 'formal' sector versus an attuned 'informal' sector', Open University, Development Policy and Practice Working Paper 35.

Abraham, Rachel 1989 'Diets and food habits in the Indian subcontinent', p. 231–34 in J.K. Cruickshank and D.G. Beevers (eds.) *Ethnic Factors in Health and Disease*, Oxford: Butterworth-Heinemann.

Achaya, K.T. 1995 *The Food Industries of British India*, Delhi: Oxford University Press.

Allison, Anne 1991 'Japanese Mothers and Obentos: the lunchbox as ideological state apparatus', p. 41-66 in *Anthropological Quarterly* 64 (1).

Amino, Yoshihiko 1994 *Nihon Shakai Seikô: ama to rettô bunka* (Rethinking Japanese Society: people of the sea and culture of the archipelago), Tôkyô: Shôgakkan.

An, Ch'on 1991 *Yosong chongch'i munhwaron* (On Women's Political Culture), Seoul: Karisani.

Anderson, Annie S. et al 1995 'Macronutrient intake in South Asian and Italian women in the west of Scotland', p. 203A in *Proceedings of the Nutrition Society* 54 (3).

Anwar, Muhammed 1985 *Pakistanis in Britain: a sociological study*, London: New Century.

Appadurai, Arjun 1981 'Gastropolitics in Hindu South Asia', p. 494–511 in *American Anthropologist* 8 (3).

—— 1986 'Theory in anthropology: center and periphery', p. 356–61 in *Comparative Studies in Society and History* 28.

—— 1988 'How to make a national cuisine: cookbooks in contemporary India', p. 3–24 in *Comparative Studies in Society and History* 13.

—— 1990 'Disjuncture and difference in the global cultural economy', p. 1–24 in *Public Culture* 2 (2).

Apte, Mahadev L. and Judit Katona-Apte 1984 'The significance of food in religious ideology and ritual behaviour in Marathi myths', p. 9–22 in A. Fenton and T. Owen (eds.) *Food in Perspective: proceedings of the International Conference on Ethnological Food Research, Cardiff 1977*, Edinburgh: Donald.

Asian Development Bank 1987 *Use of Pesticides in the Asian-Pacific Region*.

Avery, Gillian 1984 'Children's corner', p. xi-xiii in *New Society*, December 20–27.

Balarajan, Rasaratnam and L. Bulusu 1990 'Mortality among immigrants in England and Wales, 1979-83', p. 104-23 in M. Britton (ed.) *Mortality and Geography: a review in the mid-1980s*, London: HMSO.

Beardsworth, Alan and Teresa Keil 1997 *Sociology on the Menu: an invitation to the study of food and society*, London: Routledge.

Beck, Brenda 1969 'Colour and heat in South Indian ritual', p. 553-72 in *Man* 4 (4).

Bernstein, Gail (ed.) 1991 *Recreating Japanese Women, 1600-1945*, Berkeley: University of California Press.

Blanchon, Flora (ed.) 1995 *Asie III, Savourer Goûter* (Asia vol. 3: Tastes and Savours), Paris: Presses de l'Université de Paris-Sorbonne

Blaut, James M. 1993 *The Colonizer's Model of the World: geographical diffusionism and eurocentric history*, New York/London: Guilford Press.

Bodenheimer, F.S. 1951 *Insects as Human Food*, Hague: W. Junk.

Boeke, Julius H. 1931 'De economische verhouding van stad en dorp in Nederlandsch- en Britsch-Indië' (The economic relation between town and village in the Dutch East and British Indies), p. 1–23 in *Koloniale Studiën* 15.

Bourdieu, Pierre (1986) *Distinction: a social critique of the judgement of taste*, London: Routledge & Kegan Paul.

Bradby, Hannah 1996 *Cultural Strategies of Young Women of South Asian Origin in Glasgow, with Special Reference to Health*, unpublished Ph.D. thesis, University of Glasgow.

Brandt, Vincent 1971 *A Korean Village: between land and sea*, Cambridge Mass.: Harvard University Press.

Braudel, Fernand 1981-1984 *Civilization and Capitalism, 15th–18th Century* (3 Vols.), London: Collins.

Brinton, Mary 1993 *Women and the Economic Miracle: gender and work in postwar Japan*, Berkeley: University of California Press,

Brugmans, Izaak J. (1983) *Paardenkracht en mensenmacht: sociaal-economische geschiedenis van Nederland 1795-1940* (Horse Power and Poeple's Power: socio-economic history of The Netherlands 1795-1940), 's-Gravenhage: Nijhoff.

Burton, David (1993) *The Raj at Table*, London and Boston: Faver and Faber.

Bush, Helen M. and Rory G.A. Williams 1995 'Economic and cultural considerations in the food choice of South Asian and Italian women in the west of Scotland', unpublished paper presented at the Fourth Food Choice Conference, University of Birmingham, April.

Bush, Helen M. et al 1995 'Dietary change in South Asian and Italian women in the west of Scotland', MRC Medical Sociology Unit Working Paper 54.

—— 1996 'Weight consciousness and body image among South Asian, Italian and general population women in Britain', p. 600 in *Journal of Epidemiology and Community Health* 50 (5).

—— 1998 'Family hospitality and ethnic tradition among South Asian, Italian and general population women in the West of Scotland', p. 351–80 in *Sociology of Health and Illness* 20 (3).

Bynum, Caroline Walker 1992 *Fragmentation and Redemption: essays on gender and the human body in medieval religion*, New York: Zone Books.

Camporesi, Piero 1993 *The Magic Harvest: food, folklore and society*, Cambridge: Polity Press.

Cantlie, Audrey 1981 'The moral significance of food among Assamese Hindus', p. 42–62 in A. Mayer (ed.) *Culture and Morality*, Oxford: Oxford University Press.

Caplan, Pat 1985 *Class and Gender in India: women and their organisations in a South Indian city*, London and New York: Tavistock Press.

Ch'ae, Ye-sok et al 1962 'Han'guk sangyongshikp'um yongyangka chosa pogo (II)' (Studies on Nutritive Value of Korean Foods, II), p. 56–64 in *Kungnip Hwahak Yon'guso Pogo* (The Reports of National Chemistry Laboratories) 10.

Chang, K.C. (ed.) 1977 *Food in Chinese Culture: anthropological and historical perspectives*, New Haven and London: Yale University Press.

Charles, Nickie and Marion Kerr 1988 *Women, Food and Families,* Manchester: Manchester University Press.

Cheng, Sea-ling 1996a 'Consuming cosmopolitanism: Lan Kwai Fong in Hong Kong', unpublished paper presented at the Conference on Consumption in Hong Kong, University of Hong Kong, March.

—— 1996b *Food and Distinction in Hong Kong Families,* unpublished MPhil thesis, University of Hong Kong.

—— 1997 'Back to the future: herbal tea shops in Hong Kong', p. 51–76 in G. Evans and M. Tam (eds.) *Hong Kong: the anthropology of a Chinese metropolis,* London: Curzon Press.

Choe, Sang-su. 1983 *Annual Customs of Korea: notes on the rites and ceremonies of the year,* Seoul: Seomun-dang.

Choe, Young-min 1998 'Eating Habits Diverse Around World', in *Korea Times,* July 9.

Chongjo Shillok (Veritable Records of the Reign of King Chongjo) 1957, Seoul: Kuksa p'yonch'an wiwonhoe.

Chu, Yong-ha 1991 *Kimch'i: hangugin-ui mokkori: kimch'i ui munhwa illyuhak* (Kimch'i: the food of Koreans: the cultural anthropology of kimch'i), Seoul: Tosoch'ulp'an konggan.

Chungjong Shillok (Veritable Records of the Reign of King Chungjong) 1957, Seoul: Kuksa p'yonch'an wiwonhoe.

Clammer, John 1997 *Contemporary Urban Japan: a sociology of consumption,* Oxford: Blackwell Publishers.

Colpi, Terri 1991 *The Italian Factor: the Italian community in Great Britain,* Edinburgh: Mainstream.

Cook, Ian and Philip Crang 1996 'The world on a plate: displacement and geographical knowledge', p. 131–53 in *Journal of Material Culture* 1 (2).

Cottaar, Annemarie and Wim Willems 1984 *Indische Nederlanders: een onderzoek naar beeldvorming* (The Indo-Dutch: the construction of an image), Den Haag: Moesson.

Craddock, Sally 1983 *Retired Except on Demand: the life of Dr Cicely Williams,* Oxford: Green College.

Curtin, Philip D. 1984 *Cross-cultural Trade in World History,* Cambridge: Cambridge University Press.

Cwiertka, Katarzyna 1996 'Minekichi Akabori and his role in the development of modern Japanese cuisine', p. 68-80 in H. Walker (ed.) *Cooks and Other People,* Devon: Prospect Books.

—— 1997 'Domesticating western food in Japan: a comparative view', p. 64–74 in H. Walker (ed.) *Food on the Move,* Devon: Prospect Books.

—— 1999 *The Making of Modern Culinary Tradition in Japan,* unpublished Ph.D. thesis, Leiden University.

Daniel, E. Valentine 1984 *Fluid Signs: being a person the Tamil way,* Berkeley, California University Press.

David, Fred 1979 *Yearning for Yesterday: a sociology of nostalgia,* New York: The Free Press.

Davidson, Alan 1983 *Food in Motion: the migration of foodstuffs and cookery techniques,* Leeds: Prospect Books.

De Haan, Frederik 1935 *Oud Batavia* (Old Batavia), Bandoeng: A.C. Nix.

De Haas, Jaap H. 1932 *De Karo-Bataksche Zuigeling* (The Karo-Batak infant), Ph.D. thesis, Batavia: Kolff.

—— 1936 'Over zuigelingenvoeding in Nederlandsch-Indië' (On infant feeding in the Dutch East Indies), p. 627-36 in *Geneeskundig Tijdschrift voor Nederlandsch-Indië, Feestbundel* (Medical Journal of Dutch East Indies, commemorative edition).

—— 1937 'Xerophtalmie bij 6 kinderen' (Six children with xerophtalmia), p. 3043–45 in *Geneeskundig Tijdschrift voor Nederlandsch-Indië* 77.

De Vries, Jan and Ad Van der Woude 1995 *Nederland 1500-1815: de eerste ronde van moderne economische groei* (The Netherlands 1500-1815: the first round of modern economic growth), Amsterdam: Balans.

Den Hartog, Adel P. 1986 *Diffusion of Milk as a New Food to Tropical Regions: the example of Indonesia*, Wageningen: Stichting Voeding Nederland.

—— 1989 'Toward improving public nutrition: nutritional policy in Indonesia before independence', p. 105–18 in G.M. Van Heteren et al (eds.) *Dutch Medicine in the May Archipelago 1816-1940*, Amsterdam: Rodopi.

—— (ed.) 1995 *Food Technology, Science and Marketing: European diet in the twentieth century*, East Linton: Tuckwell Press.

Donath, Willem Frederik 1938 'Nogmaals afgeroomde gesuikerde melk' (Once more sweetened condensed skimmed milk), p. 1258–67 in *Geneeskundig Tijdschrift voor Nederlandsch-Indië* 78.

Driver, Christopher 1983 *The British at Table, 1940-1980*, London: Chatto and Windus.

Du Boulay, Juliet 1986 'Gifts and strangers', p. 37–53 in *Journal of Mediterranean Studies* 1.

Dupuis, Jacques 1970 'Coutumes alimentaires, sociétés et économies. Le cas de la répartition de la consommation du lait en Asie tropicale' (Food habits, societies and economies: the case of the distribution of milk consumption in tropical Asia), p. 529–44 in *Annales de Géographie* 79.

Eichinger Ferro-Luzzi, Gabriella 1977 'Ritual as language: the case of South Indian food offerings', p. 507–14 in *Current Anthropology* 18 (3).

—— 1980 'Food avoidances at puberty and menstruation in Tamilnadu', 'Food avoidances during the puerperium and lactation in Tamilnadu' and 'Food Avoidances of Pregnant women in Tamilnadu', p. 93–117 in J.R.K. Robson (ed.) *Food, Ecology and Culture*, New York: Gordon and Breach.

Elias, Norbert and John L. Scotson 1965 *The Established and the Outsiders*, London: Frank Cass and Co.

Elisseef, Danielle 1995 'L'étrange goût du chien, petites questions suggérées par l'archéologie chinoise' (The strange taste of dog), p. 83–88 in Blanchon 1995.

Evans, Grant 1997 'Ghost and the New Governor: The Anthropology of a Hong Kong Rumour', p. 267–296 in G. Evans and M. Tam (eds) *Hong Kong: the anthropology of a Chinese metropolis,* London: Curzon Press.

Evans, Grant and Maria Tam 1997 'Introduction: the anthropology of contemporary Hong Kong', p. 1–24 in G. Evans and M. Tam (eds.) *Hong Kong: the anthropology of a Chinese metropolis*, London: Curzon Press.

Fairbanks, John et al 1973 *East Asia: tradition and transformation*, Boston: Houghton Mifflin.

Fiddes, Nick 1991 *Meat: a natural symbol*, London and New York: Routledge.

Fields, George 1983 *From Bonsai to Levis*, New York: Mentor.

Foreign Agricultural Service, United States Department of Agriculture 1997 *Agricultural Situation*, annual report (KS7063), Seoul: Foreign Agricultural Service, United States Department of Agriculture, American Embassy.

Frank, Andre G. 1998 *ReOrient: global economy in the Asian age*, Berkeley/Los Angeles/ London: University of California Press.

Goodman, Roger 1990 *Japan's International Youth: the emergence of a new class of schoolchildren*, Oxford: Clarendon Press.

Goody, Jack 1982 *Cooking, Cuisine and Class: a study in comparative sociology*, Cambridge: Cambridge University Press.

—— 1996 *The East in the West*, Cambridge: Cambridge University Press.

Gourou, Pierre 1959 *The Tropical World: its social and economic conditions and its future status*, London: Longmans.

Grinker, Roy Richard 1995 'Mourning the nation: ruins of the North in Seoul', p. 192–223 in *Positions* 3:1.

Gupta, Akhil and James Ferguson 1992 'Beyond "culture": space, identity and the politics of difference', p. 6–23 in *Cultural Anthropology* 7 (1).

Hahn, Eduard 1896 *Die Haustiere und ihre Beziehungen zur Wirtschaft des Menschen, eine Geografische Studie* (Domesticated Animals and their Relationship with Human Economy. A geographic study), Leipzig: Ducker und Humbolt.

Hall, Carla 1997 'A Dialogue, Five Years Later', *Los Angeles Times*, April 27.

Hall, Rosetta S. 1933 'Korean foods for the sick', p. 187 in *Korea Mission Field* 29 (9).

Han, Kyong-ku 1994 'Otton umshig-un saenggakhagi-e chot'a: kimch'i-wa Han'guk minjoksong ui chongsu' (Some foods are good to think: kimchi and the epitomizations of national character), p. 51–68 in *Han'guk Munhwa Illyuhak* 26.

Handler, Richard 1988 *Nationalism and the Politics of Culture in Quebec*, Madison: University of Wisconsin Press.

Hannerz, Ulf 1990 'Cosmopolitans and locals in world culture', p. 237–52 in M. Featherstone (ed.) *Global Culture: nationalism, globalization and modernity*, London: Sage Publications.

—— 1992 *Cultural Complexity: studies in the social organization of meaning*, New York: Columbia University Press.

—— 1996 *Transnational Connections: culture, people, places*, London, New York: Routledge.

Harris, Marvin 1985 *Good to Eat: riddles of food and culture*, New York: Simon & Schuster.

Heer, Jean 1966 *World Events 1866-1966: the first hundred years of Nestlé*, Lausanne: Nestlé.

Hershatter, Gail 1997 *Dangerous Pleasures: prostitution and modernity in twentieth-century Shanghai*, Berkeley: University of California Press.

Hieatt, Constance B. 1997 'How Arabic traditions travelled to England', p. 120–26 in H. Walker (ed.) *Food on the Move*, Devon: Prospect Books.

Hirschon, Renee 1989 *Heirs of the Greek Catastrophe*, Oxford: Clarendon.

Ho, Ping-ti 1955 'The introduction of American food plants into China', p. 191–01 in *American Anthropologist* 57.

Ho, Chun 1975 (1613) *Tongui Pogam (Kugyok chungbo)* (Precious Mirror of Korean Medicine [with Korean translation and additions]) Seoul: Namsandang.

Hobbs, Mrs. Thomas 1929 'The Society for the Prevention of Cruelty to Animals: annual report', p. 258-260 in *Korea Mission Field* 25 (10).

Hobsbawm, Eric J. 1991 (1987) *The Age of Empire, 1875-1914*, London: Cardinal.

Hodgson, Marshall G.S. 1993 *Rethinking World History*, Cambridge: Cambridge University Press.

Holm, Lotte 1996 'Identity and dietary change', p. 95–98 in *Scandinavian Journal of Nutrition* 40.

Hong Kong Government 1938 *Hong Kong Report.*

Hong, Suk-ki 1995 'La gastronomie funéraire en Corée' (Funerary Gastronomy in Korea), p. 89-96 in Blanchon 1995.

hooks, bell 1992 *Black Looks: race and representation*, Boston, MA: South End Press.

Huitema, H. 1982 *Animal husbandry in the tropics, its economic importance and potentialities: studies in a few regions of Indonesia*, Amsterdam: Royal Tropical Institute, Agricultural Research Communication 73.

Hulbert, Homer 1969 (1906), *The Passing of Korea*, Seoul: Yonsei University Press.

Hunziker, Otto Frederick 1946 *Condensed Milk and Milk Powder: prepared for factory, school, and laboratory*, La Grange, Illinois: published by the author.

REFERENCES

Hyojong Shillok (Veritable Records of the Reign of King Hyojong) 1957, Seoul: Kuksa p'yonch'an wiwonhoe.

Im, Tong-kwon 1972 *Han'guk Seship'ungsok* (Seasonal Customs of Korea), Seoul: Somundang.

Ionescu, Sanda forthcoming 'Soka Gakkai in Germany: The story of a qualified success', in H. Befu and S. Guichard-Anguis (eds.) *Globalizing Japan*, Routledge.

Ishige, Naomichi and Tadashi Inoue (eds.) 1991 *Gendai Nihon ni okeru Katei to Shokutaku: meimeizen kara chabudai e* (Change and Transformation in Table Setting: home dining in modern Japan), Bulletin of the National Museum of Ehtnology, Special Issue 16.

Itô, Abito 1978 'Rituals at McDonald's', p. 370–386 in *Journal of American Culture* 1 (2).

——1996 *Korea*, Tôkyô: Kawade Shobô.

Japan Information and Culture Center 1997 'Convenience Stores', p. 4 in *Japan Now*, Washington D.C.: Embassy of Japan.

Jeffery, Patricia 1976 *Migrants and Refugees: Muslim and Christian Pakistani families in Bristol*, Cambridge: Cambridge University Press.

Jetro 1990 'Cereal catches on in Japan', p. 96–97 in *Tradescope* 6.

Jiménez, Michael F. 1995 'From plantation to cup: coffee and capitalism in the United States, 1830-1930', p. 38-64 in W. Roseberry et al (eds.) *Coffee, Society, and Power in Latin America*, Baltimore, MD: John Hopkins University Press.

Jobse-van Putten, Jozien 1995 *Eenvoudig maar Voedzaam: cultuurgeschedenis van de dagelijkse maaltijd in Nederland* (Simple but Nutritious: a cultural history of the daily meal in the Netherlands), Nijmegen: Sun.

Johnson, O. (ed.) 1995 *Information Please Almanac*, New York: Houghton Mifflin.

Kennard, Mary 1997 'Convenience stores', p. 12–15 in *Mangajin* 69.

Khare, Ravin S. 1976a *The Hindu Hearth and Home*, New Delhi: Vikas Publishing House.

—— 1976b. *Culture and Reality: essays on the Hindu system of managing foods*, Simla: Indian Institute of Advanced Study.

—— 1986 'The Indian meal: aspects of cultural economy and food use', p. 159–84 in R.S. Khare and M.S.A. Rao (eds.) *Food, Society and Culture: aspects in South Asian food systems*, Durham: Carolina Academic Press.

Kim, J. G. 1984 *Illustrated Natural Drugs Encyclopaedia*, Seoul: Nam San Dang Pub.

Kim, Kwang-ok 1994 'Umshik ui saengsan-gwa munhwa ui sobi: ch'ongnon' (Cultural consumption of food in contemporary Korea: an anthropological overview), p. 7–50 in *Han'guk Munhwa Illyuhak* 26.

Kim, Yang-ki 1987 (1976) *Kimuchi to Oshinko: nikkan hikaku bunka kô* (Kimch'i and Oshinko: a comparative consideration of the culture of Japan and Korea), Tôkyô: Chûô kôronsha.

Kirishima, Yoko 1995 'Revolution Begins in the Kitchen', p. 161–71 in M. White and S. Barnet (eds.) *Comparing Cultures*, Boston: Bedford Books (reprinted from *Japan Interpreter* 1975).

Lang, Graeme 1997 'Sacred power in the metropolis: shrines and temples in Hong Kong', p. 242-66 in G. Evans and M. Tam (eds.) *Hong Kong: the anthropology of a Chinese metropolis*, London: Curzon Press.

Lang, Graeme and Lars Ragvald 1993 *The Rise of a Refugee God: Hong Kong's Wong Tai Sin*, Hong Kong: Oxford University Press.

Lanser, Susan S. 1993 'Burning dinners: feminist subversions of domesticity', p. 36–53 in J.N. Radner (ed.) *Feminine Messages: coding in women's folk culture*, Champaign-Urbana: University of Illinois Press.

Leake, J. 1980 'The livestock industry', p. 65–74 in *Bulletin of Indonesian Economic Studies* 16 (1).

REFERENCES

Lee [Yi], Ch'ang-hui 1989 *Sanch'aeryu Chaebae Hyonhwang* (Mountain [wild] Vegetable Cultivation Status), unpublished report, Suwon: Rural Development Administration (Republic of Korea).

Lee, Tchang-bok [Yi, Ch'ang-pok] 1969 *Yasaeng Sigyong Singmul Togam* (Wild Edible Plants), Seoul: Forest Research Institute.

—— 1979 *Taehan Shinmul Togam* (Illustrated Flora of Korea), Seoul: Hyang Mun Sa.

Legge, James (tr.) 1885 *The Sacred Books of China* Vol. XXVII, Oxford: Clarendon Press.

Lethbridge, Henry 1969 'Hong Kong under Japanese occupation: changes in social structure', p. 77-127 in I.C. Jarvie (ed.) *Hong Kong: a society in transition*, London: Routledge & Kegan Paul.

Levenstein, Harvey A. 1985 'The American response to Italian food, 1880-1930', p. 1–24 in *Food and Foodways* 1 (1).

—— 1993 *Paradox of Plenty: a social history of eating in modern America*, New York and Oxford: Oxford University Press.

Lilley, Rozanna 1993 'Claiming identity: film and television in Hong Kong', p. 261–92 in *History and Anthropology* 6 (2-3).

Long, Susan O. 1996 'Nurturing and femininity: the ideal of caregiving in postwar Japan', p. 156-76 in A. Imamura (ed.) *Re-Imaging Japanese Women*, Berkeley: University of California Press.

Malkki, Liisa 1992 'National Geographic: the rooting of peoples and the territorialization of national identity among scholars and refugees', p. 24–44 in *Cultural Anthropology* 7 (1).

Mathews, Gordon forthcoming 'A Collision of Discourses: Japanese and Hong Kong Chinese during the Diaoyu/Senkaku Islands crisis', in H. Befu and S. Guichard-Anguis (eds.) *Globalizing Japan*, Routledge.

Mauss, Marcel 1990 *The Gift: the form and reason for exchange in archaic societies*, New York: W.W. Norton.

Mayer, Adrian 1956 'Some hierarchical aspects of caste', p. 117–44 in *Southwestern Journal of Anthropology* 12 (2).

Mayer, Philip 1971 *Townsmen or Tribesmen*, Cape Town: Oxford University Press.

McBean, L.D. and G.D. Miller 1998 'Allaying fears and fallacies about lactose intolerance', p. 671–6 in *Journal of American Dietetic Association* 98.

McDonald's Corporation 1998 *McDonald's Country Openings*, unpublished report (July 31), Oakbook, Illinois, USA.

McIntosh, Wm. Alex and Mary Zey 1989 'Women as gatekeepers of food consumption: a sociological critique', p. 317–32 in *Food and Foodways* 3 (4).

Mennell, Stephen J. 1985 *All Manners of Food: eating and taste in England and France from the Middle Ages to the present*, Oxford: Basil Blackwell.

—— 1987 'On the civilizing of appetite', p. 373–403 in *Theory, Culture & Society* 4.

—— 1989 'Voorspel: eten in de Lage Landen', p. 15–29 in *Smaken Verschillen* (Dutch edition of *All Manners of Food* 1985), Amsterdam: Bert Bakker.

—— 1990 'The globalization of human society as a very long-term social process: Elias's theory', p. 359–371 in M. Featherstone (ed.) *Global Culture: nationalism, globalization and modernity*, London: Sage.

Mennell, Stephen J. et al 1992 *The Sociology of Food: eating, diet and culture*, London/New Delhi: Sage.

Meulemans, O. and Jaap H. De Haas 1940 'Karnemelk als zuigelingenvoeding, bereiding uit ondermelk en volle melk' (Buttermilk for infant feeding prepared from skim milk and full-cream milk), p. 2465–77 in *Geneeskundig Tijdschrift voor Nederlandsch-Indië* 80.

Miles, Robert 1982 *Racism and Migrant Labour*, London: Routledge and Kegan Paul.

REFERENCES

Ministry of Agriculture, Forestry and Fisheries 1993 and 1992 *Statistical Yearbook of Agriculture, Forestry and Fisheries*, Seoul: Ministry of Agriculture, Forestry and Fisheries (Republic of Korea).

Ministry of Education 1983 *Korean Gazetteer*, Seoul: Ministry of Education (Republic of Korea).

Mintz, Sidney 1986 *Sweetness and Power: the place of sugar in modern history*, New York: Viking.

—— 1996 *Tasting Food, Tasting Freedom,* Boston: Beacon Press.

—— 1997 'Afterword: swallowing modernity', p. 183–200 in J. Watson (ed.) 1997b.

Mo, Po-il and Ho Sang-ch'on 1990 'Mettugiga toesarananda' (The mettugi revival), in *Chungang Ilbo,* October 8.

Moeran, Brian 1986 'One over the seven: sake drinking in a Japanese pottery community', p. 226–42 in J. Hendry and J. Webber (ed.) *Interpreting Japanese Society*, Oxford: JASO.

Mori, Barbara L.R. 1996 'The traditional arts as leisure activities for contemporary Japanese women', p. 117–34 in A. Imamura (ed.) *Re-Imaging Japanese Women*, Berkeley: University of California Press.

Morris, T.N. 1958 'Management and preservation of food', p. 26–52 in C. Singer et al (eds.) *A History of Technology, Vol. 5, 1850-1900*, Oxford: Clarendon Press.

Murcott, Anne 1982 'On the social significance of the "cooked dinner" in South Wales', p. 677-95 in *Social Science Information* 21 (4/5).

—— 1983a (ed.) *The Sociology of Food and Eating*, Aldershot: Gower.

—— 1983b '"It's a pleasure to cook for him": food, mealtimes and gender in some South Wales households', p. 78–90 in E. Garmarnikow et al (eds.) *The Public and the Private,* London: Heinemann.

—— 1996 'Food as an expression of identity', p. 49–77 in S. Gustavsson & L. Lewin (eds.) *The Future of the Nation State: essays on cultural pluralism and political integration*, London: Routledge and N&S Publishers.

'Nationaal rapport van Nederlandsch-Indië voor de intergouvernementeele conferentie van landen in het Verre Oosten voor de landelijke hygiëne, 3–13 augustus 1937, Volkenbond, hygiëne-organisatie' (National Report on the Dutch East Indies for the Intergovernmental Conference of Far Eastern Countries on Rural Hygiene, 3–13 August 1937, League of Nations, Hygiene Organisation), p. 99–216 in *Mededeelingen van den Dienst der Volksgezondheid in Nederlandsch-Indië* 26.

Newsreview: Korea's weekly magazine, Seoul: The Korea Herald.

Ng, Kam Yui (ed.) 1988 'Introduction', p. 10-15 in *Famous Cuisine in Hong Kong*, Food World: Hong Kong.

Nishimura, Yuko 1998 *Gender, Kinship and Property Rights: Nagarattar womanhood in South India*, Delhi: Oxford University Press.

Nonghyop Samsibonyon Sa (A History of Thirty-five Years of the Agricultural Cooperative) 1996, Seoul: Nongop hyoptong chohap chunganghoe.

Ohnuki-Tierney, Emiko 1993 *Rice as Self: Japanese identities through time*, Princeton: Princeton University Press.

Orange, Marc 1995 'En Corée, le chien se mange surtout en été' (In Korea, dog is mostly eaten in the summer), p. 373–77 in Blanchon (ed.).

Osgood, Cornelius 1951 *The Koreans and their Culture*, New York: Ronald Press.

Ōtsuka, Shigeru 1986 'Nihonshoku no seiritsu to sono ayumi: Kingendai wo chûshin ni', p. 18-25 in *Seikatsu Bunka Shi* 9.

Pemberton, Robert 1994 'The revival of rice-field grasshoppers as human food in South Korea', p. 323–27 in *Pan-Pacific Ethnopharmacology* 70.

—— 1999 'Insects and other arthropods used as drugs in Korean traditional medicine', p. 207–16 in *Journal of Ethnobiology* 65.

181

REFERENCES

Pemberton, Robert and Nam-sook Lee 1996 'Wild food plants in South Korea; market presence, new crops, and exports to the United States', p. 57–70 in *Economic Botany* 50.

Perlin, Frank 1994 *Unbroken Landscape: commodity, category, sign and identity. Their production as myth and knowledge from 1500*, Aldershot, UK: Variorum.

Pharr, Susan 1987 *Political Women in Japan: the search for a place in political life*, Berkeley: University of California Press

Pitt-Rivers, Julian 1977 *The Fate of Shechem,* Cambridge: Cambridge University Press.

Pudjilestari, Liling et al 1995 *Undernutrition in Low Income Households in Jakarta City, Indonesia: assessment of underlying factors*, Jakarta: Urban Health Study Group, Atma Jaya Catholic University.

Pyke, Magnus 1970 *Food Science and Technology,* London: John Murray.

—— 1972 *Technological Eating: or where does the fish finger point?*, London: John Murray.

Rizvi, S.M.A. 1981 Some Aspects of Industry and Social Change Among the Muslim Karkhanedars. Unpublished Ph.D. thesis, University of Delhi, cited by Murphy, C.P.H. 1986 'Piety and honor: the meaning of Muslim feasts in old Delhi', p. 85–119 in R.S. Khare and M.S.A Rao (eds.) *Food, Society and Culture*, Durham, N. Carolina: Carolina Academic Press.

Robertson, Roland 1990 'Mapping the global condition: globalization as the central concept', p. 15–30 in M. Featherstone (ed.) *Global Culture: nationalism, globalization and modernity*, London: Sage.

Roden, Claudia 1985 *A New Book of Middle Eastern Food*, London: Viking.

—— 1989 *The Food of Italy*, London: Arrow.

Romein, Jan and Annie Romein 1979 *De Lage Landen bij de Zee: een geschiedenis van het Nederlandse volk* (The Low Countries: a history of the Dutch nation), Amsterdam: Querido.

Rural Development Administration 1993 *Sanch'aeryu Chaebae Hyonhwang* (Mountain [wild] Vegetable Cultivation Status), unpublished report, Suwon: Rural Development Administration (Republic of Korea).

Said, Edward W. 1995 *Orientalism: western conceptions of the Orient*, Harmondsworth: Penguin.

Saifullah Khan, Verity 1976 'Purdah in the British situation', p. 224–45 in D.L. Barker and S. Allen (eds.) *Dependence and Exploitation in Work and Marriage*, London: Longman.

Schama, Simon 1987 *The Embarrassement of Riches: an interpretation of Dutch culture in the Golden Age,* New York: Knopf.

Scrimshaw, Nevin S. and E.B. Murray 1988 'The acceptability of milk and milk products in populations with a prevalence of lactose intolerance', p. 1083–159 in *American Journal of Clinical Nutrition* 48.

Selwyn, Tom 1980 'The order of men and the order of things: an examination of food transactions in an Indian village', p. 297–317 in *International Journal of the Sociology of Law* 8.

Sharp, Charles E. 1919 'Shall we eat Korean food?', p. 139–141 in *Korean Mission Field* 15.

Shaw, Alison 1988 *A Pakistani Community in Britain*, Oxford: Blackwell.

Shin, Chun-ho 1991 *Han'guk Minsok Taesajon I* (Dictionary of Korean Folk Customs, vol. 1), Seoul: Minjok munhwasa.

Simoons, Frederick J. 1970 'Primary adult lactose intolerance and the milking habit: a problem in biologic and cultural interrelations, a cultural, historical hypothesis', p. 695–710 in *American Journal of Digestive Diseases* 15.

—— 1971 'Antiquity of dairying in Asia and Africa', p. 431–39 in *Geographical Review* 3.

REFERENCES

Skov, Lise and Brian Moeran (eds.) 1996 *Women, Media and Consumption in Japan*, London: Curzon Press.

Smith, Joan 1998 'Guess Who's Spoiling the Dinner Party', p. 3 in the Saturday review of the *Guardian*, October 31.

Sokolov, Raymond 1991 *Why We Eat What We Eat: how the encounter between the New World and the Old changed the way everyone on the planet eats*, New York: Summit Books.

Sperl, Barbara 1974 *Tradition und Moderne in einem Koreanischen Dorf* (Tradition and Modernity in a Korean Village), Wien: Verband der wissenschaftlichen Gesellschaften Österreichs.

Swamy, D.S. and K. Singh, 1994 *Against Consensus: three years of public resistance against structural adjustment programme*, Delhi: Public Interest Research Group.

Tanaka, Norio 2000 'Shoyu: the flavor of Japan', p. 1–7 in *Japan Foundation Newsletter* 27 (2).

Tannahill, Reay 1988 *Food in History*, Harmondsworth: Penguin.

Theodoratus, Robert J. 1983 'The changing patterns of Greek foodways in America', p. 87-104 in A. Davidson (ed.) *Food in Motion: the migration of foodstuffs and cookery techniques*, volume II, Stanningley/Leeds: Prospect Books.

Tjepkema, K. 1963 *Dat is 't Kondensfabryk* (This is the Milk Condensery), Leeuwarden: Coöperatieve Condensfabriek Friesland.

Tobin, Joseph (ed.) 1992 *Re-made in Japan*, New Haven: Yale University Press.

Tolksdorf, Ulrich 1978 'Essen und Trinken in alter und neuer Heimat' (Eating and drinking in the old and new fatherland), p. 341–64 in *Jahrbuch für Ostdeutsche Volkskunde* (The Yearbook of East-German Ethnology) 21, Marburg: Erhard Riemann, N.G. Erwart Verlag.

Tomlinson, John 1991 *Cultural Imperialism: a critical introduction*, London/Washington: Pinter.

—— 1999 *Globalization and Culture*, Cambridge: Polity Press.

Toomey, Paul M. 1992 'Mountain of food, mountain of love: ritual inversion in the Annakuta Feast at Mount Goverdhan', p. 117–45 in R.S. Khare (ed.) *The Eternal Food: gastronomic ideas and ideas of Hindus and Buddhists*, Albany: SUNY Press.

Treat, John Whittier 1996 'Yoshimoto Banana's *Kitchen*, or the cultural logic of Japanese consumerism', p. 274–98 in L. Skov and B. Moeran (eds.).

Tricon Global Restaurants Inc. 1998 *Quarterly Store Count Report*, unpublished report (June 30), Louisville, Kentucky, USA.

Turner, Matthew 1994 '60's/90's Dissolving the People', Hong Kong: Hong Kong Arts Centre.

University of Birmingham 1995 *Abstracts of the Fourth International Multidisciplinary Research Conference on Food Choice*, University of Birmingham, April 24–26.

Uno, Kathleen 1991 'Good Wives and Wise Mothers in early twentieth century Japan', p. 17–41 in G. Bernstein (ed.).

Van de Burg, C.L. 1883 *De Geneesheer in Nederlandsch-Indië. Vol. 1.* (The Physician in the Dutch East Indies, vol. 1), Batavia: Ernst & Co.

Van Laanen, Jan T.M. 1979 'Het bestedingspakket van de͂Inheemse◌ bevolking op Java (1921-1931)' (Budget expenditure of the indigenous population of Java, 1921-1931), p. 133–46 in F. van Anrooij et al (eds.) *Between People and Statistics: essays in modern Indonesian history presented to Piet Creuzberg*, The Hague: M. Nijhoff.

Van Otterloo, Anneke H. 1987 'Foreign immigrants and the Dutch at table, 1945-1985: bridging or widening the gap?', p. 812–35 in *Netherlands Journal of Sociology* 4.

REFERENCES

—— 1990 *Eten en Eetlust in Nederland (1840-1990): een historisch-sociologische studie* (Eating and Appetite in the Netherlands (1840-1990): a historical and sociological study), Amsterdam: Bert Bakker.

—— 2000 'The Low Countries', p. 1232–1240 in K.F. Kiple and K.C. Ornelas (eds.) *The Cambridge World History of Food*, New York and Cambridge: Cambridge University Press.

Van Veen, Andre G. 1950a 'Nutritional studies in Indonesia before the war', p. 121–27 in *Documenta Neerlandica et Indonesica de Morbis Tropicis* 2.

—— 1950b 'Nutrition studies in Indonesia 1850-1950', p. 374–83 in *Documenta Neerlandica et Indonesica de Morbis Tropicis* 2.

Vansina, Jan 1978 *The Children of Woot: a history of the Kuba peoples*, Madison: Visconsin University Press.

Vogel, Suzanne 1978 'The professional housewife', p. 81–93 in *Japan Interpreter* (Winter).

Vuyk, Bep 1981 'De invloed van ons koloniaal verleden op ons hedendaagse eetpatroon' (The Influence of our colonial past on our contemporary eating habits), in p. 178–81 *Nederlands Tijdschrift voor Diëtisten* 36.

Vuyk, Bep 1973 *Groot Indonesisch Kookboek* (Great Indonesian Cookery Book), Utrecht/Antwerpen: Kosmos.

Warde, Alan 1997 *Consumption, Food and Taste: culinary antinomies and commodity culture*, London: SAGE.

Washida, Kiyokazu 1997 'Open all hours', p. 11–13 in *Look Japan*.

Wallerstein, Immanuel 1974-1989 *The Modern World-System* (3 Vols.), New York: Academic Press.

Watson, James 1987 'From the common pot: feasting with equals in Chinese society', p. 389–401 in *Anthropos* 82.

—— 1997a 'Introduction' p. 1–38 in J. Watson (ed.) *Golden Arches East: McDonald's in East Asia*, Stanford: Stanford University Press.

—— (ed.) 1997b *Golden Arches East: McDonald's in East Asia*, Stanford: Stanford University Press.

—— 1998 '*Puhn tsoi* in Hong Kong', unpublished paper presented at the Asian Food Workshop, Leiden University, February.

Weber, Max 1958 *The Protestant Ethic and the Spirit of Capitalism*, New York: Charles Scribner's Sons.

Werbner, Pnina 1990 *The Migration Process: capital, gifts and offerings among British Pakistanis*, New York: Berg.

Wertheim, Wim F. 1951 'De stad in Indonesië, oud Indische steden' (The town in Indonesia, old Indian cities), p. 24–40 in *Indonesië* 5.

—— 1958 'Town development in the Indies', p. 1–77 in W.F. Wertheim (ed.) *The Indonesian Town: studies in urban sociology*, The Hague: Van Hoeve.

Wheatley, Paul 1965 'A note on the extension of milking practices into Southeast Asia during the first millenium A.D.', p. 577–90 in *Anthropos* 60.

White, Merry 1992 *The Japanese Overseas: can they go home again?*, Princeton, NJ: Princeton University Press.

—— 1993 *The Material Child: coming of age in Japan and America*, New York: Free Press.

—— 1995 'Women, food and identity construction: role attenuation and elaboration in Japan', p. 379–90 in F. Blanchon (ed.).

Wiegelmann, Günter 1974 'Innovations in food and meals', p. 20–30 in *Folk Life* 12.

Williams, Brackett F. 1989 'A class act: anthropology and the race to nation across ethnic terrain', p. 401–44 in *Annual Review of Anthropology* 18.

Williams, Rory G.A. 1993a 'Health and length of residence among South Asians in Glasgow: a study controlling for age', p. 52–60 in *Journal of Public Health Medicine* 15.

REFERENCES

—— 1993b 'Religion and illness', p. 71–91 in A. Radley (ed.) *Worlds of Illness: biographical and cultural perspectives on health and disease*, London, New York: Routledge.

Williams, Rory G.A. et al 1994 'Coronary risk in a British Punjabi population: comparative profile of non-biochemical factors', p. 28–37 in *International Journal of Epidemiology*, 23 (1).

—— 1998 'Food choice and culture in a cosmopolitan city. South Asians, Italians and other Glaswegians', p. 267–84 in A. Murcott (ed.) *The Nation's Diet: the social science of food choice*, London: Addison Wesley, Longman.

Wolf, Eric 1997 *Europe and the People Without History*, Berkeley: University of California.

Wong Lo Kat Herbal Tea Corporation Ltd. 1987 *A History of the Wong Lo Kat Herbal Tea Business*, Hong Kong.

Wood, Roy C. 1995 *The Sociology of the Meal*, Edinburgh: Edinburgh University Press.

Wu, David 1996 'Chinese Cafes in Hong Kong', paper presented at International Conference on Changing Diet and Foodways in Chinese Culture, Chinese University of Hong Kong, June.

Yalman, Nur 1992 'Ningen seishin no kansei: Isuramu ni okeru chô-nashonarizumu no mondai' (The perfection of man: the question of supra-nationalism in Islam), p. 34–49 in *Shisô* 823 (January).

Yi, Sok-rae (ed.) 1974 *P'ungsok Kasa Chip* (A Collection of Kasa Poems on Customs), Seoul: Shin'gu munhwasa.

Yi, Tu-hyon et al 1974 *Han'guk Minsokhak Kaesol* (Outline of Korean Folklore), Seoul: Minjung sogwan.

Yoshimoto, Banana 1990 *Kitchen*, New York: Washington Square Press.

Yu, Eui-young 1994 'Ethnic Identity and Community Involvement of Younger-Generation Korean Americans', p. 263–282 in Dae-sook Suh (ed.) *Korean Studies: new Pacific currents*, Honolulu: Pacific Association of Korean Studies.

Yu, Pon-ye 1956 *Han'gyong Chiryak* (A Brief Description of the Capital), Seoul: Seoul t'ukpyolshi-sa p'yonch'an wiwonhoe.

LIST OF CONTRIBUTORS

Helen Bush has an interest in food which crosses several disciplines. Her doctoral research in the Department of Archaeology and Prehistory, University of Sheffield was in the field of biological anthropology. She then studied for a Master of Science degree in the Centre for Human Nutrition, London School of Hygiene and Tropical Medicine. In 1996 she was commissioned by the Department of Health, with Rory Williams, to prepare a literature review, *Opportunities for and Barriers to Good Nutritional Health in Ethnic Minorities* (1997).

Pat Caplan is Professor of Social Anthropology at Goldsmiths College, University of London, UK. Her interest in food has led to research and fieldwork in South Asia (Nepal, South India, mainly Madras City), East Africa (Tanzania), and Britain. She has written or edited several books of which the most recent are *Gendered Fields: women, men and ethnography* (1994), *Understanding Disputes* (1995), *African Voices African Lives* (1997), *Food, Health and Identity* (1997) and *Risk Revisited* (2000).

Cheng Sea-ling is a PhD candidate in Anthropology at the University of Oxford. She completed her MPhil at the University of Hong Kong. Extending her research interest from food to sex, she is completing her doctoral thesis on clubs in US military camp towns in Korea.

Katarzyna J. Cwiertka is Associate in Research at the Centre for Japanese and Korean Studies, Leiden University, The Netherlands. She received her PhD in January 1999 and is currently revising her dissertation, *The Making of Modern Culinary Tradition in Japan* for publication. She is also involved in a number of projects dealing with East-Asian food habits.

Adel P. Den Hartog is Associate Professor in Social Nutrition, Division of Human Nutrition and Epidemiology, Wageningen Agricultural University, the Netherlands. He worked as a specialist in food habits for the Food and Agriculture Organisation of the United Nations, first in West Africa and later at the FAO Headquarters, Rome, Italy. His main research interests are in the field of food habits and socio-cultural dimensions of food and nutrition, in particular Western Europe, South East Asia and tropical Africa. He published a wide range of articles and a number of books, both in English and Dutch.

Robert W. Pemberton received his PhD in Entomology from the University of California, Berkeley. He works for the Agricultural Research Service (the science branch) of the United States Department of Agriculture, Ft. Lauderdale, Florida. His research involves basic and applied ecology, including biological control of pests and the ecology of plant-insect mutualisms. He has frequently worked in Asia, including five years as the director of a US Department of Agriculture laboratory in Seoul, South Korea. For about 15 years he has done research in ethnobiology on Asian topics, including food. R.W. Pemberton may be contacted via e-mail at bobpem@eemail.com.

Anneke H. Van Otterloo is lecturing at the University of Amsterdam in the Department of Sociology and Anthropology. Her fields of research are the history and sociology of religion, worldviews and religious movements, lifestyles and (alternative) health, food and food technology. She is co-author of *The Sociology of Food: eating, diet and culture* (Sage 1992), on overview of food studies in Western languages. Since 1995 she has been involved in the interdisciplinary project: The History of Technology in the Netherlands in the Twentieth Century; editing an associated volume on agriculture and food, published in autumn 2000.

Boudewijn C.A. Walraven is Professor of Korean Language and Culture at Leiden University, and has been President of the Association for Korean Studies in Europe. Since 1991, he has also been Contributing Editor of *Korea Journal* published by the Korean National Commission for UNESCO. He is the author of *Songs of the Shaman: The Ritual Chants of the Korean Mudang* (1994) and has written on various aspects of Korean culture.

Merry White is Professor of Anthropology at Boston University, and Associate in Research at the E.O. Reischauer Institute of Japanese Studies at Harvard University. Among her published books are *Cooking for Crowds* (1973), *Noodles Galore* (1976), *The Japanese Educational Challenge* (1986), *The Japanese Overseas* (1987), and *The Material Child* (1993). She is currently finishing a manuscript on family and social change in post-war Japan, and is undertaking research on food trends in Japan.

Rory Williams is Senior Research Scientist at the Social and Public Health Sciences Unit in Glasgow University, funded by the Medical Research Council of Great Britain. He runs the Ethnicity, Religion and Health Programme at the unit, which is concerned with both black and white minorities in Britain. He is the author of *A Protestant Legacy: attitudes to death and illness among older Aberdonians* (1990) and numerous journal papers on ethnicity, religion and health.

INDEX

Note: References to illustrations are in bold type.

188